VOLUME **4**

Curriculum
Growing

RECOMMENDED CITATIONS

AEPS®-3

Bricker, D., Dionne, C., Grisham, J., Johnson, J. J., Macy, M., Slentz, K., & Waddell, M. (2022). *Assessment, Evaluation, and Programming System for Infants and Children, Third Edition (AEPS®-3)*. Brookes Publishing Co.

Volume 1 AEPS®-3 User's Guide

Bricker, D., & Johnson, J. J. (Eds.). (2022). *AEPS®-3 Volume 1: User's guide.* In D. Bricker, C. Dionne, J. Grisham, J. J. Johnson, M. Macy, K. Slentz, & M. Waddell, *Assessment, Evaluation, and Programming System for Infants and Children, Third Edition (AEPS®-3)*. Brookes Publishing Co.

Volume 2 AEPS®-3 Assessment

Bricker, D., & Johnson, J. J. (Eds.). (2022). *AEPS®-3 Volume 2: Assessment.* In D. Bricker, C. Dionne, J. Grisham, J. J. Johnson, M. Macy, K. Slentz, & M. Waddell, *Assessment, Evaluation, and Programming System for Infants and Children, Third Edition (AEPS®-3)*. Brookes Publishing Co.

Volume 3 AEPS®-3 Curriculum—Beginning

Grisham, J., & Slentz, K. (Eds.). (2022). *AEPS®-3 Volume 3: Curriculum—Beginning.* In D. Bricker, C. Dionne, J. Grisham, J. J. Johnson, M. Macy, K. Slentz, & M. Waddell, *Assessment, Evaluation, and Programming System for Infants and Children, Third Edition (AEPS®-3)*. Brookes Publishing Co.

Volume 4 AEPS®-3 Curriculum—Growing

Grisham, J., & Slentz, K. (Eds.). (2022). *AEPS®-3 Volume 4: Curriculum—Growing.* In D. Bricker, C. Dionne, J. Grisham, J. J. Johnson, M. Macy, K. Slentz, & M. Waddell, *Assessment, Evaluation, and Programming System for Infants and Children, Third Edition (AEPS®-3)*. Brookes Publishing Co.

Volume 5 AEPS®-3 Curriculum—Ready

Grisham, J., & Slentz, K. (Eds.). (2022). *AEPS®-3 Volume 5: Curriculum—Ready.* In D. Bricker, C. Dionne, J. Grisham, J. J. Johnson, M. Macy, K. Slentz, & M. Waddell, *Assessment, Evaluation, and Programming System for Infants and Children, Third Edition (AEPS®-3)*. Brookes Publishing Co.

VOLUME 4

Curriculum
Growing

edited by

Jennifer Grisham, Ed.D.
University of Kentucky
Lexington

and

Kristine Slentz, Ph.D.
Western Washington University
Bellingham

·P·A·U·L·H·
BROOKES
PUBLISHING C°®

Baltimore • London • Sydney

Paul H. Brookes Publishing Co.
Post Office Box 10624
Baltimore, Maryland 21285-0624
USA
www.brookespublishing.com

Typeset by Progressive Publishing Services, York, Pennsylvania.
Manufactured in the United States of America by Sheridan Books, Inc.

All examples in this book are composites. Any similarity to actual individuals or circumstances is coincidental, and no implications should be inferred.

To order, contact Brookes Publishing Co. or visit www.brookespublishing.com.

Please see Recommended Citations at the beginning of this book for a list of AEPS-3 volumes. Printable masters of the AEPS-3 forms are also available. All AEPS-3 materials are available from Brookes Publishing Co., P.O. Box 10624, Baltimore, Maryland 21285-0624 (800-638-3775 or 410-337-9580).

To find out more about AEPS-3, please visit www.aepsinteractive.com.

Library of Congress Cataloging-in-Publication Data

Names: Bricker, Diane D., editor. | Johnson, JoAnn, editor. | Grisham, Jennifer, editor. | Slentz, Kristine, editor.
Title: Assessment, evaluation, and programming system for infants and children / edited by Diane Bricker, JoAnn (JJ) Johnson.
Other titles: At head of title: AEPS-3
Description: Third edition. | Baltimore, Maryland: Paul H. Brookes Publishing Co., [2022] | Includes bibliographical references and index.
Contents: v. 1. User's guide / edited by Diane Bricker, JoAnn (JJ) Johnson—v. 2. Assessment / edited by Diane Bricker, JoAnn (JJ) Johnson—v. 3. Curriculum-beginning / edited by Jennifer Grisham and Kristine Slentz—v. 4. Curriculum-growing / edited by Jennifer Grisham and Kristine Slentz—v. 5. Curriculum-ready edited by Jennifer Grisham and Kristine Slentz.
Identifiers: LCCN 2021022790| ISBN 9781681255194 (v. 1; paperback) | ISBN 9781681255200 (v. 2; paperback) | ISBN 9781681255217 (v. 3; paperback) | ISBN 9781681255224 (v. 4; paperback) | ISBN 9781681255231 (v. 5; paperback)
Subjects: LCSH: Assessment, Evaluation, and Programming System. | Child development—Testing. | Child development deviations—Diagnosis.
Classification: LCC RJ51.D48 A87 2022 | DDC 618.92/0075—dc23
LC record available at https://lccn.loc.gov/2021022790

British Library Cataloguing in Publication data are available from the British Library.

2025   2024   2023   2022   2021

10   9   8   7   6   5   4   3   2   1

Contents

About the Authors

Diane Bricker, Ph.D., Professor Emerita and Former Director, Early Intervention Program, Center on Human Development, and Former Associate Dean for Academic Programs, College of Education, University of Oregon, Eugene

Dr. Bricker served as Director of the Early Intervention Program at the Center on Human Development, University of Oregon, from 1978 to 2004. She was a professor of special education, focusing on the fields of early intervention and social communication.

Her professional interests have addressed three major areas: early intervention service delivery approaches, curriculum-based assessment and evaluation, and developmental-behavioral screening. Dr. Bricker's work in early intervention approaches has been summarized in two volumes: *An Activity-Based Approach to Early Intervention, Fourth Edition* (with J. Johnson & N. Rahn; Brookes Publishing Co., 2015), and *An Activity-Based Approach to Developing Young Children's Social Emotional Competence* (with J. Squires; Brookes Publishing Co., 2007). Her work in curriculum-based assessment and evaluation has focused on the development of the *Assessment, Evaluation, and Programming System for Infants and Children* (*AEPS*®; Brookes Publishing Co., 1993, 1996, 2002, 2022). This measure and associated curricula provide intervention personnel with a system for the comprehensive assessment of young children with results that link directly to curricular content and subsequent evaluation of child progress.

Dr. Bricker has been a primary author of the *Ages & Stages Questionnaires*® (*ASQ*®; with J. Squires; Brookes Publishing Co., 1995, 1999, 2009) and has directed research activities on the ASQ system starting in 1980. *Developmental Screening in Your Community: An Integrated Approach for Connecting Children with Services* (with M. Macy, J. Squires, & K. Marks; Brookes Publishing Co., 2013) offers a comprehensive system for creating and operating communitywide developmental-behavioral screening programs for young children.

Dr. Bricker's distinctions include the Division of Early Childhood, Council for Exceptional Children Service to the Field Award, December 1992, and the Peabody College Distinguished Alumna Award, May 1995.

Carmen Dionne, Ph.D., Chairholder, United Nations Educational, Scientific and Cultural Organization (UNESCO), and Lecturer, Department of Psychoeducation, University of Québec at Trois-Rivières (UQTR), Canada

Dr. Dionne is Professor of Special Education at the University of Québec at Trois-Rivières (UQTR), where she has worked since 1997. She led the Canada Research Chair in Early Intervention from 2005 to 2015. She also served as Scientific Director of a research institute on intellectual disabilities and autism spectrum disorder. Dr. Dionne has served as Principal Investigator on numerous research studies focused on early intervention and early childhood special education. In 2016, she began work as a United Nations Educational, Scientific and Cultural Organization (UNESCO) Chair on screening and assessment of young children, collaborating with Dr. Jane Squires and colleagues from other countries. Project objectives include training graduate students and conducting research activities in early intervention for children from birth to 6 years of age who are at risk for or have disabilities.

Jennifer Grisham, Ed.D., Professor, Interdisciplinary Early Childhood Education Program, and Director, Early Childhood Laboratory School, Department of Early Childhood, Special Education, and Counselor Education, College of Education, University of Kentucky, Lexington

Dr. Grisham is Professor in the Interdisciplinary Early Childhood Education program at the University of Kentucky, Lexington. She received her doctorate in education from the University of Kentucky. She is also Faculty Director of the Early Childhood Laboratory at the University of Kentucky, an inclusive early childhood program for children from birth to 5 years of age.

Dr. Grisham has directed research projects on topics including linking assessment and instruction, early care and education program quality, and individualizing instruction for young children with disabilities. In addition, she has conducted research on the effectiveness of instructional procedures that are embedded into developmentally appropriate activities, the application of multi-tiered systems of support in early childhood settings, and coaching teachers and caregivers to implement evidence-based instructional strategies with fidelity. Dr. Grisham is Project Director for the Kentucky Deaf-Blind Project, which provides technical assistance to families and service providers of infants, toddlers, children, and youth with deaf-blindness. She coauthored a book titled *Reach for the Stars: Planning for the Future* (with D. Haynes; American Printing House for the Blind, 2013), which is used to support families of young children in planning for their children's future and articulating their priorities to educational team members, as well as *Blended Practices for Teaching Young Children in Inclusive Settings, Second Edition* (with M. L. Hemmeter; Brookes Publishing Co., 2017), and *Assessing Young Children in Inclusive Settings: The Blended Practices Approach* (with K. Pretti-Frontczak; Brookes Publishing Co., 2011). Finally, Dr. Grisham directed the nationwide field test for AEPS-3. Dr. Grisham is frequently asked to provide professional development to state departments of education, universities, and local education agencies on topics for which she conducts research throughout the country. Dr. Grisham is co-founder of a children's home and preschool program in Guatemala City, Hope for Tomorrow, where she accompanies students for the education abroad program. Dr. Grisham also works internationally in other locations to promote inclusion of young children with disabilities.

JoAnn (JJ) Johnson, Ph.D., Professor and Department Chair, Department of Child and Family Studies, College of Education, St. Cloud State University, Minnesota

Dr. Johnson is Professor in Child and Family Studies at St. Cloud State University in Minnesota, where she provides professional development education in early childhood education, early intervention, and early childhood special education. She completed her undergraduate degree in special education and elementary education at the University of Idaho and her master's and doctoral degrees in early intervention at the University of Oregon under the advisement of Dr. Diane Bricker.

Dr. Johnson has worked at University Centers for Excellence in Developmental Disabilities in Louisiana, Oregon, and Nevada as Program Coordinator, Teacher, Service Coordinator, Grant and Contract Administrator, Director, Principal Investigator, and Instructor. She served as Director of the Research and Educational Planning Center and the Nevada University Center for Excellence in Developmental Disabilities from 2001 to 2008, where she developed and administered lifespan programs, services, and supports for individuals with disabilities and their families. Her professional experiences encompass all service settings for young children, including neonatal intensive care units, pediatric intensive care units, well-baby clinics, home- and center-based programs for infants and young children (including Head Start and Early Head Start), nursing homes, supported employment, transition programs, special education schools, and university lab school programs. Much of her professional career has focused on developing and refining assessment and curriculum systems to support interventions for young children with disabilities, birth to age 6, and their families. Dr. Johnson is author, developer, and trainer of *An Activity-Based Approach to Early Intervention, Fourth Edition* (with N. Rahn & D. Bricker; Brookes Publishing Co., 2015), and the *Assessment, Evaluation, and Programming System for Infants and Children* (*AEPS*; Brookes Publishing Co., 2002, 2022) and has been involved with the system since her days as a graduate student at the University of Oregon. In her spare time, Dr. Johnson likes to read, work on home projects, observe and interact with young children, and support human and animal rights.

Marisa Macy, Ph.D., Cille and Ron Williams Endowed Community Chair for Early Childhood Education and Associate Professor, Early Childhood Education, College of Education, University of Nebraska at Kearney

Dr. Macy teaches early childhood classes at the University of Nebraska at Kearney. She does research related to young children with disabilities. Dr. Macy engages in research and outreach with the Buffett Early Childhood Institute. As the Community Chair, Dr. Macy adopts an integrated approach to early childhood education and development through theory, research, and practice that links empirical research with the creation of programs, ideas, and tools for practitioners and community members. She received master's and doctoral degrees in special education from the University of Oregon with an emphasis on early intervention and early childhood special education. Her research interests include assessment of children from birth to age 8 with delays, developmental screening, play, and personnel preparation.

Kristine Slentz, Ph.D., Professor Emerita, Department of Special Education and Education Leadership, Woodring College of Education, Western Washington University, Bellingham

Dr. Slentz began her career in early intervention and early childhood special education with home visiting and classroom teaching with infants, toddlers, and preschoolers and progressed to directing a regional home-based early intervention program in Montana. For decades, she was involved in pre-service preparation of early interventionists and early childhood special educators at the University of Oregon and Western Washington University. She also provided technical assistance and program development for Part C in Washington. She is currently Professor Emeritus in the Department of Special Education at Western Washington University.

Dr. Slentz's involvement with AEPS began with the earliest versions of the system and continues today, including development, consultation, research, and training. Her particular areas of interest and expertise are assessment and evaluation, infant development, early intervention, and working within family contexts across cultures. She has been fortunate to combine her love of travel with international training and consultation opportunities in Canada, United Arab Emirates, Singapore, and Kenya.

Misti Waddell, M.S., Senior Research Assistant and Supervisor, Early Intervention Program, College of Education, University of Oregon, Eugene

Misti Waddell is Senior Research Assistant/Project Coordinator at the Early Intervention Program at the University of Oregon. She used the *Assessment, Evaluation, and Programming System for Infants and Children (AEPS)* in classroom settings early in her career and, since the early 1990s, contributed to the development and research of the second edition of AEPS (2002), including project coordination for several field-initiated research and outreach training projects. Most recently, Ms. Waddell served as coordinator for the field testing of AEPS-3. Her professional activities in curriculum-based assessment also focus on the social-emotional development of young children. She coordinated the research study Project SEAM: Preventing Behavior Disorders and Improving Social Emotional Competence in Infants and Toddlers with Disabilities to examine the psychometric properties of the *Social-Emotional Assessment/Evaluation Measure, Research Edition (SEAM™)* (with J. Squires, D. Bricker, K. Funk, J. Clifford, & R. Hoselton; Brookes Publishing Co., 2014). She is currently part of the development team and serves as project coordinator for Project SELECT: Social-Emotional Learning in Early Childhood for Infants and Toddlers, a federally funded project to develop the curricular component of SEAM. Ms. Waddell provides training for early childhood teachers, interventionists, and parents in developmental and social-emotional screening, assessment, and intervention, including *AEPS, SEAM, Ages & Stages Questionnaires®, Third Edition (ASQ®-3),* and *Ages & Stages Questionnaires®: Social-Emotional, Second Edition (ASQ®:SE-2).*

About the Contributors

Ching-I Chen, Ph.D., Associate Professor, Special Education Department, School of Lifespan Development and Educational Sciences, Kent State University, Ohio

Dr. Chen is Associate Professor of Early Childhood Intervention at Kent State University. She is the lead translator of the traditional version of *Ages & Stages Questionnaires® in Chinese, Third Edition (ASQ®-3 Chinese)* (by J. Squires & D. Bricker; Brookes Publishing Co., 2019). She received her doctorate in early intervention/special education from the University of Oregon and was a university postdoctoral fellow at the University of Connecticut Health Center. Dr. Chen's work focuses on the development and application of culturally and linguistically relevant assessments and personnel development in early childhood intervention. She loves reading, traveling, and cats.

Naomi Rahn, Ph.D., Assistant Professor, Department of Special Education, University of Wisconsin–Whitewater

Dr. Rahn is Assistant Professor of Special Education at the University of Wisconsin–Whitewater. She completed her undergraduate degree in communicative disorders at the University of Wisconsin–Madison, her master's degree in early intervention at the University of Oregon, and her doctoral degree in special education at the University of Minnesota under the advisement of Dr. Scott McConnell. She has worked as a preschool special education teacher with children having a range of needs, including children with significant disabilities, and as an early interventionist providing services to infants and toddlers with special needs and their families. Dr. Rahn is author of *An Activity-Based Approach to Early Intervention, Fourth Edition* (with J. Johnson & D. Bricker; Brookes Publishing Co., 2015). While at the University of Oregon, she provided training on AEPS and earlier editions of *An Activity-Based Approach to Early Intervention* to programs around the country as part of an outreach training grant. Her areas of interest include naturalistic intervention strategies, early language and literacy interventions, multi-tiered systems of support, and personnel preparation. Dr. Rahn's research focuses on embedded vocabulary and language interventions for young children with disabilities and at risk for disabilities.

About EMRG

The Early Intervention Management and Research Group (EMRG) is a non-profit mutual benefit corporation that was created to manage future developments associated with linked measurement and curriculum systems designed to enhance early childhood intervention offered to young children and their families. EMRG has two general objectives: 1) oversee the future development of AEPS®, and 2) conduct descriptive and empirical research to refine and enhance AEPS.

For more information about EMRG and ongoing research, see https://aeps-emrg.weebly.com/.

EMRG BOARD MEMBERS

Diane Bricker, Ph.D.
Professor Emerita
Early Intervention Program
University of Oregon

Ching-I Chen, Ph.D.
Associate Professor
Special Education Program
Kent State University

Carmen Dionne, Ph.D.
Professor
Department of Psychoeducation
University of Québec at Trois-Rivières

Jennifer Grisham, Ed.D.
Professor, Lab School Director
Department of Early Childhood,
    Special Education and Counselor
    Education
University of Kentucky

JoAnn (JJ) Johnson, Ph.D.
Professor, Department Chair
Department of Child and Family
    Studies
St. Cloud State University

Marisa Macy, Ph.D.
Cille and Ron Williams Endowed
    Community Chair for Early
    Childhood Education
Associate Professor
Early Childhood Education
University of Nebraska at Kearney

Naomi Rahn, Ph.D.
Assistant Professor
Department of Special Education
University of Wisconsin–Whitewater

Kristine Slentz, Ph.D.
Professor Emerita
Department of Special Education and
    Education Leadership
Western Washington University

Misti Waddell, M.S.
Senior Research Assistant,
    Project Coordinator
Early Intervention Program
University of Oregon

To teachers, children, and families of the University of Kentucky Early Childhood Laboratory who conceptualized, assisted in writing, and validated the AEPS-3 Curriculum, thank you for implementing high-quality inclusive programming for ALL young children and serving as a model for the community, the state, and the nation

I

AEPS®-3 Curriculum Organization and Use

1

AEPS®-3 Curriculum Foundations and Framework

The AEPS-3 Curriculum is grounded in established contemporary early childhood developmental theory as well as recommended practices in early intervention and early childhood special education (EI/ECSE). The AEPS-3 Curriculum is a core component of AEPS-3 and a key part of the AEPS-3 *linked system*. It is specifically designed to be used as part of a multi-tiered system of support in all early childhood settings. Figure 1.1 illustrates the linked system approach that underlies AEPS-3.

As a complete system, AEPS-3 directly links the components of *assessment, goal/outcome development, teaching/intervention*, and *progress monitoring*. A linked system is one that allows practitioners to collect assessment data and use those data to develop specific developmental and academic goals, plan teaching/intervention efforts, and guide monitoring of children's progress.

AEPS-3 is such a system. Within it, the AEPS-3 Curriculum provides content for and guidance on what and how to teach individuals and groups of children (infants, toddlers, and preschoolers) who are learning at different levels and who acquire new skills and information in different ways. Throughout the AEPS-3 Curriculum, the term *children* is used to refer to the age range that includes infants, toddlers, and preschoolers. The *curriculum* content and procedures offer teachers, interventionists, and specialists detailed guidance about how to do the following:

- Collect initial assessment information to establish children's developmental skills and informational levels in all important areas.

- Use assessment data to make instructional/programming decisions about outcomes to teach within hierarchical sequences of developmental and content skills. Program development at this level provides a clear, appropriate scope and sequence of what to teach.

- Teach skills embedded within regularly occurring routines and activities at home and in classrooms or other environments, using a range of evidence-based practices. Specifically, intervention and instructional strategies show how to effectively teach

  - <u>All children</u> individually and in groups

  - <u>Some children</u> who need extra help

  - <u>Few children</u> who have specialized needs that require individual supports

- Monitor progress using the AEPS-3 Test to determine whether teaching/intervention efforts have resulted in positive outcomes for individuals and groups of children.

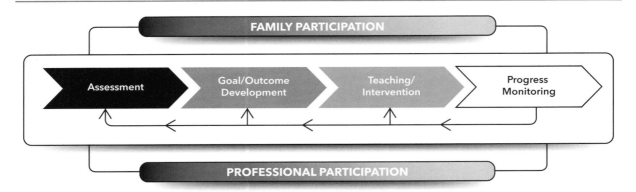

Figure 1.1. AEPS-3 Linked System Approach. This figure illustrates the conceptual framework of the AEPS-3 linked system. The arrow shapes represent the four main components of the AEPS-3 Linked System Framework: assessment, goal/outcome development, teaching/intervention, and progress monitoring. As the direction of the arrows illustrates, assessment informs goal/outcome development, goal/outcome development influences teaching/intervention, teaching/intervention informs progress monitoring, and progress monitoring then influences all three of the other parts. Participation of the family and professionals is essential throughout.

FOUNDATIONS

Designed for practitioners, the AEPS-3 Curriculum is based on three interrelated themes consistently found in recommended practices for infants and young children:

1. <u>MTSS</u>—The curriculum is organized as a *multi-tiered system of support (MTSS)* that provides specific strategies to meet the developmental needs of every child, regardless of the level of support necessary to promote effective learning.

2. <u>Blended practices</u>—The curriculum blends theory, strategies, and practices from early childhood education and early childhood special education (ECE/ECSE) to meet the needs of diverse groups of young children.

3. <u>ABI</u>—The curriculum uses *activity-based intervention (ABI)* as a strategy for providing teaching/intervention in the context of naturally occurring, *developmentally appropriate* routines and activities.

Each of these practices can support practitioners who serve infants and young children in home and classroom settings. The next section explains them in more detail.

1. Multi-tiered System of Support

The AEPS-3 Curriculum is designed to address the need for a continuum of differentiated strategies to effectively serve diverse groups of young children. Although MTSS has been around for some time as a means of offering different levels or intensities of teaching/intervention support, the notion of MTSS in early childhood emerged from discussions about how to apply response to intervention (RTI) in early childhood programs.

In 2019, the Division of Early Childhood (DEC) developed a position paper to address issues associated with MTSS in early childhood. As defined in the paper, MTSS "is a system-wide framework for delivering effective and efficient educational services and supports, matched to the needs of all learners for acquisition of essential skills, knowledge and dispositions, resulting in improved learner performance across one or more settings" (DEC, in press).

According to Carta and Miller Young (2019), the following principles characterize early childhood MTSS:

1. All children can learn and achieve when they are provided with high-quality services and supports to match their needs.

2. Instruction should focus on academic, social-emotional, and behavioral goals.

3. Children showing signs of delay should be identified as early as possible and provided with a level of instructional intensity to match their needs.

4. Interventions to address children's needs should be designed by collaborative teams that include parents, administrators, teachers, and other instructional staff. These interventions should be guided by student data and informed by evidence-based practices.

5. Children's responses to intervention should be monitored continuously, and explicit data-based decision rules should be in place for making adjustments in intervention.

6. All intervention should be based on evidence-based practice implemented with fidelity.

The AEPS-3 Curriculum is designed to meet the definition of an MTSS that helps teams differentiate approaches or levels of support for young children with diverse needs. Other widely known MTSS approaches include the Pyramid Model (Hemmeter et al., 2016), Recognition and Response (Coleman et al., 2006), and Building Blocks (Sandall et al., 2019).

2. Blended Practices

The term *blended practices* refers to "the integration of practices that can be used to address the needs of all children in inclusive settings" (Grisham-Brown & Hemmeter, 2017, p. 7). Practices that blend theories, strategies, and supports from general and special education are essential to effectively addressing the increasing diversity in contemporary early childhood settings. The AEPS-3 Curriculum draws from traditional child development theories such as Piaget's (1955) cognitive developmental theory and Bronfenbrenner's (1994) ecological systems theory, as well as behavioral principles such as Skinner's (1953) theory of behavior, that serve as the foundation for effective teaching/intervention practices in special education.

The AEPS-3 Curriculum draws on the work of Grisham-Brown and Hemmeter (2017), who proposed a curriculum framework based on identifying appropriate outcomes for all, some, and individual children. Goals/outcomes at each curriculum level are matched with detailed teaching/intervention strategies that provide increasing support:

- *Universal strategies* appropriate for teaching all children

- *Focused strategies* for targeted instructional outcomes

- *Specialized strategies* for children who require individualized support

The curriculum framework suggests a set of practices that serves as the foundation in any early childhood setting for helping children acquire common outcomes such as early learning standards—practices that rely on positive interactions between children and adults, a well-organized learning environment, and young children's hands-on learning.

3. Activity-Based Intervention

The AEPS-3 Curriculum includes an emphasis on delivering intervention/instruction that is derived largely from the four basic elements of ABI (Johnson et al., 2015):

1. ABI makes use of three types of activities:

   - Child-initiated activities, such as learning centers and free play

   - Regularly occurring routines, such as meals and transitions

   - Small-group activities that adults plan and guide, such as storytime

2. ABI encourages multiple and varied learning opportunities so that teaching occurs with sufficient frequency and across a variety of people and materials to support generalization of skills.

3. Functional and generative goals increase children's independence and allow them to use a variety of responses across settings.

4. ABI uses consequences that are natural or logical to the task to provide immediate and relevant feedback as children learn new skills.

Table 1.1. Evidence-based practices and skill areas

Evidence-based practice	Skill area(s) aligned with practice
Differential reinforcement	Play, engagement, and appropriate behavior
Correspondence training	Engagement, play, academic skills, and health/safety skills
High-probability requests	Request-following, social skills, and communication skills
Modeling, mand-modeling, incidental teaching, and naturalistic time delay (milieu teaching)	Requesting, choice making, saying/signing single/multiple words, play expansions, and responding to questions
Graduated guidance	Safety skills, feeding self, and dressing
System of least prompts	Play skills and dressing
Constant time delay Progressive time delay	Play skills, academic skills (counting, reading), prewriting, engagement, peer imitation, and communication skills
Simultaneous prompting	Play skills and home skills
Peer-mediated instruction	Social skills

Other Evidence-Based Practices (EBP)

The AEPS-3 Curriculum incorporates a variety of evidence-based teaching/intervention practices in ECE/ECSE, defined as "practices and programs shown by high-quality research to have meaningful effects on student outcomes" (Cook & Odom, 2013, p. 135). The AEPS-3 Curriculum uses principles and research-based strategies associated with such evidence-based practices as embedded instruction, *data-driven decision making (DDDM)*, and specific systematic instruction, each of which is addressed in the paragraphs that follow. Table 1.1 lists the strategies identified throughout the AEPS-3 Curriculum along with the skills that are best aligned with each strategy.

Embedded Instruction. Embedded instruction occurs when a child is engaged in preferred activities and an adult intentionally uses that activity as an opportunity to practice or demonstrate a target skill by expanding, modifying, or taking a logical next step with the skill. The activity itself provides feedback based on the child's response. Embedded instruction, which is an underlying process of ABI, has been shown repeatedly to be an effective method for helping infants and young children with and without disabilities acquire or expand skills. Embedded instruction has been used successfully to teach preacademic, social, communication, motor, adaptive, and cognitive skills to young children. The AEPS-3 Curriculum embeds all AEPS-3 Test items in commonly occurring routines and activities that take place at home or in center-based environments such as child care and pre-K classrooms.

Data-Driven Decision Making. Data on individual children's performance levels are the best source of information for selecting appropriate teaching/intervention goals and effective teaching strategies matched to support needs. AEPS-3 is structured to provide evidence to guide decision making at each step in the linked system. Observing young children as they engage in daily activities yields a vast amount of information about what a child knows and is able to do over time. The AEPS-3 Test provides precise performance data to inform decisions about the most appropriate goals and objectives for each child. Likewise, data collected during teaching/intervention reveal information that is critical for adjusting outcomes and modifying teaching strategies. Progress monitoring data also provide updates to the assessment data from the test, forming a comprehensive profile of skills acquired across all areas of development.

Specific Systematic Instruction. The teaching strategies in the AEPS-3 Curriculum were selected because evidence demonstrates that they result in positive outcomes for young children who have disabilities or are at risk. Emerging evidence also indicates that some strategies (such as peer-mediated instruction and system of least prompts) are effective in teaching high-priority skills to children without disabilities.

CURRICULUM FRAMEWORK

The AEPS-3 Curriculum is designed intentionally to coordinate and integrate recommended practices and evidence-based research into a coherent, easy-to-use framework by suggesting differentiated instruction similar to an MTSS model, using evidence-based practices from both ECE and ECSE, and embedding those practices into home and classroom routines and activities. The sections that follow provide details about the curriculum's central elements and characteristics.

Inclusive of All Children From Birth to 6 Years, With and Without Disabilities

The AEPS-3 Curriculum makes it possible to teach critical early skills to all children. It should be useful for individual children in Early Head Start, children in Part C Early Intervention home settings, and groups of young children in preschool classrooms (blended, inclusive, or self-contained), including those with developmental and early academic problems who have not yet been formally identified for special services.

Based in Routines and Activities

The AEPS-3 Curriculum focuses on teaching during regularly occurring routines and activities at home and in the classroom. The curriculum is organized into 18 routines and activities (see Box 1.1 for a complete list) and emphasizes play and young children's successful participation in homes and classrooms. Practitioners use evidence-based strategies to teach specific developmental skills without removing young children from their daily routines and ongoing interactions with peers and family members.

Active & Outdoor Play	Field Trips
Arrival & Departure	Math
Art	Meals & Snacks
Bath Time	Music & Movement
Blocks	Nap & Sleep
Circle Time	Science (in Growing and Ready levels)
Diapering, Toileting, & Handwashing	Sensory
Dramatic Play	Technology (in Growing and Ready levels)
Dressing	Writing

Box 1.1   AEPS-3 Curriculum Routines and Activities

Organized Around Three Skill Ranges—Beginning, Growing, and Ready

In the curriculum, AEPS-3 items are grouped into three levels, making it possible to teach infants and young children developmental skills that are embedded in a consistent set of daily routines and activities. In early development, the times at which specific skills emerge differ from child to child, and some skill areas may develop more quickly than others for any given child.

The AEPS-3 Curriculum includes one complete volume for each skill level. Taken together, the three curriculum volumes provide comprehensive strategies for teaching developmental skills in each of the eight AEPS-3 areas to children who function developmentally between the ages of birth and 6 years.

- The Beginning level (Volume 3) includes foundational skills that *typically developing* children acquire in the first year to 18 months of life.

- The Growing level (Volume 4) generally covers those skills that require children to combine and apply earlier skills. These skills typically appear during the toddler years, from 18 months to 3 years of age.

- The Ready level (Volume 5) has more complex developmental and early academic skills that are typical of preschool-age children and considered important for success in school.

Tiered for Differentiated Teaching

The AEPS-3 Curriculum is arranged in differing tiers of support to help match teaching strategies to children's support needs. A central feature of the curriculum, this tiered model accommodates the varying rates at which young children learn skills in different developmental areas. This three-tiered model provides increasingly intensive intervention/instruction to help ensure the level of support needed for each child to participate successfully at home, in classrooms, and in community settings.

Each of the curriculum's three tiers of support—universal, focused, and specialized—contains a variety of suggestions for specific teaching strategies that are appropriate for children with and without disabilities. Figure 1.2 shows the tiered model of the AEPS-3 Curriculum framework in more detail, indicating for whom that tier's strategies are intended, the types of strategies the tier includes, and the frequency of data collection. As the figure shows, data collection occurs least frequently in Tier 1, more frequently in Tier 2, and most frequently in Tier 3. Refer to Figure 1.2 in the discussion that follows. The teaching strategies in Tier 1 are for all young children in high-quality early childhood learning environments. The teaching strategies in Tier 2 are for some children who need extra help, and those in Tier 3 are for the few children who need individual help.

Tier 1: Universal Support   The support strategies in Tier 1 reflect best practices in caregiving and teaching. They are designed to provide safe, healthy learning environments and high-quality, developmentally appropriate curriculum for ALL young children. Within the universal support tier, developmental skills constitute core curriculum content for infants and young children. Daily routines and activities provide meaningful teaching and learning contexts for every young child with or without disabilities. Each of the curriculum's routines and activities lists suggestions for the following:

- Arranging daily routines and activities
- Facilitating appropriate, positive social interactions
- Selecting materials

Universal strategies may not work well for every child, and some children may need alternatives that require more input and structure to learn specific skills.

Tier 2: Focused Support   The strategies within Tier 2 build on the routines and activities of the universal tier and involve relatively minor modifications and adaptations for SOME children who need extra help to ensure more frequent and focused learning opportunities. The AEPS-3 Curriculum offers a range of specific strategies for the following:

- Identifying targeted outcomes
- Adapting and modifying routines, activities, and environments

Figure 1.2.   Tiered Model of the AEPS-3 Curriculum Framework. This illustration depicts the three tiers of the AEPS-3 Curriculum (universal, focused, and specialized teaching strategies), indicates for whom the strategies are intended, and briefly describes the types of strategies included at that tier. Data are collected with increasing frequency the higher the tier.

- Incorporating child preferences, family priorities, and peer supports

- Selecting specialized materials

- Modifying teacher prompts

Tier 3: Specialized Support   Tier 3's specialized support strategies are for the FEW individual children who need intensive supports to address their unique learning goals, such as those found on IFSPs and IEPs. Specialized strategies build upon, rather than replace, universal and focused levels of teaching. Strategies at the specialized tier are individualized to help children acquire prerequisite and foundational skills more quickly and thus increase their participation in high-priority routines and activities. Specialized strategies emphasize the following:

- Suggestions for selecting high-priority skills to teach that emphasize positive *caregiver*–child relationships and promote peer interactions

- Specific individualized prompts and cues

- Materials and interactions that are specific to children with a variety of identified disabilities

Designed for Continuous Monitoring and Evidence-Based Decision Making

Monitoring children's progress is a central element of the AEPS-3 Curriculum, especially as they learn new skills. Monitoring children's progress is important for both teachers and parents and provides the necessary basis for making teaching decisions. Chapter 5 in this volume provides specific directions for matching how often to collect progress monitoring data with the level of teaching/intervention support provided (with data collected more often as the support level increases). The AEPS-3 Test's scoring system and organization are designed to allow you to monitor and track progress with precision as new skills emerge and children master them.

Data that show children's progress (or lack thereof) are essential for determining the level of support children need to learn new skills. For efficiency's sake, it is important to move to new outcomes as soon as children master skills. Likewise, when progress monitoring data indicate progress is not occurring or is slower than desired, it is necessary to modify outcomes and/or teaching strategies. In the AEPS-3 linked system, assessment data are used to make decisions about selecting learning outcomes and goals for individual children, and progress monitoring data are used to move to new outcomes and goals and different teaching/intervention strategies.

2

AEPS®-3 Curriculum Content and Organization

The AEPS-3 Curriculum covers eight developmental areas across the age range from birth to 6 years: Fine Motor, Gross Motor, Adaptive, Social-Emotional, Social-Communication, Cognitive, Literacy, and Math. The skills included in each *area* of development are the same for the AEPS-3 Test and Curriculum components. The curriculum embeds specific skills from each developmental area into routines and activities for teaching at home and in classrooms.

CURRICULUM LEVELS

For ease of use, the AEPS-3 Curriculum is organized in three separate volumes by developmental age or skill range: **Beginning, Growing,** and **Ready.** When selecting which curriculum level is appropriate, it is important to use AEPS-3 Test results to select the developmental content that is appropriate for each child.

Beginning Level (Volume 3)

Volume 3 contains the Beginning level curriculum. It includes developmental skills typically expected for infants and young children from birth to 18 months. The Beginning level contains the earliest skills in each of the eight areas, with a strong emphasis on early motor, social-communication, and interaction skills. Skills at the Beginning level are primarily foundational skills that are components of later, more complex skills. Following are some examples:

- Rolls from stomach to back

- Uses finger to touch or point

- Uses consistent approximations for words or signs

- Responds appropriately to soothing by adults

- Imitates familiar vocalizations

Volume 3 is a curriculum resource for practitioners working with infants and toddlers or older children who have significant disabilities. It is an ideal resource for professionals such as Early Head Start home educators and early intervention home visitors, who will find valuable strategies for teaching infants and toddlers with and without disabilities in the context of family routines and activities. As noted, the Beginning level also is recommended to meet the needs of early childhood special educators who serve chronologically older children who are eligible for services under Part B, Section 619, in blended, inclusive, and self-contained classrooms. The tiered, activity-based curriculum framework is effective for teaching a range of specific, developmentally early goals to very young children being served in a range of early childhood environments (such as child care). As a result, Volume 3 is a valuable resource for teachers and interventionists who are looking for help organizing routines, planning activities, arranging environments, selecting materials, and teaching specific skills in their infant classrooms and in infants' homes.

Growing Level (Volume 4)

Volume 4 contains the Growing level curriculum. It includes skills expected for typically developing older toddlers and young children, as well as older children with significant disabilities who are functioning at a developmental level from 18 months to 3 years. The Growing level includes the expanding, middle-range skills in each of the eight AEPS-3 areas and emphasizes social-emotional, early cognitive, adaptive, social-communication, and early literacy skills. Skills at the Growing level are basic, building on the earlier foundational and prerequisite skills targeted in Volume 3. Following are some examples:

- Jumps up and down in place

- Scribbles

- Uses 50 single words, signs, or symbols

- Meets behavioral expectations in familiar environments

- Indicates need to use toilet

- Identifies common concepts

Volume 4 is a curriculum resource for practitioners who work with older toddlers in home and classroom settings. Early Head Start home educators and Part C Early Intervention home visitors will find valuable strategies for teaching functional basic skills to young children with and without disabilities in the context of play and family routines and activities. The AEPS-3 Curriculum has been specifically designed to meet the needs of preschool special educators who serve diverse groups of developmentally younger eligible children under Part B, Section 619, in blended, inclusive, and self-contained classrooms. The tiered, activity-based curriculum framework is effective for teaching a range of specific, developmentally early goals and for improving the quality of routines and activities in any early childhood environment. Volume 4 is also a valuable resource for teachers and other providers who work with toddlers and who are looking for help organizing routines, planning activities, arranging environments, selecting materials, and teaching specific skills in their classrooms and in children's homes.

Ready Level (Volume 5)

Volume 5 contains the Ready level curriculum. It includes skills expected for typically developing preschoolers or children who are functioning in the 3- to 6-year developmental age range. Skills at the Ready level are the most difficult in each of the eight AEPS-3 areas and emphasize cognitive, social-communication, math, and literacy skills necessary for success in school. These skills tend to be complex combinations of basic skills contained in Volume 4. Following are some examples:

- Rides and steers tricycle

- Uses conversational rules

- Responds appropriately to warnings

- Counts forward to 10

- Names 12 frequently occurring letters

Volume 5 is a curriculum resource for preschool and kindergarten teachers who serve developmentally diverse groups of young children. AEPS-3 Curriculum strategies are especially useful for blended or inclusive classrooms that serve children with and without identified disabilities. The tiered, activity-based curriculum framework is effective for teaching a range of specific preschool goals and is designed to prepare children for kindergarten programs that follow developmentally appropriate practices. Because the curriculum strategies are equally appropriate for home and classroom use, the same skills can be addressed in the context of play, routines, and activities both at home and at school, promoting home–school coordination. Volume 5 is a valuable resource for classroom teachers who are looking for help organizing routines, planning activities, arranging environments, selecting materials, and teaching specific preschool skills in their classrooms and in children's homes.

CURRICULUM ROUTINES AND ACTIVITIES

The AEPS-3 Curriculum is organized into **18 routines and activities.** With the exception that the Beginning level does not include Science or Technology, the same routines and activities are included in the Beginning, Growing, and Ready levels:

- Active & Outdoor Play
- Arrival & Departure
- Art
- Bath Time
- Block Play
- Circle Time
- Diapering, Toileting, & Handwashing
- Dramatic Play
- Dressing
- Field Trips
- Math
- Meals & Snacks
- Music & Movement
- Nap & Sleep
- Science
- Sensory
- Technology
- Writing

For purposes of the AEPS-3 Curriculum, **routines** are common sequences of behavior that occur every day in homes and early childhood classrooms. Routines include Arrival & Departure; Bath Time; Diapering, Toileting, & Handwashing; Dressing; Meals & Snacks; and Nap & Sleep. **Activities** are more likely to be planned or facilitated by caregivers in specific locations and with specific materials and equipment. Activities include Active & Outdoor Play, Art, Block Play, Circle Time, Dramatic Play, Field Trips, Math, Music & Movement, Science, Sensory, Technology, and Writing.

Early childhood education can take place in many different settings, such as homes and classrooms, and AEPS-3 Curriculum strategies are appropriate for most settings. Some caregiving routines are equally relevant at home and at school, such as dressing, meals and snacks, and nap and sleep. Other routines are more common at home, such as bath time. Some occur most often in classrooms, such as science and math, although families can facilitate these activities at home. Others can occur at the playground or park, such as running and jumping (active and outdoor play). The AEPS-3 Curriculum emphasizes routines and activities that are meaningful and functional and focuses on teaching specific skills that promote participation and inclusion of all children.

Caregiving routines are highlighted in each curriculum volume and include Bath Time; Meals & Snacks; Dressing; Diapering, Toileting, & Handwashing; and Nap & Sleep. These routines are grounded in adult–child interactions during caregiving activities and are important to family life and sometimes to daily classroom schedules. Home educators and early interventionists often select caregiving routines that are high priority for parents as the context to address targeted skills. Specifically, in early intervention, caregiving routines serve as the foundation for developing *individualized family service plan (IFSP)* outcomes for young children with disabilities. In classrooms, caregiving routines often are closely related to program health and safety requirements and family-identified needs.

When children have difficulty participating in caregiving routines, the impact is generally high because of the importance of caregiver–child interactions, the high frequency of the routines, and the complexity of skills involved. Teachers in classrooms that have infants, toddlers, or older children with significant disabilities spend a considerable amount of time engaged in caregiving each day and need strategies for how to teach new skills in the context of routines. Children in preschool classrooms who can participate independently in eating, dressing, toileting, and naptime will have more time to devote to learning skills across other areas.

It is important to recognize the great variation among families in caregiving practices for eating, sleeping, dressing, and toileting routines, including but not limited to terminology and materials used and cultural traditions. Working on caregiving routines with parents at home means using as your teaching context the routines, terminology, and materials that are culturally appropriate for each family. Working in classrooms means knowing similarities to and differences between children's home routines and classroom expectations, as well as coordinating goals and strategies with parents.

Common routines and activities in early childhood classrooms tend to focus on prerequisite and early academic skills that are often addressed in learning centers and planned activities. Many of the AEPS-3 *Curriculum routines and activities* serve as the core of center-based classroom schedules, learning centers, and planned activities—for example, Arrival & Departure, Math, Science, Art, Writing, and Block Play. These are designed with emphasis on skills that promote success in school.

The 18 routines and activities in Volumes 3, 4, and 5 follow a consistent format:

- Name of the routine or activity

- Description of the routine or activity, including

  - How the routine or activity typically unfolds at home and school

  - Relevant developmental information across AEPS-3 areas

- Skill level/age range (Beginning, Growing, or Ready)

- List of *concurrent skills* by AEPS-3 area, with embedded learning opportunities as functional examples

- Narrative sections include the following:

  - **Universal Strategies**—Best practices for all children; Universal Strategies also includes two subsections, Interactions (useful teaching suggestions for all children) and Environment and Materials (overall suggestions for structuring the classroom environment and including materials that may be useful in teaching).

  - **Focused Strategies**—Strategies for teaching children who are struggling with a component of an outcome or whose development is stalled; these include a variety of relatively minor adaptations or modifications to help children catch up or keep up.

  - **Specialized Strategies**—Strategies for teaching children who need intensive support; these include a variety of specialized, individualized, and precise strategies.

Appendix A in this volume, Resources for AEPS-3 Curriculum Routines and Activities, provides additional resources to support the curriculum. The first section of this appendix presents lists of general resources to complement the curriculum, including books, journals, and web sites. The second part of the appendix is organized by the 18 routines and activities and includes lists of numerous complementary resources that are specific to each routine, such as articles and other readings, books, activities and ideas to try, and videos.

The AEPS-3 Skills Matrix in Appendix B spotlights individual skills by showing functional application across all routines and activities. Each skills matrix (there are eight total, one for each of the test's eight developmental areas) allows you to quickly and easily locate routines and activities that address specific AEPS-3 Test items. Ready-Set items are marked with a yellow flag.

In each skills matrix, the letter *B* corresponds with the Beginning level (Volume 3), *G* corresponds with the Growing level (Volume 4), and *R* corresponds with the Ready level (Volume 5). For example, the Fine Motor skills matrix indicates that AEPS-3 *goal* FM B1 (Activates object with finger) appears as a concurrent skill in 11 routines and activities. Most test items are linked to curriculum content in multiple routines and activities, which supports flexibility and opportunities for embedded learning. In this example, Active & Outdoor Play addresses the test item at both the Beginning and the Growing levels, as do several other routines and activities. Some items appear in more than one curriculum level because the emergence and growth of the skill occurs across a developmental span. As you plan teaching/intervention efforts, consider which level and which routines and activities offer content best suited to children's needs.

Some test items on the skills matrix, such as the one in the example above, also have *Foundation Steps* (denoted by *FS*) that break a skill into discrete component skills. For children who have difficulty learning new skills at the level of individual AEPS-3 Test items, the Foundation Steps provide an even more granular breakdown of component subskills that are either a sequence of developmental precursors or steps in task analyses.

AEPS-3 CURRICULUM QUICK START

The AEPS-3 Curriculum is a go-to resource for dynamic, creative, differentiated early childhood education strategies. It helps practitioners

- Design routines and activities that use best practices at the <u>universal tier</u>.

- Plan and apply adaptations and modifications for children who need extra help learning at the <u>focused tier</u>.

- Implement specialized teaching for children who need intensive help to participate in ongoing routines and activities at the <u>specialized tier</u>.

The curriculum covers Fine Motor, Gross Motor, Adaptive, Social-Emotional, Social-Communication, Cognitive, Literacy, and Math areas across the age range from birth to 6 years. The skills included in each area are the same for both the AEPS-3 Test and Curriculum. The curriculum embeds specific skills from each of these developmental areas into routines and activities for teaching and intervening across multiple environments.

Following are the basic steps for choosing the appropriate curriculum level, identifying initial routines and activities, and identifying any supports that might be needed within each.

Step 1

Select the curriculum level that matches the developmental level of the children on your caseload or in your classroom, identifying whether you might need other levels for children who have more or less advanced learning needs:

- <u>Volume 3, Beginning</u>: Addresses early foundational skills (birth to 18 months developmentally)

- <u>Volume 4, Growing</u>: Addresses expanding skills (18 months to 3 years developmentally)

- <u>Volume 5, Ready</u>: Addresses complex, coordinated preschool and school readiness skills (3 to 6 years developmentally)

Step 2

Identify the routines and activities in the volume(s) that are **priority contexts in which children need to learn new skills.** Begin with those that

- Have been identified by parents and caregivers as difficult times in the daily schedule at home, in the classroom, or in other environments (such as a community outing).

- Contain skills from developmental areas that commonly interfere with children's learning (motor, cognitive, communication, social).

- Will help children with specific disabilities be more independent at home or in the classroom.

Step 3

- Identify any supports required for individual or groups of children within each routine or activity (the expectation is that at any given time, you may be implementing strategies from all three tiers). Keep in mind that universal strategies are appropriate for <u>all children</u>—children with and without disabilities, at home and in classrooms. The Universal Strategies section in each routine or activity chapter provides suggestions to help improve the flow of routines and the quality of planned activities. For example, this section addresses the best ways to set up diapering routines at home and in classrooms.

- Focused strategies are beneficial for <u>some children who need extra help with specific skills</u> at home or school, and for small groups of children in classrooms. The Focused Strategies section in each routine or activity provides suggestions that can help children catch up and increase successful participation. For example, this section suggests changes in materials, supplies, and interactions during art activities to address social-emotional, social-communication, cognitive, and literacy skills.

- Specialized strategies are individualized for <u>children who need intensive support</u> and focus on increasing access to and participation in home and classroom routines and activities. The Specialized Strategies section in each routine or activity chapter provides information about prompting, positioning, and adaptive equipment to address the needs of children who have specific disabilities. For example, this section suggests adaptive utensils to use during meals for children who have motor impairments.

In summary, AEPS-3 Curriculum aligns with AEPS-3 Test items across eight developmental areas at three developmental levels. It identifies concurrent AEPS-3 skills that can be addressed efficiently using 18 routines and activities that occur regularly within the lives of young children. The curriculum also provides detailed suggestions and examples for three tiers of teaching/intervention strategies within the context of the routines and activities. The remaining chapters guide providers in making decisions about what young children need to learn and how to teach and monitor progress toward acquiring and using targeted skills.

3

Deciding What to Teach

Selecting goals and outcomes—deciding what each child needs to learn—is the second component of the AEPS®-3 linked system. AEPS-3 gives you flexibility in identifying goals and outcomes for young learners. This chapter offers ideas for using the components of AEPS-3, such as the test and the *Family Assessment of Child Skills (FACS)*, to help you decide **what to teach.** Both the test and the FACS have their own instructions, which Volume 2 discusses in detail, so this chapter focuses on briefly describing how to use them to select teaching/intervention outcomes. As you read the suggestions offered, consider your particular program's assessment requirements. For example, some programs require providers to complete an entire *curriculum-based assessment* two or three times a year on all children, whereas others may require more frequent data collection but only in the areas of concern for individual children.

The AEPS-3 Curriculum's organization into routines and activities is designed to provide a range of flexible options for selecting goals or outcomes. The way the curriculum is used will vary depending on a program's philosophy, design, the population served, regulations, and the context in which services are provided. For example, if you are an early intervention home visitor or a Head Start home educator, for individual children, you will identify routines that occur regularly in the home and that are a priority for the family. In contrast, if you work in a blended/inclusive preschool classroom, you will select developmentally appropriate routines and activities that occur in your classroom setting, such as those for Circle Time & Storytime and Writing included in these volumes.

The AEPS-3 Curriculum is designed to allow professionals to address the learning needs of classroom groups of children, small groups of children, and individual children. In addition, the curriculum can be used as a standalone resource for any practitioner who is interested in implementing intentional strategies to teach developmental or content goals in the context of ongoing routines and activities, across a variety of settings.

DECIDING WHAT TO TEACH FOR ALL CHILDREN

Because AEPS-3 Test items align with many states' early learning standards and other program standards and outcomes, such as the Head Start Early Learning Outcomes Framework, implementing the AEPS-3 Curriculum allows programs to address important federal, state, and program goals and outcomes for specific groups of children such as children from birth to 3 years old who are receiving special education services or all 3- and 5-year-olds. To ensure that you are basing decisions about what to teach on sound assessment practices, AEPS-3 offers several strategies:

- **Use the concurrent skills for routines and activities:** One way to determine what to teach is to select outcomes from the list of concurrent AEPS-3 skills that appears near the beginning of each curriculum routines and activities chapter. Concurrent skills are AEPS-3 skills that can be easily embedded and taught during regular occurrences of each particular routine or activity. You can select what to teach from the concurrent skills lists, based on your program's standards and outcomes. For example, if you are required to address early literacy skills with all children in your program, you would identify the routines and activities that address specific AEPS-3 literacy skills (such as Art, Circle Time & Storytime, and Arrival & Departure) and focus on teaching those outcomes whenever the appropriate routines and activities occur during the day.

- **Use the AEPS-3 Test goals data:** Some programs require providers to collect assessment information on all children in their program. Completing the AEPS-3 Test can be challenging for providers who serve large numbers of children. Although some programs require providers to complete the entire AEPS-3 Test on all children, it may be appropriate to collect data at the goal level only, rather than including all the associated objectives. AEPS-3 Test goals can prove useful in making decisions about what to teach children who are typically developing when you have no concerns about their development—for example, typically developing children in blended/inclusive classrooms or infants and toddlers in Early Head Start.

- **Use the AEPS-3 Ready-Set:** The *Ready-Set* assessment contains developmental and content-specific skills that children need for success in early primary programs. You can use it to efficiently assess all children in their final year of preschool or first year of kindergarten. Select learning outcomes for groups of 4- to 6-year-olds from the Ready-Set skills the majority of children need to master.

- **Use the AEPS-3 Family Report and FACS:** The routines and activities reflected in the *Family Report* and FACS include the same skills around which the curriculum is organized. A routines and activities–based approach can help you select learning goals for any child at home or in a classroom group. As part of the outcome development process, you can engage families in conversations about the routines and activities that are priorities and concerns for them at home and in the community. First, locate the corresponding priority routine or activity in the curriculum, and then identify the specific skills children need to participate successfully in each routine or activity of interest.

DECIDING WHAT TO TEACH FOR CHILDREN WHO DO NOT MAKE EXPECTED PROGRESS

As you implement the AEPS-3 Curriculum, you may notice that some children are unable to participate fully in the routines and activities or that their mastery of one or more associated skills appears to have stalled. To identify teaching outcomes to address these children's needs, you will first need to collect additional assessment information. Following are suggestions for pinpointing focused intervention/instruction to help some children learn specific skills:

- **Use the AEPS-3 Test:** If you have assessed only the AEPS-3 goals, conduct a more in-depth assessment by testing the objectives associated with the goals on which the child's development is not progressing. The child may need to learn a specific component skill before learning the more difficult goal. Conducting a fine-tuned assessment will help identify the specific skill components a child might be missing.

- **Use the Scoring Notes:** Go back to the developmental area(s) of the AEPS-3 Test where the child is not making expected progress and carefully review or collect precise data using the Scoring Notes. Some recurring issues associated with the skills might be causing the child trouble. For example, the child might be able to perform a skill only with particular people and materials or only in certain places. Or, the child might need a high level of assistance to perform skills correctly. Another possibility is that the child performs a skill, but the quality of performance is unacceptable. In each of these scenarios, you would need to focus your teaching/intervention on the aspect of the skill that is causing the problem (generalization, more independence, improved quality) rather than teaching a new or different skill.

- **Use the AEPS-3 FACS:** You can help caregivers complete the FACS in the areas(s) where the child is struggling to function and participate and then use information from the FACS to identify skills the family considers critical for successful participation in home and community routines and activities. Intervention/instruction can then focus on the specific skills both the professional and the family identify to give the child additional practice and support.

- **Group children with similar goals and outcomes:** You can use the assessment information from the AEPS-3 Test to identify small groups of children who may need to learn the same skill(s). By analyzing test data across groups of children, you are likely to see patterns that can help you design intentional small-group activities to focus on the skill(s) that several children need to learn.

DECIDING WHAT TO TEACH
FOR INDIVIDUAL CHILDREN WHO NEED SPECIALIZED SUPPORT

Some children may face significant challenges, such as the following, in acquiring the developmental goals and outcomes that all children need to learn:

1. Gaps in important milestones that same-age peers learned at an earlier age

2. Missing prerequisite skills that are components of more advanced skills

3. Issues that must be addressed before the child can move forward with learning new skills (specific disabilities or health issues, language differences, behavior challenges, food insecurity)

Children who are eligible for special services will have IFSPs or IEPs that list individualized goals or outcomes. It is essential that the team assigned to the child and family work together to develop a coordinated plan of intervention that addresses the child's disability, as discussed in Volume 1, Chapters 4 and 6. However, children not identified for special education services also may be missing prerequisites or developmental milestones, or they may have significant barriers to learning that must be addressed. The following sequence of steps will help you identify appropriate priorities for individual children. *Please note that these are steps in a sequence—NOT separate intervention options for determining learning outcomes.*

1. **Complete the AEPS-3 Family Report and FACS:** *Interview* the family to determine the routines and activities that are of highest priority in their family life. If the family has also completed the FACS, facilitate a discussion with caregivers to identify the specific skills the child needs to participate in difficult routines, and consider these skills when determining individual learning goals.

2. **Complete the entire AEPS-3 Test:** Assess all goals and objectives in the appropriate skill range across all eight areas of development, using the 3-point scoring system. The complete assessment will identify skills the child has **mastered** (those with a score of 2), skills that are **emerging** (score of 1), and skills **not yet in the child's repertoire** (score of 0). Analyze the results of the child's assessment data to identify any skills scored 1 or 0 over a period of time, and consider them as potential individual learning goals.

Occasionally, you may have difficulty identifying individual goals that are developmentally appropriate for children who learn new skills slowly or those who require specialized modifications and adaptations. For example, it might be difficult to identify specific AEPS skills to teach children with multiple disabilities (physical disabilities, sensory impairments). In those circumstances, **use the AEPS-3 Foundation Steps** to identify the incremental skills and behaviors that fall between AEPS-3 goals and objectives, and target those skills as individualized outcomes. These can be found in Volume 2, Chapter 3, as well as in the skills matrix in Appendix B.

3. **Cross-reference the AEPS-3 Test with data from the Family Report and FACS:** The Family Report identifies routines and activities that are priorities for the family, and the FACS identifies skills the child needs to participate in them. Compare the results of your AEPS-3 data analysis from step 2 with the results of the Family Report and FACS to identify two or three high-priority, maximum-impact goals and outcomes that meet all of the following criteria:

   - The goal is a priority for the family.

   - The goal will allow the child greater independence in daily routines and activities.

   - The child has not mastered the goal according to the AEPS-3 *criterion* (the child scored a 1 or 0 on the goal).

If both the professional and the family identify a skill as a priority, the child is likely to have many opportunities both at home and at school to learn and practice it.

4

Deciding How to Teach

Teaching/intervention is the third component of the AEPS-3 linked system. Practitioners who work in early childhood settings make a multitude of large and small teaching decisions each day, because individual infants and young children learn differently from one another. The AEPS-3 Curriculum provides practical, specific resources that match a full range of teaching/intervention strategies with infants' and young children's individual needs. The AEPS-3 Curriculum is designed to include children with and without delays and disabilities and is designed for practitioners working in both home and classroom settings.

TIERED TEACHING/INTERVENTION STRATEGIES

The curriculum organizes AEPS-3 skills in 18 routines and activities, with each routine or activity further organized in three teaching/intervention tiers, as introduced in Chapter 1 (see Figure 1.2), that match specific teaching/intervention strategies to individual children's needs:

- Tier 1, Universal Support: Strategies at this tier generally entail best practices in early childhood education (ECE) for ALL children.

- Tier 2, Focused Support: This tier's strategies offer suggestions for relatively minor modifications and adaptations, often temporary, to help SOME children whose progress is falling behind their peers at Tier 1.

- Tier 3, Specialized Support: Strategies at this tier offer more intensive and individualized teaching techniques that are necessary for the relatively FEW children who are learning prerequisite or foundational skills or who are not progressing adequately with support of Tier 2 strategies.

Overall, teaching/intervention strategies become more intensive and intentional at each tier, beginning with a strong foundation of teaching for all children and progressing to more specialized and individualized interventions for children who need higher levels of support.

Several assumptions underlie this tiered arrangement:

- All children require a high-quality early childhood program with environments, materials, schedules, and interactions that facilitate learning (Tier 1).

- The teaching/intervention strategies suggested for Tiers 2 and 3 are cumulative—they do not replace the strategies at earlier levels. Tier 2's focused support strategies build on the foundation of Tier 1's universal support strategies, and Tier 3's specialized support strategies build on the strategies in Tiers 1 and 2.

- Children's problems acquiring skills and behaviors are identified early and targeted for specific teaching interaction, regardless of the types or levels of need.

- As much as possible, children with disabilities should be taught using strategies similar to those used for their peers and should be included in routines and activities with their peers to the greatest extent possible.

- Monitoring progress toward learning goals and outcomes becomes more frequent and specific as interventions become more intensive (see Chapter 5 for details).

The AEPS-3 Curriculum

- Provides increasingly frequent opportunities to learn within routines and activities for children who need extra practice to acquire skills both at home and in classrooms.

- Arranges more specific teaching interactions within routines and activities to match needs for increased structure both at home and in classrooms.

- Emphasizes adult–child interactions at home and at school and peer interactions in classrooms.

- Organizes teaching strategies for large groups, small groups, and individual teaching interactions in classrooms.

UNIVERSAL STRATEGIES

Based on child development and learning theories, the National Association for the Education of Young Children (Copple & Bredekamp, 2009) and the Division for Early Childhood Recommended Practices (Division for Early Childhood, 2014) have developed recommended guidelines for educating young children:

1. Young children learn best in the context of engaging interactive routines and activities.

2. The design of early childhood activities is most effective when it addresses young children's preferences and interests.

3. A program's sensitivity to the cultural and linguistic backgrounds of young children and their families is foundational for educational success.

4. Curriculum content and strategies should accommodate young children who are developing typically, those who are at risk, and those who have identified disabilities.

Universal teaching involves designing environments, activities, and interactions that create opportunities to learn skills that are important for success in present and future environments. Universal strategies in Tier 1 emphasize broad goals and outcomes, such as state ECE standards, that all children need to learn. At the universal support level, the AEPS-3 Curriculum provides recommendations for designing learning environments, selecting materials and equipment, and supporting social interactions. The Tier 1 recommended strategies embed a core set of early childhood goals and objectives in play, daily routines, and activities.

Physical and Learning Environments

Young children need a **schedule** of routines and activities that incorporates their learning needs. An ideal classroom schedule includes

- Opportunities for child-initiated and adult-guided activities

- Balance between movement and quiet activities

- Brief, focused activities

- Planned transition times when children are alerted to upcoming events

Consistent, predictable daily home schedules are beneficial and should include both ample opportunities for child-initiated activities and structure for learning during caregiving routines such as eating, bathing, and sleeping. Transition times at home also tend to go more smoothly when caregivers alert children to upcoming events that are outside of the typical daily routine. Children learn best when daily schedules are taught directly and implemented with consistency. In classrooms, a copy of the daily schedule should be posted, reviewed regularly, and referred to often. As at home, children should be alerted about transitions and unexpected schedule changes, such as those for an upcoming field trip.

Physical environments at home and in the classroom are best organized to allow children easy access to activities and materials while also maintaining health and safety standards. In classrooms, teachers generally create learning centers to cover all content areas, including art, blocks, dramatic play, math, music, sensory table, science, and writing. Learning centers should be designed around the interests of all children in the classroom, contain sufficient materials for multiple children to use the center at one time, and be arranged so noisy centers are separated from quiet ones. There should also be clear physical areas and visual boundaries for learning centers and limits on the number of children allowed to use a center at one time. Although families are unlikely to set up formal learning centers in their homes, young children still benefit from having access to learning experiences that include art activities, opportunities to engage with manipulatives, interactions with print material, and opportunities to express themselves through music, movement, and drama. In home and classroom environments, children need opportunities for active play activities both indoors and outdoors.

Materials

Developmentally appropriate materials give children opportunities to engage with their environments in ways that let them practice emerging skills and learn new skills. For young children, selecting and using learning materials can be a fun, dynamic endeavor that springs from everyday events and happenings. Following are some general suggestions:

- **Select materials that are based on children's immediate interests.** Children are more likely to interact with materials that reflect and expand on the most interesting aspects of their daily lives. For example, when children notice and talk about construction equipment near their homes or classrooms, adults can find books about construction and construction equipment, place toy construction trucks in play areas, or use simple art supplies (empty boxes, pipe cleaners, papers) to make construction sites.

- **Rotate learning materials regularly to provide novelty and increase engagement.** Children's interests change frequently, and when interest in a topic or materials fades, it is time for new supplies and activities.

- **Make sure enough materials are available for several children to play with preferred items at the same time.** When you realize a toy or material is a favorite, consider getting multiples of the item to prevent arguments, promote imitation, and encourage communication.

- **Choose objects that promote positive social interactions between and among children.** Young children can learn about turn-taking on a toy such as a rocking boat that safely holds only two at a time, whereas older children might take turns in a simple board game. Siblings can take turns helping set the table. Children will learn to cooperate if given opportunities to do so, such as by creating a shared art collage on a large piece of butcher paper.

- **Stock plenty of open-ended materials that allow children to use their creativity.** Young children do not need expensive toys to experiment, create, and manipulate. Scraps of material, empty containers, cardboard rolls, baskets, boxes, clothing that no longer fits, leaves, pinecones, shells, wallpaper scraps, and colored paper can offer endless opportunities for young children to engage in a variety of activities.

Social Interactions

One of the most prominent and pervasive aspects of universal teaching/instruction is the social interaction that occurs between children and adults and among peers. The ways adults interact with young children and support peer interactions create an important framework for young children's overall development. Positive interaction between young children and caregivers is one of the best predictors of later social competence with peers, and positive interactions with peers is a critical element of success in classrooms.

Positive Adult-Child Interactions   Trusting relationships with familiar adults encourage children to take chances in new learning situations and initiate their own learning opportunities. Strategies for developing nurturing relationships very early in life include

- Being responsive to infants' cues for attention, caregiving, and soothing
- Directing children's attention
- Naming and describing events, objects, and people in the environment
- Redirecting children rather than correcting them.
- Focusing on positive behaviors

Parallel strategies, once children develop language, are

- Following children's leads
- Having meaningful conversations
- Talking with each child at their own level
- Discussing topics that are of interest to each child
- Acknowledging children's efforts
- Giving children choices

To support a young child's learning, adults can engage in supportive practices that are known to encourage early learning, including teaching early concepts, providing feedback, and modeling language. Adults can promote concept development by asking children questions to encourage problem solving, creating opportunities for them to explore new ideas, and letting children try out their own solutions to common problems. Adults also hold the important role of providing ongoing, quality feedback, using whatever level of support each child needs to be successful and expand learning. Some of the most effective, convenient supports for learning at the universal tier are language modeling strategies that include conversations, open-ended questions, repetition and extension, self- and parallel talk, and introduction of new vocabulary.

Positive Child-to-Child Interactions　　Teaching positive interactions between and among children is another important element of the universal tier. One way adults can support these interactions is to arrange for children who are less socially competent to engage in activities alongside children who are more socially competent. Adults can also create opportunities for conversation among children during routine activities such as meals and snacks. Playing simple games such as I Spy or asking open-ended conversation starters such as "Tell me about what you did this weekend" can create natural opportunities for children to converse with one another. In most situations, children will talk more to each other if adults act as participant observers, being in the immediate vicinity and keeping careful watch rather than being directive. When communication is not taking place, adults can briefly model what a child might say to another child ("Ask your friend if you can play") or provide a hint about what a child needs to say or do to interact appropriately with a peer or sibling ("What should you say to your sister when you want to play with a toy she has?").

To promote a positive early childhood social environment, it is essential for caregivers who interact with young children to have consistent social expectations. Experts agree that these expectations should be expressed as brief positive statements of what the *caregiver* wants children to do, limited in number, and focused on behaviors that promote and support a positive learning environment. Here are some examples of appropriate rules for young children at home or in classrooms: "Walk in the hallway." "Use your inside voice." "Be kind to each other." "Tell your friends 'good morning!'"

FOCUSED STRATEGIES

When a child's development is not progressing or the child is struggling to learn some component of a goal, you may need teaching/intervention strategies at the focused tier to provide more frequent, intentional learning opportunities. Focused strategies may also be necessary when families have concerns about a specific skill on which a child needs continuous practice or when a teacher becomes aware that a child is falling behind or is not performing a skill as expected. In the AEPS-3 Curriculum, the strategies identified as focused are temporary in nature rather than permanent modifications in teaching/intervention. This means that a provider might use them only until a child acquires a targeted outcome and then revert to more universal strategies. Some focused strategies can be used with small groups of children who experience learning challenges, thereby increasing the efficiency of instruction.

It is important to remember that focused teaching/intervention is delivered in addition to, and within the framework of, universal strategies, such as when a child fails to make progress and needs focused strategies in some areas but continues to learn much of what they need to know through the universal curriculum. The AEPS-3 Curriculum offers the following focused tier strategies to supplement high-quality universal strategies.

Using Embedding Schedules

When you need additional opportunities for teaching targeted skills, one of the best ways to ensure that children get additional learning opportunities is to create an **embedding schedule:** a matrix that depicts specific opportunities to practice the targeted outcome(s) throughout the day. An embedding schedule lists each targeted goal/outcome, along with information about how the outcome will be embedded into each routine or activity in a child's daily home and/or school schedule. Figure 4.1 presents a sample blank embedding schedule that can be used for individual children or small groups, in home and classroom settings. Take these steps when using the embedding schedule:

1. Identify the desired outcomes from assessment data.

2. Clearly define each desired goal/outcome and write a concise description of it in the space provided in the box at the top of each column on the sample blank schedule.

3. List all or a portion of the daily schedule in the boxes in the left column of the blank schedule.

4. Find where the child's or group's targeted goal/outcome intersects with an activity in the daily schedule. In the corresponding box on that row of the blank schedule, add a bullet that concisely describes the focused strategy adults will deliver to create an embedded learning opportunity.

Providers may develop embedding schedules for groups of children who are working on similar outcomes but perhaps different specific skills. A common example is when all children are working on identifying letters but each child is working on the letters in their own name.

Creating Easy, Effective Adaptations and Modifications

For children who need extra help, providing adaptations and modifications can increase attention, improve ability to follow directions, and promote independent participation. Following are some examples:

- If a child fails to pay attention during long activities, you might increase the child's chances for success by preparing shorter versions of the activities in advance.

- If a child has difficulty processing information when you provide task directions, consider giving the child additional time to respond after each direction.

- To simplify a task for a child or increase their independence in completing it, make available easier-to-use materials such as adapted scissors, chunky crayons, or puzzles with handles.

- Visual schedules can also provide children with information about what comes next in the day or the correct sequence of steps to complete tasks such as putting away materials or washing hands.

- Some children may be able to pay attention longer and participate more fully in activities when they have access to special equipment—for example, special seating such as a sensory seat, ball chair, rocker, or floor sitter.

- Other children might perform adaptive skills more independently if they can use adapted eating utensils such as bowls, spoons, or cups or if their clothing has elastic waistbands and Velcro fasteners to make dressing easier.

- Assistive technology can also increase children's independence—for example, the variety of available adapted switches allows young children to independently use battery-operated toys, small electronics, and computers.

Embedding Schedule

DIRECTIONS: This template can be used for individual children or small groups of children, in home and classroom settings. Follow these steps:

1. Identify targeted goals or outcomes from the assessment data.
2. Clearly define each desired goal/outcome, and write a concise description of each one in the blanks provided at the top of each column (one goal or outcome per column).
3. List all or a portion of the daily schedule in the boxes in the left column of the template.
4. Find the blank box in the template where the targeted goal/outcome from the top row intersects with an activity in the daily schedule column at left. In that box, write a bullet point that concisely describes the focused strategy adults will deliver to create an embedded learning opportunity.

Daily Schedule	Goal/Outcome: _____ Focused Strategy	Goal/Outcome: _____ Focused Strategy	Goal/Outcome: _____ Focused Strategy

Assessment, Evaluation, and Programming System for Infants and Children, Third Edition (AEPS®-3), by Bricker, Dionne, Grisham, Johnson, Macy, Slentz, & Waddell. © 2022 Brookes Publishing Co. All rights reserved.

Figure 4.1. Sample blank embedding schedule. An embedding schedule is a matrix (table) that shows opportunities to practice targeted goals or outcomes throughout the day. It lists each targeted goal/outcome, along with information about how the outcome will be embedded in each routine or activity in a child's daily home or school schedule.

- For children who cannot communicate their wants and needs verbally, a wide array of augmentative and alternative communication (AAC) devices is available ranging from general use items such as iPads to specially designed Tobii Dynavox AAC devices. A variety of communication applications is available for the iPad, such as Proloquo2Go, iCommunicate, and Voice4u.

Forming Small Groups

Small groups are another effective focused strategy:

- For children whose learning has not progressed, a small group can be designed to provide efficient teaching opportunities in which each child receives a minimum of six learning opportunities in sessions lasting no longer than 10 minutes. Ideally, children in small groups should participate in random order, with no one child receiving more than two learning opportunities in a row in order to maintain children's attention.

- Small groups are also useful for children who are struggling to learn a similar skill—for example, several children who are learning the letter A.

- You may also use a small group to teach different skills to each child in a common activity—for example, when one child is learning to identify the letters in their name and another child is working on writing the letters in their name while engaged in an art activity.

- You can teach different skills to different children in the group—for example, during a literacy activity, one child may be working on letter identification while another is working on numbers.

Among the advantages of small-group teaching are that

- Children may also learn nontargeted skills from their peers in the group

- It is an efficient use of a teacher's instructional time

- Children may learn social behaviors that are useful in other early childhood play and learning environments, such as waiting for a turn, interacting with other children, and paying attention within the context of group activities

Using Peer-Mediated Instruction

With peer-mediated instruction, a competent peer shows a child how to perform a communication or social skill and reinforces the desired targeted outcomes. This strategy can provide assistance and motivation to children who are working on learning particular skills. Considerations for implementing peer-mediated instruction include ensuring that the peer has already learned the skill being taught, planning motivating activities that are of interest to the children, and training and supporting the peer. For example, if a child needs to be reminded to stay seated and remain on task during a large-group activity, a peer might be taught to tap the child on the shoulder and show a visual cue, such as a picture of a child sitting down, to remind the other child to stay in place during the activity. Another example is if a child needs to learn to take turns, a more socially competent peer could be taught to verbally and physically support the other child in taking turns.

Scaffolding

The focused strategy of **scaffolding** involves providing targeted assistance to children and then fading the support as the child no longer needs it. Scaffolding techniques include hinting, explaining, modeling, and questioning. For example, if a child's goal is to follow a social routine, the caregiver or teacher may give hints such as asking questions to help a child remember the next step ("What comes next?"). To ensure that scaffolding is effective, teachers must provide only the support necessary for the child to grasp a new concept or learn a new skill and then gradually withdraw that support when the child no longer needs it. To accomplish this, teachers need to make moment-to-moment decisions about how much support each child needs and when to withdraw it.

SPECIALIZED STRATEGIES

When children have needs that cannot be addressed with strategies from the universal or focused tiers, strategies from the specialized tier are needed. These strategies build upon, rather than replace, universal and focused strategies.

Specialized strategies are designed individually to address foundational and prerequisite skills or to address unique barriers to learning that prevent children from learning new skills. Many children with individualized family service plan (IFSP) outcomes and *individualized education program (IEP)* goals need specialized support strategies to make adequate progress. At times, young children without disabilities might also need specialized strategies to acquire a concept or learn a skill. For example, for children who have short attention spans, it is necessary to teach attention to task before teaching concepts such as color or shape identification that are taught to all young children in early learning settings. Similarly, children must learn pincer grasp and wrist rotation before they can feed themselves independently. Here are some helpful suggestions for selecting specialized strategies:

- Complete an AEPS-3 Test on the child. **Results from the assessment will help you identify appropriate individualized goals and skill sequences for teaching them.**

- Gain a thorough understanding of each child's specific disabilities and the implications of their effects on the child's development. Physical and sensory impairments alter how children receive, process, and respond to intervention. Providers should be aware of how specific diagnoses such as autism, Down syndrome, or cerebral palsy affect children's learning, as well as the specific interventions and strategies that have proved effective for children with those diagnoses.

- Get to know each child's learning preferences. This will help you choose individualized prompts, cues, and materials that will motivate the child to learn. Some other important elements to consider include

  - The ways in which the child prefers to receive new information and explore new materials (auditory, visual, tactile)

  - Appropriate wait times before expecting a response from the child

  - The most effective and appropriate modes of response (physical, verbal, technological)

  - Types of reinforcement that most effectively motivate the child's persistence, engagement, and skill mastery

ABC Design for Individualized Teaching/Intervention

Specialized teaching strategies require careful attention to three elements of each teaching interaction:

1. Antecedents (the conditions that set the occasion for a child to demonstrate the skill)

2. Well-defined behaviors and responses expected from the child

3. Consequences (the results of correct and incorrect responses)

Together, these three elements constitute **ABC design** (Antecedents, Behavior, Consequences) for individualized teaching/intervention.

Antecedents   **Antecedents** are the many varied circumstances that set the occasion for a child to demonstrate a desired skill or behavior. Providers need to determine ahead of time where to teach, when to teach, and what materials are best to use. Ideally, antecedents for teaching individual outcomes are integrated within existing environments and ongoing activities at home and in the classroom. In addition, the most effective individual teaching interactions include antecedents for establishing joint attention, delivering task directions, and determining how long to wait for the child to respond. Once the child is paying attention, keep task directions short, clear, and direct, with the general intent to decrease the length of time it takes a child to respond.

Specific Behaviors   Another factor to consider before using a specialized strategy is the **specific behaviors** that define correct and incorrect responses, including criteria for acceptable and unacceptable responses. For consistency's sake, it is essential for all the adults who use a specialized strategy to have a shared understanding about what constitutes an acceptable and an unacceptable response. For example, if a goal is to have a child initiate a social interaction, the provider needs to indicate which of the child's behaviors would be considered correct (extending a toy to a friend, saying, "Play with me"; verbally greeting a peer) and which would be considered incorrect (grabbing a toy from another child; hitting a child and saying, "Mine!"). Specialized strategies can be used to address all AEPS-3 Test items, because each goal and *objective* is written as an observable behavior with specific criteria and examples.

For children who have IEP/IFSP goals and outcomes that fall between goals and objectives in the AEPS-3 sequences, use the AEPS-3 Foundation Steps for functional and developmental task analyses that identify specific incremental skills and behaviors. These can be found in Volume 2, Chapter 3, as well as in the AEPS-3 Skills Matrix in Appendix B of this volume, where they are indicated by the marker *FS*.

Consequences and Feedback   **Consequences** are what happens after the child responds. The child should receive immediate **feedback** for demonstrating the expected response, ideally because the environment is arranged so the child attains the goal via natural consequences. For example, if the child is supposed to say "more milk" and does so, receiving more milk is the natural consequence of demonstrating the expected response. If the child does not demonstrate the correct response, the teacher's role is to provide additional support to help the child demonstrate the expected behavior. For example, if the child doesn't say "more milk," the child's mother might verbally model the correct response and use a variety of prompts. These include but are not limited to

- Indirect verbal prompts (asking, "What should you do next?")

- Direct verbal prompts (saying, "Turn on the water")

- Gestures (pointing to the correct item)

- Visual or physical modeling (demonstrating how to write a letter)

- Pictorial prompts (showing pictures of the sequences of steps in a task)

- Partial or full physical prompts (putting a hand over or under the child's hand to perform a manual task)

Developing Intervention Plans

An **intervention plan** is a tool for designing specialized instruction. Specifically, the intervention plan

- Ensures that ABC sequences are embedded into ongoing home and classroom routines and activities

- Describes when, where, and with what the child will learn the priority skill and how to set the occasion for the learning (antecedent)

- Provides a clear definition of correct and incorrect responses (behaviors)

- Details what the environment, teacher, or peer is supposed to do if the child demonstrates a correct response (provide reinforcement) or an incorrect response (provide additional support or consequences). Figure 4.2 presents an example of a completed intervention plan, and Figure 4.3 provides a blank template to be filled in with the ABC sequence information needed to deliver specialized instruction. (See also AEPS-3 Forms USB for a blank template.)

Evidence Base for Specialized Strategies

A great deal of research has been conducted on teaching/intervention strategies at the specialized tier, demonstrating that the practices are effective and efficient for teaching children from birth to age 6 years, with and without disabilities. Generally, evidence-based strategies fall into three broad categories:

1. Consequence strategies

2. Enhanced milieu teaching

3. Response prompting procedures

Intervention Plan

aeps·3

Date(s) completed: _3/3/22_   Person completing form: _Maria_

Program: _Bright Beginnings Preschool_

Child's name: _Alex_

Skill: _Initiate social interactions using tablet computer communication application_

Before (A = Antecedent)	Possible Behavior Responses (B = Behavior)	After (C = Consequence)
1. **When:** *Free choice* 2. **Where:** *Student-chosen classroom activity center (blocks area, library, etc.)* 3. **With what:** *Student-chosen materials (blocks, books, tablet with GoTalkNow app, etc.)* 4. **How:** • **Establish joint attention:** *Join the child in play by taking turns with the activity (take turns stacking blocks in a tower and knocking it down, take turns turning pages in a book, etc.).* • **Establish a topic:** *Talk with the child about the activity using target verbs (teacher says, "Let's build," "Put the block on," "Push it down," "Read the book," "Turn the page," etc.).*	**Correct response (+)** *Alex presses the correct button on the tablet to initiate the correct verb within 5 seconds.*	**Correct response (+)** *Teacher continues play with the action Alex requested and provides verbal feedback specific to the request ("Okay, I will build a tower").*
• **Make a request in a format the child can understand:** *Interrupt the play routine and look expectantly at the student.* • **Wait for the child to process:** *Wait 5 seconds for the child to initiate using the iPad.*	**Incorrect responses (−)** • *Alex does nothing within 5 seconds.* • *Alex reaches for the toy but does not initiate with the button on the tablet.* • *Alex presses the button for an incorrect verb (selects READ while playing in the blocks area).*	**Incorrect responses (−)** • *Teacher models the correct response (pushes the correct button) and says, "Do this."* • *Teacher waits 5 seconds for Alex to imitate.* • *If Alex does not imitate, teacher provides physical prompt.* • *Teacher continues playing and provides verbal feedback specific to the task ("You want to build").*

Assessment, Evaluation, and Programming System for Infants and Children, Third Edition (AEPS®-3),
by Bricker, Dionne, Grisham, Johnson, Macy, Slentz, & Waddell. © 2022 Brookes Publishing Co. All rights reserved.

Figure 4.2. Sample completed intervention plan. An intervention plan is a tool for designing specialized instruction. It ensures that ABC (Antecedent, Behavior, Consequence) sequences are embedded in ongoing routines and activities; describes when, where, and with what the child will learn the priority skill and how to set the occasion for the learning (Antecedent); clearly defines correct and incorrect responses (Behavior); and specifies what the environment, teacher, or peer should do when the child responds correctly and incorrectly (Consequence). The sample plan shown here for a child named Alex focuses on initiating social interactions using an app on a tablet computer.

Intervention Plan

Date(s) completed: _____   Person completing form: _____

Program: _____

Child's name: _____

Skill: _____

Before (A = Antecedent)	Possible Behavior Responses (B = Behavior)	After (C = Consequence)
1. When: 2. Where: 3. With what: 4. How: • Establish joint attention: • Establish a topic:	Correct response (+)	Correct response (+)
• Make a request in a format the child can understand: • Wait for the child to process:	Incorrect responses (−)	Incorrect responses (−)

Figure 4.3. Sample blank intervention plan. This template is designed to be filled in with the ABC (Antecedent, Behavior, Consequence) sequence information needed to deliver specialized instruction.

It is beyond the scope of this curriculum to describe every one of the specialized instructional strategies associated with each of these categories. Collins (2022) and Grisham-Brown and Hemmeter (2017) offer detailed descriptions, and Table 4.1 provides an overview of specific teaching/intervention strategies for the specialized tier.

Specialized strategies also are available for working with children who have specific disabilities. Table 4.2 presents a partial list of disability-specific strategies. The curriculum also suggests specialized, assistive, and adaptive equipment and materials associated with each specific routine or activity.

Table 4.1. Teaching/intervention strategies for specialized tier

Category	Strategy	Use of strategy	Process
Consequence strategies	Differential reinforcement	Used alone or in combination to increase positive behaviors and decrease negative or undesired behaviors	• Reinforce the desired behavior and ignore undesired behaviors. • Reinforce an incompatible behavior—any positive behavior the child cannot physically do at the same time as the undesired behavior. • Reinforce a positive alternative behavior—any behavior other than the undesired behavior. • Reinforce the omission of the behavior, providing reinforcement when the child is not engaging in the undesired behavior for a specified period of time. • Reinforce a lower rate of the undesired behavior, providing reinforcement whenever the child engages in the negative behavior fewer times than previously.
	Correspondence training	Used to reinforce a child for verbalizing and carrying out a plan of engagement	• Prompt the child initially to verbalize how they will engage in an activity. • Reinforce the child for verbalizing their plan, and then reinforce again for actually engaging in the activity as verbalized.
	High-probability requests	Used to increase rate of appropriate responding	• Make three to five high-probability requests (requests the child is likely to follow). • Make one lower-probability request (a request the child is less likely to follow). • Make all requests in rapid succession.
Enhanced milieu teaching/ naturalistic language intervention	Responsive interaction	Used in combination to support language production during interactions between peers/ teachers and children with language delays	• Follow a child's lead when they look, point, move toward, or comment. • Comment on what the child is doing. • Respond to and expand upon the child's attempts to communicate. • Provide language models that are somewhat more difficult than the child's current level.
	Environment arrangement techniques	Used to increase opportunities and motivation to communicate	• Limit access to an activity or material (place it out of reach or in a sealed container) until the child communicates. • Perform an unexpected event or create a spectacle. • Provide insufficient materials for a child to engage in an activity.
	Prompting strategies	Used in various combinations to promote new skills in communication or expand on current levels of communication	• Provide models for the specific words, gestures, or signs a child is learning (modeling). • Give the child a direction to say or tell, and then model the response (mand model). • Wait a specific period of time for the child to communicate before providing a model/mand model (time delay). • Be aware and take advantage of a child's interests, preferences, and engagement to motivate communication (incidental teaching).

Category	Strategy	Use of strategy	Process
Response prompting procedures	Graduated guidance	Used to support performance of motor tasks by providing dynamic levels of physical support	• Provide physical prompts as needed on a moment-by-moment basis. • Provide the minimum amount of prompting needed to support the child in performing a task. • Increase physical support as soon as the child begins to make mistakes. • Decrease physical support as soon as the child begins to perform the task independently.
	Most to least prompting	Used to teach new and unfamiliar fine and gross motor skills	• Begin by using the most intrusive prompt a child needs to perform a new skill. • Gradually reduce support by using less intrusive prompts as the child begins to perform the new skill with full support. • Remove prompts entirely when the child can perform the skill independently.
	System of least prompts	Used to teach new skills when the child performs some parts or steps of the task more independently than other parts or steps	• Allow time initially for the child to perform the task, or a step in the task, independently. • Provide the least amount of assistance possible for the child to perform the task or step successfully if the child does not perform it after a specific wait time. • Gradually increase the level of support for each task or step after each wait period. • Use a fully controlling prompt, if necessary, to ensure that the child performs the expected response.

	Time delay	Used to promote a child's ability to initiate and complete tasks	• Provide a task direction and immediately provide a prompt that ensures that the child completes the task (0 second delay).
			THEN
			• Provide a task direction and wait a period of time before prompting the response by either:
			    Waiting a consistent number of seconds before providing the controlling prompt (constant time delay).
			        OR
			    Gradually increasing the amount of time between the task direction and a prompt (progressive time delay).

	Simultaneous prompting	Used to ensure correct responses by interspersing training trials for skills with probes	• Provide a task direction and immediately provide a controlling prompt that ensures that the child performs the expected response. • Prompt the child to complete the task during all training trials • Conduct probe trials in which no prompting is provided (before and/or after training trials) to see how well the child can perform the skill independently.

Table 4.2. Specialized strategies for working with specific disabilities

Disability	Specialized strategies
Physical disabilities	• Positioning equipment (floor sitters, standers, side-lying support devices) • Proper positioning techniques • Adapted eating utensils and writing utensils • Nonslip mats to secure materials on surfaces • Sign language • Oral-motor techniques (consult occupational therapist or speech-language pathologist) • Accessible environments • Augmentative and alternative communication (AAC) devices • Assistive technology
Visual impairments	• Materials with olfactory or tactile features • Accessible environments • Tactile symbols and books • Objects with contrasting colors • Slant boards • Assistive technology • Hand-under-hand prompting • Extra time to process information
Hearing impairments	• Sign language • Frequency modulation (FM) system • Preferential seating • Picture schedule to assist with transitions
Deafness-blindness	• Calendar system to assist with transitions • Object and tactile cues • Tactile books • AAC devices • Assistive technology • Tactile signing • Haptics • Extra time to process information
Autism	• Picture schedule to assist with transitions • Social Stories • Noise-reducing headphones • AAC devices • First-then boards
Intellectual disabilities	• Extra time to process information • Picture schedule to assist with transitions • Social Stories • AAC devices • Assistive technology • First-then boards

5

Progress Monitoring

Progress monitoring is the fourth component of the AEPS-3 linked system and refers to the ongoing evaluation of teaching/intervention effectiveness with individuals and groups of children. Progress monitoring data are used to inform future decisions about all facets of teaching/intervention.

Following teaching/intervention, teams need to determine its impact by collecting information to monitor progress. The AEPS-3 Curriculum is a tiered model of teaching/intervention with a tiered progress monitoring approach that requires more frequent and intense data collection as teaching strategies move from universal to focused to specialized support tiers. See Figure 5.1 for an overview of AEPS-3 progress monitoring. The sections that follow discuss the collection of progress monitoring data at each teaching/intervention tier.

UNIVERSAL (TIER 1) PROGRESS MONITORING

AEPS-3 offers several options for collecting progress monitoring data at the universal tier.

- States and programs typically align test items with state or agency outcomes and standards. Therefore, to monitor progress against state or agency outcomes, one option is to readminister all areas of the AEPS-3 Test two or three times a year. Because test content is aligned with state early childhood outcomes, progress on AEPS-3 Test items that were initially scored 0 or 1 and later scored 2 indicates progress toward state and agency outcomes.

- If your program does not require you to collect data on all state/agency outcomes or standards, and/or you are using AEPS-3 for children who are developing typically, you may readminister the AEPS-3 goals only or the Ready-Set two or three times a year.

- If you are a home visitor monitoring progress of children in homes, you may wish to readminister the AEPS-3 Family Report or Family Assessment of Child Skills (FACS) two or three times a year to get a sense of how parents perceive their children's progress toward participating in family routines and activities.

Data collected at the universal tier can be used to show children's growth over time as well as to determine which children need more intensive teaching/intervention and which skills or outcomes need the most attention. Teachers can use data collected at this tier to move children from universal to focused strategies on skills where an individual child or group of children is not making expected progress toward a targeted skill or concept. In summary, when using universal teaching/intervention, teachers or interventionists may readminister the entire AEPS-3 Test or Ready-Set, or use the Family Report or FACS to gather information about progress toward outcomes.

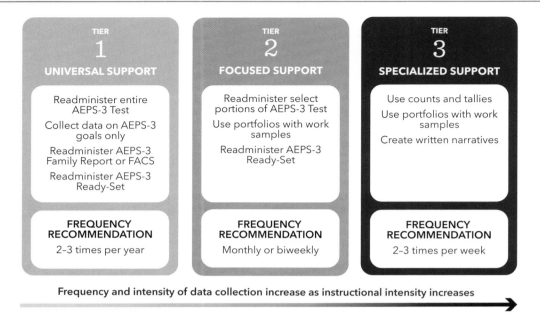

Figure 5.1. Overview of AEPS-3 Progress Monitoring. This graphic summarizes the general guidelines and frequency recommendations for progress monitoring at all three tiers of the AEPS-3 Curriculum (Tier 1–Universal, Tier 2–Focused, Tier 3–Specialized).

FOCUSED (TIER 2) PROGRESS MONITORING

When teachers or interventionists use focused strategies, they are providing more intensive intervention than that in Tier 1 to support a child or small group of children whose development is not meeting expectations or who are not acquiring targeted outcomes at the expected rate. Using a focused strategy requires data to be collected more frequently and intensively than for universal strategies. The AEPS-3 Test is organized to facilitate data collection on specific skills at various levels of specificity and intensity. Following are some possibilities for monitoring progress when using Tier 2 strategies:

- When monitoring performance on targeted test goals or *strands* of skills over time, conduct a probe at least bimonthly or monthly. Figure 5.2 shows a sample AEPS-3 Test goal for alphabet knowledge that could be used as a probe for continuous monitoring.

- Another way of monitoring progress on targeted outcomes is to use permanent products (described in more detail on page 37) assembled in a **child portfolio.** Child portfolios can be an excellent way to document change and show qualitative aspects of developmental change—for example, the quality of a child's movement, or the time lapse between an adult's direction and the child's performance of the expected behavior. A provider addressing the alphabet knowledge goal shown in Figure 5.2 might collect work samples of the letters a child can write. A home visitor working with an infant might collect photos or videos of the infant using a targeted motor skill. It is important that any work samples in the portfolio include an anecdotal note stating the date of data collection and a description of the targeted skill.

- A teacher who is tracking the progress of a child's early school readiness skills could readminister Ready-Set. Done on a regular basis, this can provide information about targeted outcomes that continue to require focused strategies. As the child acquires the skills in Ready-Set, the teacher then incorporates those skills into teaching at the universal tier and collects data less frequently.

Data collected at the focused tier can also be used to make decisions about what level of ongoing support a child needs:

- If the child is making expected progress on a skill and further progress is still needed, the teacher can continue the focused strategy.

- If the child has mastered the targeted outcome, the teacher can discontinue the focused strategy.

- If the child is not making expected progress, the teacher can try other focused support strategies or consider designing more intensive strategies at the specialized tier to help the child learn the skill.

Strand C Alphabet Knowledge

RS 29 **GOAL 1** **Names all uppercase and lowercase letters of alphabet Ⓡ**

CRITERION: Child correctly states or signs letter name of all handwritten or printed uppercase <u>and</u> lowercase letters in English or other alphabet, presented separately in random sequence.

Example: When presented with random upper- and lowercase letters, child correctly names each letter in alphabet in upper- and lowercase.

Note: Items in this strand may be modified for other languages. Criteria can be adjusted up or down depending on the number of letters in the alphabet of child's language.

Figure 5.2. Sample AEPS-3 Literacy Area Goal for Progress Monitoring. The sample goal shown here could be used as a probe for continuous monitoring.

In summary, when implementing focused teaching/intervention, professionals may collect data more often by using AEPS-3 Test strands, Ready-Set, and/or child portfolios.

SPECIALIZED (TIER 3) PROGRESS MONITORING

Strategies at the specialized tier are used to help children learn foundational, prerequisite skills needed to acquire learning goals for the general curriculum and participate in daily routines and activities. At this tier, data must be collected frequently to determine whether a particular specialized strategy is effective.

For each goal taught using specialized strategies, target collecting data a minimum of two or three times a week. Three broad techniques used to collect the data are permanent products, written descriptions, and counts and tallies.

Permanent Products

Permanent products include items such as photos, videotapes, and written documents. Such products can be catalogued to evaluate changes in a child over time. For example, photos of a child sitting in a chair might reveal changes in how the child sits when physical support is reduced, and videotapes collected over time might demonstrate changes in how a child interacts with peers.

Written Descriptions

A **running record** documents all behaviors the child performs over a short period of time. This data collection method often is used when providers are interested in a child's social development—for example, teachers may observe a child interacting with a peer or sibling and record social-emotional and play skills. Running records also are used frequently when documenting children's language development. Teachers or interventionists may write down everything a child says while interacting with others during play or a routine activity.

Professionals also may write **anecdotal notes** based on observing the child demonstrating a particular goal during a specific event or activity. Anecdotal notes should be accurate, include the context in which the behavior is observed, and focus on the specific behavior. Teachers might use sticky notes or adhesive labels or make notes on an electronic tablet.

Counts and Tallies

Four types of counts and tallies help in collecting progress data on the effectiveness of specialized strategies:

- **Checklists** record whether a child performed the skill (marked with a + symbol) or did not perform it (– symbol). Take care not to overuse this common strategy because checklists often lack the detail necessary for making informed decisions. Customized data collection sheets are available for many specialized strategies, including time delay, system of least prompts, and mand model. Specialized checklists collect data at a detailed level, such as the exact prompt a child needs to perform a skill or whether the child demonstrates the behavior before or after a prompt. Such detailed data can be useful when making adjustments to strategies at the specialized tier.

- **Event sampling** is used to determine how frequently a child performs a skill when given an appropriate opportunity—for example, it is an efficient way to tally how many times a child initiates a social interaction or how many steps a child takes. When there is a need for more specific information than a simple frequency count would yield, the scoring notes from the AEPS-3 Test can be valuable. These notes can be used in several ways:

  - To describe a child's performance when skill quality is problematic

  - To identify when a child needs help to complete the goal

  - To specify when a child's behavior interferes with performing the skill

  - To determine when a modification is necessary to address specific learning problems

- **Time sampling** is used to observe behaviors that occur with high frequency. To determine whether a child has engaged in a behavior or performed a skill, the teacher or interventionist may divide the *observation* period into small increments and collect data at the end of each interval. For example, if the goal is to have a child participate with other children during small-group time, the teacher could set a timer to observe the child's behavior every 30 to 60 seconds.

- **Rubrics** help measure a child's generalized use of skills taught using specialized strategies. For each skill, a rubric usually provides descriptors at three to five different levels of successful performance. Table 5.1 shows a sample progress monitoring rubric that measures four performance levels (novice, apprentice, proficient, distinguished) and five criteria (performance, setting, material, people, embedded learning opportunities performed correctly).

Table 5.1.   Sample progress monitoring rubric for a child's outcome

	1 Novice	2 Apprentice	3 Proficient	4 Distinguished
Performance	Struggling to meet expectations (baseline)	Approaching expectation	Meeting expectation (criterion)	Exceeding expectation
Setting	Across 1 or no settings	Across 2 settings **OR**	Across 3 settings **AND**	Across 4 or more settings **AND**
Material	With 1 or no materials	With 2-3 materials **OR**	With 4 materials **AND**	With 5 or more materials **AND**
People	With 1 or no people	With 2 people **OR**	With 3 people **AND**	With 4 or more people **AND**
Embedded learning opportunities performed correctly	25% or less	50% or less	90% or less	100%

With specialized strategies, it is necessary to collect progress monitoring data frequently, intensely, and precisely to allow team members to detect whether the strategies are effective. Teachers and interventionists should be prepared to continue using specialized strategies that help children make progress and to move to more advanced skills once children attain the criteria on skills that require specialized strategies. Conversely, teachers should be prepared to modify and replace specialized strategies if children are not making adequate progress.

In summary, permanent products, written descriptions, and counts and tallies are useful for monitoring progress when specialized teaching/intervention is employed.

AEPS-3 progress monitoring data collection provides information at each level of tiered teaching/intervention that informs every other component of the AEPS-3 linked system. Ongoing data collection accomplishes several things:

1. Updates initial assessment results

2. Indicates when goals/outcomes have been mastered or need to be adjusted

3. Informs providers and parents about the relative success of specific teaching/intervention strategies

As teaching/intervention strategies become more intensive and frequent, data collection also is increased in frequency and detail to match the level of effort and specificity invested to support each child's progress.

II

AEPS®-3 Curriculum Growing Routines and Activities

6

Active & Outdoor Play

Active & Outdoor Play includes children's participation in activities that help develop and use balance and mobility to acquire a vast array of motor skills (climb, ride, walk, run, jump, throw, kick, roll, swing, catch). The routines change significantly over time as young children become more aware of their environment (surfaces, toys, people, spaces) and interested in using materials in their active play, such as push and pull toys, riding toys, and playground equipment (balls, jump ropes, hoops and rings, climbing and hanging bars, slides and tunnels, swings, teeter-totters, merry-go-round, balance beam). The AEPS-3 Growing level of Active & Outdoor Play uses skills from eight developmental areas.

Concurrent Skills

The following concurrent skills are AEPS-3 skills that can be easily embedded and taught during regular occurrences of Active & Outdoor Play.

FINE MOTOR Growing Skills

B 1   Activates object with finger

B 2   Rotates wrist to manipulate object

B 3   Manipulates object with two hands, each performing different action

B 3.2 Aligns objects

Embedded Learning Opportunities

- *Rotates wrist while playing with toy, such as swinging baseball bat in circles*

- *Aligns cups by placing them side by side in the sandbox or lines up vehicles to make a train*

- *Manipulates object with both hands by digging in sand while holding bucket in one hand and shovel in other hand*

- *Holds chalk using three fingers to write or draw on sidewalk*

GROSS MOTOR Growing Skills

B 3   Walks avoiding people, furniture, or objects

B 3.1   Walks without support

B 4   Alternates feet going up and down stairs

B 4.1   Walks up and down stairs using support

B 4.2   Moves up and down stairs

B 4.3   Gets up and down from low structure

B 5   Runs while avoiding people, furniture, or other objects

B 5.1   Runs

B 5.2   Walks fast

B 6   Jumps forward

B 6.1   Jumps up and down in place

B 6.2   Jumps down from low structure

C 1.2   Bounces ball with two hands

C 1.3   Catches ball

C 1.4   Kicks ball

C 1.5   Throws ball overhand at target with one hand

C 1.6   Throws or rolls ball at target with two hands

C 2.2   Climbs play equipment

C 2.3   Goes down small slide

C 3.1   Pedals and steers bicycle with training wheels

C 3.2   Pedals and steers tricycle

C 3.3   Pushes riding toy with feet while steering

Embedded Learning Opportunities

■ *Walks around outside play structure without bumping into it*

■ *Walks using two hands to hold onto an adult*

■ *Walks up and down steps of slide or stairs alternating feet to get to playground*

■ *Jumps forward with both feet landing on the ground at same time*

■ *Hops forward on one foot while playing Hopscotch*

■ *Bounces playground ball with one or two hands*

■ *Throws basketball at goal overhand*

■ *Uses feet to pedal tricycle and hands to steer tricycle*

■ *Uses hands to hang on play equipment with bars, such as holding bar above slide to swing in air before sliding down*

■ *Climbs ladders on play equipment using both hands and feet*

ADAPTIVE Growing Skills

B 1.1   Indicates need to use toilet

B 1.2   Has bowel and bladder control

B 1.3   Indicates awareness of soiled and wet pants or diapers

D 1   Takes independent action to alleviate distress, discomfort, and pain

D 1.1   Communicates internal distress, discomfort, or pain to adult

D 3.1   Responds appropriately to warnings of dangerous conditions or substances

Embedded Learning Opportunities

■ *Says "I need to go to the bathroom," "I had an accident," or "My pants are wet" while on playground*

■ *Resolves issue of distress, discomfort, or pain while on playground by walking away from friend hitting them or telling teacher "I hurt my leg"*

■ *Complies with playground rules: Goes down slide on bottom, stops at gate labeled with stop sign, or rides bicycle only on designated path*

■ *Avoids strangers and busy roads while playing outside*

■ *Tells teacher "Mary push me" or "Bob said he's not my friend" when outside on playground*

SOCIAL-EMOTIONAL Growing Skills

B 1   Responds appropriately to others' emotions

B 1.1 Identifies/labels emotions in others

B 1.2 Identifies/labels own emotions

B 2   Uses appropriate strategies to manage emotional states

B 2.1 Responds appropriately to soothing by peer

B 3   Makes positive statements about self or accomplishments

B 3.1 Explains or shows others how to do tasks mastered

B 3.2 Shares accomplishment with familiar caregiver

C 1   Maintains interaction with peer

C 1.1 Initiates social behavior toward peer

C 1.2 Responds appropriately to peer social behavior

C 3.1 Initiates cooperative activity

C 3.2 Joins others in cooperative activity

D 1   Interacts appropriately with others during small-group activities

D 1.2 Responds appropriately to directions during small-group activities

D 1.3 Remains with group during small-group activities

D 2.2 Responds appropriately to directions during large-group activities

D 2.3 Remains with group during large-group activities

D 3.1 Responds to request to finish activity

D 4   Resolves conflicts using negotiation

D 4.1 Uses strategies to resolve conflicts

E 1.1 Meets internal physical needs of hunger and thirst

E 2.1 Meets behavioral expectations in familiar environments

E 2.2 Adjusts behavior based on feedback from others or environment

E 3.1 Seeks adult permission when appropriate

E 3.2 Follows established social rules in familiar environments

Embedded Learning Opportunities

- ■ *Says "Are you OK?" to friend who got hurt on the playground*

- ■ *Says "I'm sad" after falling down*

- ■ *Shares accomplishments with adult, such as "I slid down the big slide!" after doing it for first time*

- ■ *Pretends to be pirate sailing on ship while climbing play structure*

- ■ *Drinks from water fountain at park when thirsty*

- ■ *Says "I do NOT like the sand box, but I like the castle"*

SOCIAL-COMMUNICATION Growing Skills

B 2 Locates common objects, people, or events

B 3 Follows multistep directions without contextual cues

B 3.1 Follows multistep directions with contextual cues

B 3.2 Follows one-step direction without contextual cues

B 3.3 Follows one-step direction with contextual cues

B 4.1 Answers *who*, *what*, and *where* questions

C 1 Produces multiple-word sentences to communicate

C 1.1 Uses two-word utterances

C 1.2 Uses 50 single words, signs, or symbols

C 2 Uses plural pronouns to indicate subjects, objects, and possession in multiple-word sentences

C 2.1 Uses irregular plural nouns in multiple-word sentences

C 2.2 Uses regular plural nouns

C 3 Uses helping verbs

C 3.2 Uses regular past tense of common verbs

C 3.3 Uses *to be* verbs

C 4 Asks questions using inverted auxiliary

C 4.1 Asks *wh-* questions

D 1 Uses language to initiate and sustain social interaction

D 1.1 Follows social conventions of language

D 2 Provides and seeks information while conversing using words, phrases, or sentences

D 2.1 Asks questions to obtain information

D 2.2 Describes objects, people, and events as part of social exchange

D 3.3 Responds to topic initiations from others

D 3.4 Alternates between speaker and listener roles during conversations with others

D 3.5 Responds to contingent questions from others

Embedded Learning Opportunities

- *Points to ball, dog, or truck when adult names object*
- *Follows directions to clean up toys and then line up or wait at door to go inside*
- *Answers comprehension questions such as "Why do you think it's going to rain?" with "Because the clouds are gray"*
- *Uses two-word utterances while talking about playing: "I play," "You jump," "We slide"*

COGNITIVE Growing Skills

B 1   Imitates novel coordinated motor actions

B 3.1 Relates recent events without contextual clues

C 1.1 Locates object in second of two hiding places

C 2   Uses object to represent another object

C 2.1 Recognizes symbols

C 3.1 Classifies according to function

C 3.2 Classifies according to physical attribute

C 3.3 Discriminates between objects or people using common attributes

C 4   Uses early conceptual comparisons

C 4.1 Identifies common concepts

C 4.2 Identifies concrete concepts

D 1.1 Uses part of object or support to obtain another object

E 1.1 Uses simple tools to gather information

E 2.2 Demonstrates knowledge about natural happenings

E 3.2 Manipulates materials to cause change

Embedded Learning Opportunities

■ *Imitates adult's motor actions, such as standing on one foot*

■ *Locates an object in a second hiding place during scavenger hunt—when doesn't find ball in one spot, looks in second spot to find it*

■ *Recognizes stop sign posted on gate outside*

■ *Identifies correct position in line when adult says to stand between Carmen and Diane*

■ *Gathers information by using shovel to figure out what is under grass*

■ *Makes observations about natural happenings outdoors by saying "I think it's going to rain because the sky is dark"*

LITERACY Growing Skills

A 3.2 Recognizes common signs and logos

B 1.2 Participates in repetitive verbal play

E 2.1 Makes representational drawings

Embedded Learning Opportunities

■ *Recognizes signs and logos, such as stop sign at park*

■ *Enjoys verbal play with teacher and peers by playing Duck Duck Goose or Ring Around the Rosie*

MATH Growing Skills

A 1   Counts out 3 items

A 1.1 Counts 3 items to determine "How many?"

Embedded Learning Opportunities

■ *Counts and says how many bubbles are floating in the air: "I see one, two, three bubbles; there's three"*

TIER 1

■ UNIVERSAL STRATEGIES

These are best practices for ALL young children, with attention to meeting learning outcomes within daily routines and activities of family life and early childhood classrooms while promoting positive adult-child relationships and peer interactions.

Children's participation in active and outdoor play at the Growing level continues to increase balance and mobility skills (jumping, hopping, climbing, running, using play materials like balls, bicycles, tricycles). Active and outdoor play allows for advancement on cognitive skills, such as identifying common and concrete concepts, using simple tools to gather information, making observations, and demonstrating knowledge about natural happenings. Socially, children are building their language skills to communicate effectively and functionally with others by using conversational rules during play, providing and seeking information, and communicating their likes and dislikes. Fine motor skills increase when children have opportunities to rotate their wrist to manipulate an object, to explore manipulating objects with two hands, or to write using a three-finger grasp. By the toddler years, children are becoming less dependent on adults because they want to complete tasks by themselves.

Interactions

Positive interactions with adults are crucial for all children, including toddlers who are beginning to develop peer relationships and who are often enthusiastic about becoming independent and guiding their own play. As they become older and more inquisitive, children begin asking questions, and active and outdoor play can stimulate these inquiries. Following are some suggested interactions for the Growing level of this routine:

▲ Remain patient, provide acceptable choices, answer questions using a calm tone of voice, and smile.

▲ Ensure safety while allowing exploration of indoor and outdoor environments.

▲ Guide toddlers to try to figure out answers to their own questions.

▲ Respond to explorations with additional questions to extend inquiry and learning.

▲ Encourage toddlers to play together, imitate one another, and answer one another's questions.

▲ Ensure enough wait time for children to answer questions before prompting them or providing answers.

▲ Remember that children are learning how to interact with others by watching how adults initiate and respond to them; adults are important role models!

Environment and Materials

As children get older, adult assistance decreases during active and outdoor play. However, for safety reasons, adults need to be aware of children's physical capabilities and stay alert to what they are doing. Any physical environment is possible for active and outdoor play as long as there is adequate space for children to move and stay safe (away from moving vehicles, with landing zones, under sufficient adult supervision). Following are some suggestions for environment and materials at the Growing level:

▲ Consider active and outdoor play environments such as parks, playgrounds, yards, driveways, sidewalks, classrooms, indoor open spaces (areas for dance, stepping stones, balance beams), gyms, or even the beach.

▲ Include materials for active indoor play such as plastic basketball goals and balls, indoor slides, music for dancing, riding toys (small tricycles, scooters), small balls and containers to throw them into, and hoops and rings.

▲ Include materials for outdoor play such as baseball bats, a wide variety of balls (basketballs, soccer balls, kickballs, baseballs, whiffle balls), containers and other targets, riding toys, tricycles, bubbles, chalk, and hula hoops.

▲ Vary the choice of materials for outdoor play based on location (playgrounds may include sand, playground equipment, bike paths).

▲ Follow children's leads and interests while remaining aware that there is no need to spend a lot of money on special materials.

▲ Model active play (climbing, walking, running, swimming) to help get children moving.

■ FOCUSED STRATEGIES

These strategies are for teaching SOME children who are struggling with a component of a skill or whose development is stalled and who need extra help to catch up or keep up. The strategies include a variety of minor adaptations or modifications to daily routines, activities, and environments to meet targeted outcomes at home and in classrooms.

▲ Give children a chance to practice, practice, practice. Repetition is important when mastering new skills, so be sure children have plenty of opportunities to practice (if the skill is throwing, let children continue to practice that skill until they have mastered it to their developmental capability, then introduce a new skill).

▲ Incorporate multiple opportunities throughout each day for children to practice skills they need for active and outdoor play:

△ Provide children who are cruising and taking steps with support but not yet walking with more opportunities to walk independently rather than picking them up.

△ Allow extra wait time for children to get to their destination.

▲ Use peer models to teach some active and outdoor play skills (throwing balls, climbing steps or ladders, using chalk).

▲ Shorten the length of activities as needed for emerging skills so the child does not get frustrated and quit.

▲ Vary the environments where active and outdoor play occurs, using settings of interest to children to encourage them to practice their skills.

▲ Vary the materials used, giving children time to explore new items before starting to use them in active and outdoor play, if possible.

▲ Model how to use materials, if necessary, to help children become interested in using them.

▲ Group children together on the basis of their skill levels to work on a specific skill with the group.

▲ Learn to recognize children's cues and preferences.

▲ Teach children who cannot speak to use simple signs (MORE, ALL DONE) so they can communicate their preferences.

▲ Pair sign language with spoken words for children who are nonverbal or who have hearing impairments.

■ SPECIALIZED STRATEGIES

These strategies for teaching the FEW children who need intensive supports include a variety of specialized, individualized, precise evidence-based strategies to meet children's unique goals/outcomes:

▲ Plan ahead for access to active and outdoor play areas for children who use wheelchairs or mobility devices:

△ Establish an alternative gate or route for navigating outdoors to a playground.

△ Make sure there is an elevator or ramp available as an alternative to stairs when accessing both indoor and outdoor activity spaces.

△ Make additional adult assistance available as needed to ensure that ratios are met for all children while in transit.

▲ Provide adaptive play materials for accessibility:

△ For children who need extra support for reclining or additional arm or leg support,

▷ Use an adaptive swing such as a Jensen ADA swing.

△ For children in wheelchairs,

▷ Use an adaptive swing such as a Playaway toy toddler swing, bean bag chairs for comfortable seating, or tumble mats for rolling, crawling, or wiggling.

▷ Use raised sand and water tables or gardens for easier access.

△ For children who have low leg muscle control,

▷ Use learn-to-pedal/glider bikes or other adaptive bikes.

▲ For children who are unable to communicate their preferences, likes, and dislikes during play,

△ Teach sign language, use picture cards, or use technology apps.

△ Teach children simple signs (MORE, ALL DONE).

△ Pair sign language with spoken words.

▲ Provide differential reinforcement of other behaviors for children who have concerning behaviors. For example, if a child continuously hits a peer while on the playground, reinforce the child for any behavior other than hitting.

▲ Use most-to-least prompts or graduated guidance to teach children advanced play skills (riding a bike with training wheels, climbing playground equipment, sliding down a slide). For example,

△ If teaching a child to ride a bike, start with fully supportive training wheels, and raise the training wheels in small increments as the child gains balance on two wheels.

△ If teaching a child to throw into a container, start with a large container and gradually reduce the container's size as the child's accuracy improves.

AEPS-3 Curriculum Resources (Appendix A)

Appendix A in this volume contains numerous additional resources to supplement the AEPS-3 Curriculum. The first part of the appendix presents a list of general curriculum resources, and the second part provides lists of supplementary resources for each individual routine and activity.

AEPS-3 Skills Matrix (Appendix B)

The AEPS-3 Skills Matrix in Appendix B of this volume spotlights individual skills by showing functional application across all routines and activities. Each skills matrix (there are eight total, one for each of the test's eight developmental areas) allows you to select individual AEPS-3 items for children who require an intensive focus on a few skills across routines and activities. For children who have difficulty learning new skills at the level of individual AEPS-3 items, the Foundation Steps (*FS*) provide an even more granular breakdown of component subskills that are either a sequence of developmental precursors or steps in task analyses.

7

Arrival & Departure

Arrival & Departure includes the activities children participate in when arriving at and departing from a location for caregiving, visiting, socializing, and receiving services, such as health care, therapy, and instruction, with the intention of interacting and sharing space with others. Children arrive and depart in many ways: being carried, walking, using riding toys or being pushed in wheelchairs. This routine changes over time as children's motor, adaptive, cognitive, and social-emotional skills develop. Children perform this routine ranging from twice a day to several times a day, depending on how often they enter or exit new environments. The AEPS-3 Growing level of Arrival & Departure uses skills from eight developmental areas.

Concurrent Skills

The following concurrent skills are AEPS-3 skills that can be easily embedded and taught during regular occurrences of Arrival & Departure.

FINE MOTOR Growing Skills

B 1   Activates object with finger

B 2   Rotates wrist to manipulate object

B 3   Manipulates object with two hands, each performing different action

C 1.4   Scribbles

Embedded Learning Opportunities

- *Pushes button on elevator to go to classroom*
- *Holds jacket with one hand while using other hand to manipulate zipper*
- *Opens door to enter classroom*
- *Uses scribble writing to sign self in*

GROSS MOTOR Growing Skills

B 3   Walks avoiding people, furniture, or objects

B 3.1   Walks without support

B 4   Alternates feet going up and down stairs

B 4.1   Walks up and down stairs using support

B 4.2   Moves up and down stairs

B 4.3   Gets up and down from low structure

B 5   Runs while avoiding people, furniture, or other objects

B 5.1   Runs

B 5.2   Walks fast

Embedded Learning Opportunities

■ *Runs or walks from car to classroom*

■ *Climbs in and out of car seat when preparing for departure and arrival*

■ *Walks up or down stairs with or without support to get to classroom*

■ *Enters classroom and avoids bumping into other children, teachers, or furniture*

ADAPTIVE Growing Skills

B 1.1   Indicates need to use toilet

B 1.2   Has bowel and bladder control

B 1.3   Indicates awareness of soiled and wet pants or diapers

B 2.2   Washes and dries hands

C 1.2   Takes off pullover clothing over head

C 1.3   Takes off front-opening coat, jacket, or shirt

C 2.2   Puts on front-opening clothing

C 2.3   Puts on pullover clothing

C 2.4   Puts on pull-up clothing

C 2.5   Puts on socks

C 2.6   Puts on shoes

D 1   Takes independent action to alleviate distress, discomfort, and pain

D 1.1   Communicates internal distress, discomfort, or pain to adult

D 3.1   Responds appropriately to warnings of dangerous conditions or substances

Embedded Learning Opportunities

■ *Indicates need to use toilet upon arrival or before leaving*

■ *Washes and dries hands upon arriving at home or school*

■ *Puts on shoes and socks before departure*

■ *Seeks familiar adult when distressed over parent's leaving*

■ *Responds when adult makes request to hold hand or walk more slowly*

SOCIAL-EMOTIONAL Growing Skills

A 3.1   Initiates next step of familiar social routine

A 3.2   Follows familiar social routines with familiar adults

B 1   Responds appropriately to others' emotions

B 1.1   Identifies/labels emotions in others

B 1.2   Identifies/labels own emotions

B 2   Uses appropriate strategies to manage emotional states

B 2.1   Responds appropriately to soothing by peer

B 3   Makes positive statements about self or accomplishments

B 3.1   Explains or shows others how to do tasks mastered

B 3.2   Shares accomplishment with familiar caregiver

C 1   Maintains interaction with peer

C 1.1   Initiates social behavior toward peer

C 1.2   Responds appropriately to peer social behavior

D 3   Initiates and completes independent activities

D 3.1   Responds to request to finish activity

D 3.2   Responds to request to begin activity

D 3.3   Entertains self by playing with toys

D 4.2   Claims and defends possessions

E 2.1   Meets behavioral expectations in familiar environments

E 2.2   Adjusts behavior based on feedback from others or environment

E 3.1   Seeks adult permission when appropriate

E 3.2   Follows established social rules in familiar environments

E 4.3   Provides given name or nickname of self and others

Embedded Learning Opportunities

■ *Says goodbye to parent and washes hands with teacher*

■ *Takes off coat and immediately walks to sink to wash hands*

■ *Puts on headphones for music to calm down immediately after parent leaves*

■ *Shows adult they finished an activity*

■ *Says peer is sad and walks over to give hug at arrival*

■ *Joins other peers in play after being dropped off at school or child care*

■ *Plays independently with toys while waiting for adult to arrive*

■ *Stays next to adult without running or wandering away*

SOCIAL-COMMUNICATION Growing Skills

B 2   Locates common objects, people, or events

B 3   Follows multistep directions without contextual cues

B 3.1   Follows multistep directions with contextual cues

B 3.2   Follows one-step direction without contextual cues

B 3.3   Follows one-step direction with contextual cues

B 4.1   Answers *who*, *what*, and *where* questions

C 1   Produces multiple-word sentences to communicate

C 1.1   Uses two-word utterances

C 1.2   Uses 50 single words, signs, or symbols

C 2   Uses plural pronouns to indicate subjects, objects, and possession in multiple-word sentences

C 2.1   Uses irregular plural nouns in multiple-word sentences

C 2.2   Uses regular plural nouns

C 3   Uses helping verbs

C 3.2   Uses regular past tense of common verbs

C 3.3   Uses *to be* verbs

C 4   Asks questions using inverted auxiliary

C 4.1   Asks *wh-* questions

D 1   Uses language to initiate and sustain social interaction

D 1.1   Follows social conventions of language

D 2   Provides and seeks information while conversing using words, phrases, or sentences

D 2.2   Describes objects, people, and events as part of social exchange

D 3.4   Alternates between speaker and listener roles during conversations with others

D 3.5   Responds to contingent questions from others

Embedded Learning Opportunities

■ *Locates teachers and children within classroom at arrival*

■ *Responds to adult when asked questions such as "Who brought you to school today?" or "Where is your coat?"*

■ *Follows multistep directions such as "Take your coat off, wash your hands, then pick an activity when you come into the room"*

■ *Asks if another child is absent: "Is Sinde sick today?"*

■ *Describes breakfast food or weekend events and tells what they want to do next day*

COGNITIVE Growing Skills

B 1   Imitates novel coordinated motor actions

B 2   Imitates novel words

B 3.1 Relates recent events without contextual cues

B 3.2 Relates recent events with contextual cues

B 3.3 Relates events immediately after they occur

C 2.1 Uses object to represent another object

C 4   Uses early conceptual comparisons

C 4.1 Identifies common concepts

C 4.2 Identifies concrete concepts

D 4.1 Draws conclusions about causes of events based on personal experience

E 1   Expands simple observations and explorations into further inquiry

E 2.2 Demonstrates knowledge about natural happenings

Embedded Learning Opportunities

- *Imitates new morning song words and movements upon arrival*
- *Tells adult about exciting vehicle they just saw*
- *Notices object in classroom and talks about similar object at home*
- *Tells adult about weather upon arriving from outdoors*

LITERACY Growing Skills

A 3.1 Recognizes own first name in print

A 3.2 Recognizes common signs and logos

B 1.2 Participates in repetitive verbal play

Embedded Learning Opportunities

- *Recognizes own name label on cubby or locker*
- *Knows to halt at stop sign; recognizes box for favorite cereal at snack*
- *Recognizes own name card and places with names of other students in attendance*

MATH Growing Skills

A 1   Counts out 3 items

A 1.1 Counts 3 items to determine "How many?"

B 1.3 Uses quantity comparison words

Embedded Learning Opportunities

- *Counts outdoor wear hanging on hooks at door and compares to number of peers present*
- *Counts number of children at circle time and says how many are present*

TIER 1

■ UNIVERSAL STRATEGIES

These are best practices for ALL young children, with attention to meeting learning outcomes within daily routines and activities of family life and early childhood classrooms while promoting positive adult–child relationships and peer interactions.

As children's minds and bodies grow, independent participation in arrival and departure grows with them. In the Growing level of the AEPS-3 Curriculum, children become more mobile (walking with and without support, running, jumping, hopping), relying less on adults to carry them to or from different environments. Cognitive skills increase, too, as children begin to make observations and transfer knowledge learned previously to current situations. Toddlers are aware that when it is time to leave, they must put on their coats, for example. Socially, children are using language skills to effectively and functionally communicate their needs and wants using appropriate conversational rules, especially when they want to go somewhere of their own choosing. Fine motor skills also improve, making buttoning and zipping of outwear more independent. Math and literacy skills also continue to develop, allowing children to associate specific letters, numbers, logos, and words with destinations. Young children generally become motivated to complete tasks by themselves, including all aspects of arrival and departure.

Interactions

As young children become motivated to complete more tasks by themselves (may no longer want help getting their coats on when departing), adults need to be patient and allow additional time for transitions, arrivals, and departures. Interactions with adults present useful opportunities to teach new skills and send a positive message to children that they matter. The way adults respond to children is important—children notice and incorporate it into the ways they are learning to respond to others. Adults will often hear young children repeat their own words. Following are some suggested interactions for the Growing level of this routine:

▲ Use arrival and departure as a teaching opportunity by modeling how to put on a coat and using parallel talk.

▲ Incorporate math and literacy:

△ Count or sing the alphabet during various parts of the routine.

△ Ask children questions about the routine ("What do we do after we put on our coat?" "Why do we wear coats?").

▲ Give children options for acceptable choices whenever possible ("Do you want to walk to the car holding my hand, or do you want to jump to the car holding my hand?").

▲ Follow children's leads during transitions when it's possible and safe to do so. (If a child chooses to put on their shoes before their coat, let them complete the task as time allows. However, if they want to put on their shoes before their socks, an adult will need to teach the skill of dressing the feet.)

▲ Teach the steps of arrival and departure directly once young children can follow the sequence of routines:

△ Use picture schedules to teach groups of children the sequence of the major tasks associated with the routines in each setting.

▲ Take as much time as possible during arrival and departure to listen to children and talk to them, and respond patiently to specific questions and bids for attention.

▲ Smile and speak at children's level, using a calm voice, especially when asking and answering questions.

▲ Give positive feedback immediately when children's behavior warrants it, and be specific (after a child walks to the door to leave, say "Alex, you used your walking feet to get to the door. Good job, buddy!").

Environment and Materials

As young children become more independent, the number of destinations in their lives expands, and they may regularly be arriving at or departing from home, school, child care, the grocery store, peers' and relatives' homes, doctors' offices, and community activities. Some children ride in car seats, some are held or sit on an adult's lap on a bus, and others may be pushed in strollers or pulled in wagons. Most young children at the Growing level prefer to receive less and less help from adults. Safety remains a basic concern for arrival and departure, so it is important to follow car seat and any other necessary safety guidelines and to be aware of each child's physical and cognitive abilities while teaching associated skills.

Arrival and departure routines generally do not require additional materials for children beyond those that adults already have available. Materials and supplies to help ensure smooth arrivals and departures will vary among families. Many young children take an interest in what goes into the diaper bag when an adult packs it, and materials packed specifically for arrival and departure might include outerwear, travel toys, books, comfort blankets, and snacks. When arriving at child care or school, children may be expected to put away their outerwear and wash their hands, but the destination will have materials and equipment (soap; cubbies and hooks) to facilitate arrival procedures.

TIER 2

■ FOCUSED STRATEGIES

These strategies are for teaching SOME children who are struggling with a component of a skill or whose development is stalled and who need extra help to catch up or keep up. The strategies include a variety of minor adaptations or modifications to daily routines, activities, and environments to meet targeted outcomes at home and in classrooms.

▲ Keep routines for arrival and departure consistent and predictable. Use the same words and actions each time very young children arrive at and depart from a particular destination, and give alerts in advance of leaving.

▲ Help parents make transport time a positive, fun experience, because arriving at child care and separating from parents is often more stressful than departing from home. This helps keep young children from negatively associating departure and transport with arrival and separation.

▲ Encourage adults to say a quick goodbye as they leave, and reassure children about the adults' return. Simultaneously, distract children who are anxious when they arrive by using parallel talk and questions to describe peers, objects, and activities in the room:

△ "I see your favorite truck right here."

△ "Let's see what Alejandro is building in the block area."

△ "Come with me to look out the window at the birds."

▲ Provide a listening center with soothing music, picture books, favorite audio stories, and engaging toys to help children who are upset calm themselves after parents leave.

▲ Incorporate extra time into daily arrivals and departures for children who become easily distracted or take a long time to get ready to leave.

▲ Read stories that address arrival and departure activities.

▲ Use picture schedules that illustrate the arrival or departure routine, or use first-then boards to show children what they need to do:

△ "First you put on your coat, then you'll go bye-bye with Mommy."

▲ Use a timer to help children transition from one activity to another:

△ In the car, an adult might use a phone timer and tell the child that when the timer goes off, it's time to walk into the school.

▲ Offer multiple opportunities during daily routines for children to practice parts of arrival and departure:

△ Provide outerwear, toy vehicles, and the like to use in pretend arrivals and departures.

△ Have children take off their own shoes at naptime, and when they wake up, allow time for them to try to put on their own shoes.

▲ Provide verbal prompts to encourage children to put on their coats or shoes at departure. If verbal prompts do not work, use gestures, models, and hand-over-hand physical prompts to help children get dressed while talking about what is happening.

▲ If possible, use peers or older siblings as buddies to model arrival and departure behaviors. Many young children learn most easily by watching and imitating other children who can perform arrival and departure tasks.

▲ Focus on the main steps when teaching arrival and departure routines at home and school:

△ Concentrate on teaching a child how to put on and take off their coat, while continuing to help the child with other parts of the routine.

▲ Provide appropriate directions for children to follow immediately upon arriving and before departing:

△ "Sign in on the attendance list."

△ "You can play in the block area."

△ "Put your coat in your cubby and wash your hands."

▲ Provide materials that will ease children's transition from one environment to another. Some young children want a security blanket from home, and others prefer a favorite book or toy.

▲ Teach children to use simple signs (MORE, ALL DONE) so they can communicate their preferences.

▲ Pair sign language with spoken words for children who are nonverbal or who have hearing impairments.

▲ Learn to recognize children's cues and preferences.

◼ SPECIALIZED STRATEGIES

TIER 3

These strategies for teaching the FEW children who need intensive supports include a variety of specialized, individualized, precise evidence-based strategies to meet children's unique goals/outcomes:

▲ Make sure each destination is accessible to children who have specialized physical and communication needs (ensure the presence of wheelchair ramps, braille on doors and elevators, wide doors, assistive communication devices).

▲ Work with home caregivers to develop specific, consistent arrival and departure procedures that address family priorities and concerns and match children's changing skills.

▲ If children cannot walk or crawl during arrival and departure, provide desirable, adaptable materials for transport:

△ Use a wagon, riding toy, or stroller to take the child from their transport to their destination, or vice versa.

▲ Adapt home and classroom environments to make them accessible for all children:

△ Move furniture around ahead of time as needed to make extra room for children who are just learning to use a walker or wheelchair.

▲ Make available to families a "lending library" of specialized equipment for transport and transition, or provide information about community resources for equipment loan.

▲ Work with motor therapists to modify transportation equipment for children with specialized fine and gross motor needs to improve their participation and independence.

▲ Provide alternative ways to communicate for children who are nonverbal or are unable to speak and those who have hearing impairments:

△ Use consistent gestures or sign language for greetings and farewells.

△ Use picture cards or technology apps to help communicate about the school day.

▲ Have a communication board ready with classroom activities so the child can point to their favorite part of the day:

△ Use individualized gestures and verbal prompts to help children understand what they should be doing during each step of the routine.

▲ Describe various environments in detail for children with vision impairments:

△ Assign and use a specific name and routine for each destination so children know where they are and what to expect.

▲ Keep aspects of arrival environments as consistent as possible:

△ If changes in child care classrooms are necessary, familiarize children who have vision impairments with new furniture arrangements, materials, equipment, and supplies in advance.

△ Introduce new toys and peers individually using touch and sound.

▲ Use sign language with children who have hearing impairments, and make sure they can see you when you give alerts and instructions about upcoming transitions.

AEPS-3 Curriculum Resources (Appendix A)

Appendix A in this volume contains numerous additional resources to supplement the AEPS-3 Curriculum. The first part of the appendix presents a list of general curriculum resources, and the second part provides lists of supplementary resources for each individual routine and activity.

AEPS-3 Skills Matrix (Appendix B)

The AEPS-3 Skills Matrix in Appendix B of this volume spotlights individual skills by showing functional application across all routines and activities. Each skills matrix (there are eight total, one for each of the test's eight developmental areas) allows you to select individual AEPS-3 items for children who require an intensive focus on a few skills across routines and activities. For children who have difficulty learning new skills at the level of individual AEPS-3 items, the Foundation Steps (FS) provide an even more granular breakdown of component subskills that are either a sequence of developmental precursors or steps in task analyses.

8

Art

Art activities can vary by a number of elements, such as materials, medium, location, and participants, and they use children's creativity and imagination to create projects both indoors and outdoors in the home, child care, or classroom setting. Art is not limited to permanent product projects (coloring pages, step-by-step paintings) or activities that limit creativity, as it can include any aspect of art. In early childhood, art is more about the process than the product. This routine changes across the skill areas as young children's motor, cognitive, and social skills increase, and art can address a number of developmental skills depending on the theme. The AEPS-3 Growing level of Art uses items from eight developmental areas.

Concurrent Skills

The following concurrent skills are AEPS-3 skills that can be easily embedded and taught during regular occurrences of Art.

FINE MOTOR Growing Skills

B 2	Rotates wrist to manipulate object
B 3	Manipulates object with two hands, each performing different actions
C 1.1	Writes or draws using mixed strokes
C 1.2	Writes or draws using curved lines
C 1.3	Writes or draws using straight lines
C 1.4	Scribbles

Embedded Learning Opportunities

- *Rotates wrist to twist caps on and off of art materials (dot markers)*
- *Holds glue stick while pulling off lid*
- *Grasps art utensils to write or draw on paper*

GROSS MOTOR Growing Skills

B 3	Walks avoiding people, furniture, or objects
B 3.1	Walks without support
B 4.3	Gets up and down from low structure

Embedded Learning Opportunities

- *Walks with and without support to art table*
- *Sits down and gets up from chair at art table*

ADAPTIVE Growing Skills

B 2.2 Washes and dries hands
C 1.2 Takes off pullover clothing over head
C 1.3 Takes off front-opening coat, jacket, or shirt
C 2.2 Puts on front-opening clothing
C 2.3 Puts on pullover clothing

Embedded Learning Opportunities

■ *Washes hands to remove paint, dirt, soil after finishing activity*

■ *Puts on or takes off front-opening or pullover garment, such as paint shirt or smock, when beginning or finishing art activity*

SOCIAL-EMOTIONAL Growing Skills

A 3.1 Initiates next step of familiar social routine
A 3.2 Follows familiar social routines with familiar adults
B 3   Makes positive statements about self or accomplishments
B 3.1 Explains or shows others how to do tasks mastered
B 3.2 Shares accomplishment with familiar caregiver
C 1   Maintains interaction with peer
C 1.1 Initiates social behavior toward peer
C 1.2 Responds appropriately to peer social behavior
C 3.1 Initiates cooperative activity
C 3.2 Joins others in cooperative activity
C 3.3 Shares or exchanges objects
D 1   Interacts appropriately with others during small-group activities
D 1.1 Interacts appropriately with materials during small-group activities
D 1.2 Responds appropriately to directions during small-group activities
D 1.3 Remains with group during small-group activities
D 3   Initiates and completes independent activities
D 3.1 Responds to request to finish activity
D 3.2 Responds to request to begin activity
D 3.3 Entertains self by playing with toys
D 4.2 Claims and defends possessions
E 2.1 Meets behavioral expectations in familiar environments
E 2.2 Adjusts behavior based on feedback from others or environment
E 3.1 Seeks adult permission when appropriate
E 3.2 Follows established social rules in familiar environments
E 4.3 Provides given name or nickname of self and others

Embedded Learning Opportunities

■ *Initiates next step of familiar art routine, such as picking up paintbrush after adult helps them put on smock*

■ *Works on collage with peer*

■ *Approaches another child at art table and says "This is how you paint"*

■ *Walks to sink and washes hands after adult says "Your hands have paint on them; please go wash your hands"*

■ *Says "That's my painting!" after adult holds up a painted picture and says "Whose is this?"*

■ *Says "Can I paint a picture with my friend?" to gain adult permission for art activity*

■ *Independently chooses to participate in art activities (painting at art easel)*

■ *Tells adult name to be written on painting or labels family members in painting*

SOCIAL-COMMUNICATION Growing Skills

B 2 Locates common objects, people, or events

B 3.1 Follows multistep directions with contextual cues

B 3.2 Follows one-step direction without contextual cues

B 3.3 Follows one-step direction with contextual cues

C 1 Produces multiple-word sentences to communicate

C 1.1 Uses two-word utterances

C 1.2 Uses 50 single words, signs, or symbols

C 2 Uses plural pronouns to indicate subjects, objects, and possession in multiple-word sentences

C 2.1 Uses irregular plural nouns in multiple-word sentences

C 2.2 Uses regular plural nouns

C 3 Uses helping verbs

C 4 Asks questions using inverted auxiliary

C 4.1 Asks *wh-* questions

D 2 Provides and seeks information while conversing using words, phrases, or sentences

D 2.1 Asks questions to obtain information

D 2.2 Describes objects, people, and events as part of social exchange

D 3.3 Responds to topic initiations from others

D 3.5 Responds to contingent questions from others

Embedded Learning Opportunities

■ *Locates additional paint for painting when none is left and adult directs child to get more*

■ *Complies when adult gives one- to three-step directions ("Take off your smock and go wash your hands")*

■ *Describes picture using multiple-word sentences ("That my mommy, daddy, brother, and puppy")*

■ *Uses two-word utterances, such as "Me done" to indicate their desire to stop working on art project*

■ *Asks adult about art materials presented to them ("Why doesn't the glue work?")*

■ *Answers adult when asked to describe picture*

COGNITIVE Growing Skills

B 1 Imitates novel coordinated motor actions

B 2 Imitates novel words

B 3.1 Relates recent events without contextual cues

B 3.2 Relates recent events with contextual cues

B 3.3 Relates events immediately after they occur

C 4 Uses early conceptual comparisons

C 4.1 Identifies common concepts

C 4.2 Identifies concrete concepts

E 3.2 Manipulates materials to cause change

Embedded Learning Opportunities

■ *Completes art project (paints/draws picture, makes collage) about book read at circle time and describes picture to adult*

■ *Identifies common concepts by referring to item in painting that is available to five senses, such as apple, guitar, soft grass, hard table, dog*

■ *Observes and describes similarities and differences between their artwork and artwork of others*

■ *Manipulates materials to cause change (mixes paint)*

LITERACY Growing Skills

A 3.1   Recognizes own first name in print

A 3.2   Recognizes common signs and logos

D 1.3   Matches pictures to actual objects, people, or actions

D 2   Retells simple story

D 2.3   Tells story associated with series of pictures

D 3   Demonstrates understanding of abstract story vocabulary

E 1.1   Dictates description of drawing

E 1.2   Verbally labels representational drawings

E 1.3   Verbally labels nonrepresentational drawings

E 2.1   Makes representational drawings

Embedded Learning Opportunities

■ *Recognizes first name when adult writes it on artwork*

■ *Makes drawing of person to represent self, verbally labels it by saying "This is me!" and tells story to go along with it*

MATH Growing Skills

A 1   Counts out 3 items

A 1.1   Counts 3 items to determine "How many?"

B 1.3   Uses quantity comparison words

Embedded Learning Opportunities

■ *Counts out 3 art materials (feathers, stickers, buttons) to determine how many are on their artwork*

■ *Uses quantity comparison words: Looks at peer's artwork and says "Taylor has more paint than me" or "I have less materials!"*

TIER 1

■ UNIVERSAL STRATEGIES

These are best practices for ALL young children, with attention to meeting learning outcomes within daily routines and activities of family life and early childhood classrooms while promoting positive adult–child relationships and peer interactions.

As children grow older, art routines become less of a sensory experience and provide more opportunity for toddlers and preschoolers to explore different types of art. In the process of exploring, children increase their fine motor, adaptive, communication, literacy, and math skills. Children begin to learn how to hold their writing or drawing utensil using a fisted or palmar grasp to draw, paint, or color art projects. Their writing begins to mature from scribbling to writing, drawing, or painting straight and curved lines. Many toddlers begin to form a few letters by accident, such as X and O, and participate in pretend writing. Children begin to understand the difference between drawing a picture and writing words and begin to produce letters from their names. They can recognize their own first name, count the number of letters, and make a comparison with the number of letters in a peer's name. They are able to draw or paint a picture and verbally assign a meaningful story to it. At this level, children's compliance with safety rules and context-specific rules increases, as does their willingness to make teachers or adults aware of rule breakers. For example, toddlers may begin to tell their teacher when a peer is not walking carefully with a pair of scissors. Their adaptive skills are increasing, so they should be able to put on a smock or paint shirt over their shirt. Children at this stage of development need guidance and interactions from adults in order to continue to increase skill levels during art routines and activities.

Interactions

At the Growing level, adults can continue to support art activities. It continues to be important at this level for adults to model different types of art projects while using parallel talk. Toddlers may ask adults for help creating art. It is important for adults to understand that art is a learning process and is likely to be messy. Following are some suggested interactions for this level:

▲ Provide developmentally appropriate opportunities for children to experience art both indoors and outdoors, multiple times throughout each day:

△ Leave safe materials (children's scissors, small pieces of paper, easy-to-open markers, crayons, colored pencils) out for children to use throughout the day.

△ Allow children to write or paint their names on pieces of paper or draw with chalk on a sidewalk or driveway.

▲ Give children choices of different ways to use the routine so that art is always open ended ("Do you want to draw, or paint?").

▲ Ask children open-ended questions about their art or make open-ended statements about it ("Tell me about your picture").

▲ Give children an opportunity to ask their own questions.

▲ Give children an opportunity to think creatively when they ask questions about art rather than doing it for them:

△ Respond with a return question that encourages their creativity.

△ Respond with an answer such as "Let's think of the parts of a bunny. What body parts do they have?"

▲ Provide stencils to serve as models for children who are learning to create representational art.

▲ Maintain positive interactions with children (smile; use pleasant tone of voice; give immediate, specific feedback).

▲ Allow adequate time for young children to experiment with and explore art materials, while encouraging them to observe other children (peers and older) as they draw, paint, color, and so forth.

Environment and Materials

This activity may be implemented both indoors and outdoors. Indoors, children are usually seated at a table or standing at an art easel, whether at home or in the classroom. Outdoors, art activities may take place on a sidewalk, driveway, or any other hard surface, such as a child-size picnic table. The materials needed will vary depending on the location and type of art children are creating. The possibilities for materials to use in open-ended art activities are nearly endless (collage materials, watercolors, egg cartons, boxes, crayons, paper). Indoor art materials may include various types of paint (watercolors, finger paint, tempera), paint daubers, stickers, playdough, clay, collage materials, markers, crayons, colored pencils, and pencils. Other materials may include large or small paper, scissors, glue, paper plates, napkins, paintbrushes, stamps, sponges, rulers, and stencils (letters, numbers, pictures). Some suggestions for environment and materials follow:

▲ Stay alert to safety concerns (cars, bicycles, pedestrians) when completing this routine outdoors.

▲ Remember that both indoor and outdoor materials should be used in an open-ended manner.

▲ Encourage and promote creativity (avoid requiring children to produce a specific outcome, such as making a picture with a blue sky).

▲ Ensure that all products available to children are nontoxic (for safety reasons) and washable (for easy cleanup).

▲ Check all ingredients in art materials before using them, especially if children who have allergies are present.

■ FOCUSED STRATEGIES

These strategies are for teaching SOME children who are struggling with a component of a skill or whose development is stalled and who need extra help to catch up or keep up. The strategies include a variety of minor adaptations or modifications to daily routines, activities, and environments to meet targeted outcomes at home and in classrooms.

▲ Offer multiple opportunities to repeat the same type of project. Repetition is an important way children learn how to do one particular kind of art, such as painting with watercolors.

▲ Use materials that are adaptable for children who have disabilities or developmental delays (adapted chairs with trays; large-size paintbrushes, sponges, crayons).

▲ Use songs to help children remember the steps for a particular kind of art (painting with watercolors):

△ Use the tune of a familiar song ("The Hokey Pokey") and come up with words related to watercolor painting.

▲ Use a verbal prompt and visual timer to alert children to when they will be transitioning from one activity to another.

▲ Use a visual schedule to make children aware of what will happen next in their day:

△ Let children put a check mark next to ART on their schedule after they complete it, and then move on to the next task on their schedule.

▲ Use peer modeling for art activities, since young children will often follow another child's lead more readily than they will follow an adult's lead.

▲ Plan art activities intentionally into daily routines and activities at home, at school, or in community locations:

△ Let children make creations with modeling clay at school.

△ Invite children to draw with washable markers in the bathtub at home.

△ Provide a paint and water mix in a spray bottle to use on sidewalks at a park.

▲ Allow extra time to complete projects for children who become easily distracted or take longer to complete an activity.

▲ Use a tablet with children to create art if they have allergies or sensitivities to art materials.

▲ Learn to recognize children's cues and preferences.

▲ Teach children to use simple signs during art activities (such as ART, PAPER, CRAYONS, PAINT, MORE, ALL DONE) to communicate their preferences.

▲ Pair sign language with spoken words for children who are nonverbal or who have hearing impairments.

■ SPECIALIZED STRATEGIES

These strategies for teaching the FEW children who need intensive supports include a variety of specialized, individualized, precise evidence-based strategies to meet children's unique goals/outcomes.

▲ Provide adaptable materials for children to use:

△ Offer oversized paintbrushes and jumbo crayons that are easier to hold.

△ Use hook-and-loop fasteners to adapt additional art supplies so children can hold them in their hands.

▲ For children who are unable to speak their wants and needs, support nonverbal participation and selection of preferences:

△ Allow children to lead you to their preferred activity.

△ Teach children to point to their preferred materials.

△ Use picture cards or technology apps.

▲ Use system of least prompts to teach children how to hold art materials:

△ Teach the child to reach for the paintbrush, then to grasp it, then to touch it to the paper, then to stroke the brush to make lines on the paper.

△ Let the child perform each step independently, and then provide increasing support as needed (modeling, then hand-over-hand).

▲ Use a picture schedule to show the sequence of an art project.

▲ Use first-then boards to show children what they need to do (with finger painting, first put hands in paint, then put hands on paper to paint).

▲ Use video modeling to demonstrate how to use age-appropriate art materials.

▲ For children who have visual impairments,

△ Use tactile or olfactory materials (gak with uncooked rice in it, scented markers).

▲ For children who have physical disabilities,

△ Ensure appropriate positioning (hips flexed, feet on floor, chest supported) so the child can use their arms and hands more effectively.

▲ For children who become easily distracted or take extra time to complete an activity, incorporate extra time to complete projects.

AEPS-3 Curriculum Resources (Appendix A)

Appendix A in this volume contains numerous additional resources to supplement the AEPS-3 Curriculum. The first part of the appendix presents a list of general curriculum resources, and the second part provides lists of supplementary resources for each individual routine and activity.

AEPS-3 Skills Matrix (Appendix B)

The AEPS-3 Skills Matrix in Appendix B of this volume spotlights individual skills by showing functional application across all routines and activities. Each skills matrix (there are eight total, one for each of the test's eight developmental areas) allows you to select individual AEPS-3 items for children who require an intensive focus on a few skills across routines and activities. For children who have difficulty learning new skills at the level of individual AEPS-3 items, the Foundation Steps *(FS)* provide an even more granular breakdown of component subskills that are either a sequence of developmental precursors or steps in task analyses.

9

Bath Time

Bath Time includes not only the time spent washing in the bathtub or shower but also the skills used before and after bathing (getting into and out of the tub or shower, using soap, drying off). As motor and adaptive skills increase, children's independence in this routine also increases at the Growing level. Bath time generally takes place in children's homes and might occur several times a day or several times a week, depending on both adults' preferences and children's need for a bath (after a messy diaper, before going to bed). The AEPS-3 Growing level of the Bath Time routine uses skills from eight developmental areas.

Concurrent Skills

The following concurrent skills are AEPS-3 skills that can be easily embedded and taught during regular occurrences of Bath Time.

FINE MOTOR Growing Skills	Embedded Learning Opportunities
B 2 Rotates wrist to manipulate object	■ *Helps adult turn on bathwater*
B 3.2 Aligns objects	■ *Aligns foam letters and numbers on side of tub*
C 1.1 Writes or draws using mixed strokes	■ *Uses bath crayons to scribble and write on tub wall*
C 1.2 Writes or draws using curved lines	
C 1.3 Writes or draws using straight lines	
C 1.4 Scribbles	

GROSS MOTOR Growing Skills	Embedded Learning Opportunities
B 5.2 Walks fast	■ *Walks or jumps forward to get to bathroom for bath time*
B 6 Jumps forward	

ADAPTIVE Growing Skills

A 6.1 Pours liquid into variety of containers

B 1.1 Indicates need to use toilet

B 1.2 Has bowel and bladder control

B 1.3 Indicates awareness of soiled and wet pants or diapers

B 2.1 Washes and dries face

B 3.1 Completes some steps to brush teeth, comb hair, and wipe nose

C 1.2 Takes off pullover clothing over head

C 1.3 Takes off front-opening coat, jacket, or shirt

C 1.4 Takes off pants

C 2.3 Puts on pullover clothing

C 2.4 Puts on pull-up clothing

C 2.5 Puts on socks

D 1 Takes independent action to alleviate distress, discomfort, and pain

D 1.1 Communicates internal distress, discomfort, or pain to adult

Embedded Learning Opportunities

■ *Pours water from one container into another while playing in tub*

■ *Expresses need to use potty before bath or (if not yet potty trained) states they have wet or soiled diaper*

■ *Helps adult comb hair after taking bath and having hair washed*

■ *Brushes teeth after taking bath*

■ *Takes off clothing for bath time; puts on clothing after bath is complete*

■ *Tells adult when water is too hot or cold*

SOCIAL-EMOTIONAL Growing Skills

A 3 Participates in familiar social routines with caregivers

A 3.1 Initiates next step of familiar social routine

A 3.2 Follows familiar social routines with familiar adults

B 1 Responds appropriately to others' emotions

B 1.1 Identifies/labels emotions in others

B 1.2 Identifies/labels own emotions

B 2 Uses appropriate strategies to manage emotional states

B 3.1 Explains or shows others how to do tasks mastered

B 3.2 Shares accomplishment with familiar caregiver

D 3.1 Responds to request to finish activity

D 3.2 Responds to request to begin activity

D 3.3 Entertains self by playing with toys

E 2.1 Meets behavioral expectations in familiar environments

E 2.2 Adjusts behavior based on feedback from others or environment

E 3.1 Seeks adult permission when appropriate

Embedded Learning Opportunities

■ *Pulls tub drain when adult says "It's time to get out of the bathtub"*

■ *Says to adult "I climbed out of the bathtub all by myself!"*

■ *Says "I'm a boy like my daddy!"*

■ *Plays game (I Spy, Simon Says) with adult while in tub*

■ *Puts bath toys in basket when adult says it's time to get out of tub*

■ *Asks adult for permission to let water out of tub*

SOCIAL-COMMUNICATION Growing Skills

B 2　　Locates common objects, people, or events

B 3　　Follows multistep directions without contextual cues

B 3.1　Follows multistep directions with contextual cues

B 3.2　Follows one-step direction without contextual cues

B 3.3　Follows one-step direction with contextual cues

B 4.1　Answers *who*, *what*, and *where* questions

C 1　　Produces multiple-word sentences to communicate

C 1.1　Uses two-word utterances

C 1.2　Uses 50 single words, signs, or symbols

C 2　　Uses plural pronouns to indicate subjects, objects, and possession in multiple-word sentences

C 2.1　Uses irregular plural nouns in multiple-word sentences

C 2.2　Uses regular plural nouns

C 3　　Uses helping verbs

C 3.2　Uses regular past tense of common verbs

C 3.3　Uses *to be* verbs

C 4　　Asks questions using inverted auxiliary

C 4.1　Asks *wh-* questions

D 1　　Uses language to initiate and sustain social interaction

D 1.1　Follows social conventions of language

D 2　　Provides and seeks information while conversing using words, phrases, or sentences

D 2.2　Describes objects, people, and events as part of social exchange

D 3.4　Alternates between speaker and listener roles during conversations with others

D 3.5　Responds to contingent questions from others

Embedded Learning Opportunities

■ *Follows all directions when adult says "Go to your bedroom, get your pajamas, and bring them to the bathroom"*

■ *Answers "My brush is in my room" when adult asks "Where is your brush?"*

■ *Says "I am done" when finished with bath*

■ *Asks "Where is my boat?"*

■ *Takes turns talking and listening with adult about what they did that day*

■ *Asks adult why bubbles disappear into water*

COGNITIVE Growing Skills

B 1 Imitates novel coordinated motor actions

B 2 Imitates novel words

B 3.1 Relates recent events without contextual cues

B 3.2 Relates recent events with contextual cues

B 3.3 Relates events immediately after they occur

C 2 Uses object to represent another object

C 3.1 Classifies according to function

C 3.2 Classifies according to physical attribute

C 3.3 Discriminates between objects or people using common attributes

C 4 Uses early conceptual comparisons

C 4.1 Identifies common concepts

C 4.2 Identifies concrete concepts

D 1.1 Uses part of object or support to obtain another object

E 1 Expands simple observations and explorations into further inquiry

E 2.1 Generates specific questions for investigation

Embedded Learning Opportunities

■ Sings songs with movements during bath time

■ Sorts foam animal shapes from foam people in tub

■ Asks to make bubbles in tub and watches what happens when bubble bath is added to water

■ Asks "Where did the water go?" when water is being drained

LITERACY Growing Skills

A 2 Demonstrates understanding that text is read in one direction and from top to bottom of page

A 2.1 Turns pages of book from beginning toward end

A 2.2 Holds book or other printed material with pictures correctly oriented

A 3.1 Recognizes own first name in print

B 1.2 Participates in repetitive verbal play

D 1 Demonstrates understanding that pictures represent text

D 1.1 Labels familiar people, actions, objects, and events in picture books

D 1.2 Locates familiar objects, people, events, and actions in picture books

D 2 Retells simple story

E 1.1 Dictates description of drawing

E 1.2 Verbally labels representational drawings

E 1.3 Verbally labels nonrepresentational drawings

E 2.1 Makes representational drawings

Embedded Learning Opportunities

■ Uses finger to point to text in sequence when "reading" with a bath book

■ Points to and names letters in own name after adult writes child's name on tub using bath crayons (for name Lily, child points out both Ls)

■ Draws picture (with bath crayons) of two people and says "Me and my dad"

■ Retells story to adult while in tub

MATH Growing Skills

A 1   Counts out 3 items

A 1.1   Counts 3 items to determine "How many?"

Embedded Learning Opportunities

■ *Puts three toys in tub when asked to pick three for bath time from basket full of bath-safe toys*

TIER 1

■ UNIVERSAL STRATEGIES

These are best practices for ALL young children, with attention to meeting learning outcomes within daily routines and activities of family life and early childhood classrooms while promoting positive adult–child relationships and peer interactions.

At the Growing level, children can participate in bath time more independently than at the Beginning level. Now children can walk, hop on one foot, and jump forward to get to the bathroom. Not only can they manipulate their clothing to undress for bath, but they also have the skills to complete related personal hygiene tasks (brushing teeth, combing hair), get dressed after the bath, and express the need to use the toilet before bath. Cognitively, children are able to use bath time to group toys according to function, color, shape, and size, as well as to imitate new words and movements adults use. Socially, children use more complex language to ask questions, initiate and sustain interactions using socially appropriate conversation rules, and respond to others' emotions. They have the skills to communicate their likes and dislikes, participate in imaginary play, and engage in games with rules. Math and literacy skills continue to expand as adults embed math and literacy concepts in bath time routines (reading bath books, counting bath toys).

Interactions

At the Growing level, adult–child interactions remain an important component of bath time. Most important, make sure bath time is a safe, positive experience. Adults should remain with children at all times during bath time. Because children may already know the steps in the actual bath time routine, adults can make use of bath time in many different ways. Following are some suggested interactions for the Growing level of this routine:

▲ Work on increasingly complex language skills with children (explain what children are doing, use new vocabulary, allow the child to ask and answer questions).

▲ Help children classify toys according to color, size, shape, and texture.

▲ Model writing letters, numbers, and shapes on the tub using bath crayons or bubble bath suds.

▲ Give children opportunities to imitate adults' writing, using calm words of encouragement if they become frustrated that their letters do not look like adults' letters.

▲ Model how to draw curved or straight lines.

▲ Draw and narrate pictures.

▲ Incorporate foam letters and numbers into tub play to build literacy and math skills enjoyably.

▲ Use foam numbers to show how to count using one-to-one correspondence.

▲ Talk about the child's age while showing the corresponding foam number.

▲ Spell out children's names with foam letters and talk about the names of the letters.

▲ Read bath books aloud and use them to help children learn and talk about their own physical characteristics and those of others around them.

▲ Use bath time to teach children the names of body parts.

▲ Talk about bathtub rules and what could happen if children don't follow the rules (could slip and fall if too much water gets splashed on the floor).

Environment and Materials

Materials needed include soap, shampoo, washcloth, towel, and tub-safe bath toys (foam letters and numbers, plastic cups, bath books). Following are some suggestions for the Growing level of this routine:

▲ Use bath crayons, bubble bath, and bathtub paints to encourage children to write letters and numbers and draw pictures.

▲ Consider using common unbreakable household items (plastic cups, measuring cups, measuring spoons) as bath toys.

▲ Confirm that all bath materials are easily accessible from the bathing area before putting a child into the bath water.

■ FOCUSED STRATEGIES

These strategies are for teaching SOME children who are struggling with a component of a skill or whose development is stalled and who need extra help to catch up or keep up. The strategies include a variety of minor adaptations or modifications to daily routines, activities, and environments to meet targeted outcomes at home and in classrooms.

▲ Allow extra time for children to answer questions during conversations at bath time.

▲ Use first-then boards to show children what they need to do (first you wash your body, then you play with toys).

▲ Simplify activities during bath time (when offering foam letters, give only letters in the child's name).

▲ Work on one specific skill at a time (if you want to focus on numbers and counting during bath time, offer only foam numbers and put away foam letters and other toys before the child sees them).

▲ Give children who have difficulty with transitions adequate advance notice that they will be taking a bath, and set a visual timer or let children set it ("Bath time is in 5 minutes. Do you want me to set the timer, or do you want to set it?"). Give a similar alert shortly before time to get out of the bath.

▲ Give children choices related to the routine ("Do you want daddy to give you a bath, or mommy?")

▲ Teach children who cannot speak to use simple signs (MORE, ALL DONE) so they can communicate their preferences.

▲ Learn to recognize children's cues and preferences.

▲ Pair sign language with spoken words for children who are nonverbal or who have hearing impairments.

■ SPECIALIZED STRATEGIES

These strategies for teaching the FEW children who need intensive supports include a variety of specialized, individualized, precise evidence-based strategies to meet children's unique goals/outcomes:

▲ Make accommodations for children who are unable to sit independently because of a physical disability:

△ Make sure children are stable and feel secure when sitting in the tub.

△ Use an adapted bath seat.

△ Make sure the water in the tub is shallow.

▲ Adapt the routine and materials for children who have sensory integration issues:

△ Shorten the time the child is in the bathtub.

△ Change the type of fabric used for drying off.

▲ Use positive reinforcement to increase children's willingness to take a bath:

△ Allow children to choose an additional book to read at the end of the routine as a reward.

▲ Use naturalistic language strategies such as mand modeling (Chapter 4) to encourage children to ask for what they want and to minimize protests:

△ Model saying "More" to encourage children to request what they want more of.

△ Say "All done" to help reduce protests.

△ When children want more of something (such as splashing) or want to get out of the tub, ask what they want and wait for them to sign or use a word to say "More" or "All done." If children do not do so, verbally or physically model doing so for them, and then give them an opportunity to make the request.

▲ Break bathing into steps and start by teaching the critical skill of washing the body parts they can see.

▲ Use system of least prompts to teach children how to wash themselves:

△ Teach a child to first wash the body parts they can see.

△ Let the child wash their legs and feet, hands and arms, and stomach independently.

△ Then provide increasing support (specific verbal cues, modeling, and then hand-over-hand prompts) to complete washing as needed.

▲ Save complicated skills (turning water on and off, adjusting water temperature) until children have mastered washing.

AEPS-3 Curriculum Resources (Appendix A)

Appendix A in this volume contains numerous additional resources to supplement the AEPS-3 Curriculum. The first part of the appendix presents a list of general curriculum resources, and the second part provides lists of supplementary resources for each individual routine and activity.

AEPS-3 Skills Matrix (Appendix B)

The AEPS-3 Skills Matrix in Appendix B of this volume spotlights individual skills by showing functional application across all routines and activities. Each skills matrix (there are eight total, one for each of the test's eight developmental areas) allows you to select individual AEPS-3 items for children who require an intensive focus on a few skills across routines and activities. For children who have difficulty learning new skills at the level of individual AEPS-3 items, the Foundation Steps (*FS*) provide an even more granular breakdown of component subskills that are either a sequence of developmental precursors or steps in task analyses.

10

Block Play

Block Play consists of playing with blocks made from different materials, in a variety of shapes, sizes, and colors. This activity may also include other toys to combine with block play (cars, people, animals, trains, town blocks). Children's participation in block play changes over time as fine motor and cognitive skills increase and play becomes more purposeful and active. This routine can take place at home, at child care, or in school and may occur several times a day depending on children's interest level and schedule. The AEPS-3 Growing level of Block Play covers eight developmental areas.

Concurrent Skills

The following concurrent skills are AEPS-3 skills that can be easily embedded and taught during regular occurrences of Block Play.

FINE MOTOR **Growing Skills**

B 2 Rotates wrist to manipulate object

B 3 Manipulates object with two hands, each performing different action

B 3.1 Assembles toy

B 3.2 Aligns objects

B 3.3 Fits variety of shapes into corresponding spaces

Embedded Learning Opportunities

- *Rotates wrist to turn blocks to see what is on front, turns car to drive down road on mat*

- *Fits different shapes of blocks into corresponding slots on shape sorter*

GROSS MOTOR Growing Skills

B 3   Walks avoiding people, furniture, or objects

B 3.1 Walks without support

B 4.3 Gets up and down from low structure

C 1.6 Throws or rolls ball at target with two hands

Embedded Learning Opportunities

■ *Walks to blocks area to play*

■ *Gets up and down from small bench at block table*

ADAPTIVE Growing Skills

D 1   Takes independent action to alleviate distress, discomfort, and pain

D 1.1 Communicates internal distress, discomfort, or pain to adult

Embedded Learning Opportunities

■ *Tells teacher when self or peer is injured*

■ *Moves independently away from peer who is bothering them*

■ *Leaves block area and goes to quiet area when not feeling well*

SOCIAL-EMOTIONAL Growing Skills

A 3.2   Follows familiar social routines with familiar adults

B 1   Responds appropriately to others' emotions

B 1.1   Identifies/labels emotions in others

B 1.2   Identifies/labels own emotions

B 2   Uses appropriate strategies to manage emotional states

B 2.1   Responds appropriately to soothing by peer

B 3   Makes positive statements about self or accomplishments

B 3.1   Explains or shows others how to do tasks mastered

B 3.2   Shares accomplishment with familiar caregiver

C 1   Maintains interaction with peer

C 1.1   Initiates social behavior toward peer

C 1.2   Responds appropriately to peer social behavior

C 3.1   Initiates cooperative activity

C 3.2   Joins others in cooperative activity

C 3.3   Shares or exchanges objects

D 1   Interacts appropriately with others during small-group activities

D 1.1   Interacts appropriately with materials during small-group activities

D 1.2   Responds appropriately to directions during small-group activities

D 1.3   Remains with group during small-group activities

D 3   Initiates and completes independent activities

D 3.1   Responds to request to finish activity

D 3.2   Responds to request to begin activity

D 3.3   Entertains self by playing with toys

D 4   Resolves conflicts using negotiation

D 4.1   Uses strategies to resolve conflicts

D 4.2   Claims and defends possessions

E 1.1   Meets internal physical needs of hunger and thirst

E 2.1   Meets behavioral expectations in familiar environments

E 2.2   Adjusts behavior based on feedback from others or environment

E 3.1   Seeks adult permission when appropriate

Embedded Learning Opportunities

■ *Knocks over a peer's block creation by accident and responds to peer's crying by saying "I can help you rebuild!"*

■ *Says "I did it!" or "My castle all done!"*

■ *Cooperates with peer on activity such as building block creation*

■ *Negotiates with peer to resolve conflict (child takes block that peer was playing with, hands peer different block, and says "You can have this one")*

■ *Hands blocks to peers instead of throwing them when teacher says "Please do not throw blocks"*

SOCIAL-COMMUNICATION Growing Skills

B 2   Locates common objects, people, or events

B 3   Follows multistep directions without contextual cues

B 3.1   Follows multistep directions with contextual cues

B 3.2   Follows one-step direction without contextual cues

B 3.3   Follows one-step direction with contextual cues

B 4.1   Answers *who*, *what*, and *where* questions

C 1   Produces multiple-word sentences to communicate

C 1.1   Uses two-word utterances

C 1.2   Uses 50 single words, signs, or symbols

C 2   Uses plural pronouns to indicate subjects, objects, and possession in multiple-word sentences

C 2.1   Uses irregular plural nouns in multiple-word sentences

C 2.2   Uses regular plural nouns

C 3   Uses helping verbs

C 3.2   Uses regular past tense of common verbs

C 3.3   Uses *to be* verbs

C 4   Asks questions using inverted auxiliary

C 4.1   Asks *wh-* questions

D 1   Uses language to initiate and sustain social interaction

D 1.1   Follows social conventions of language

D 2   Provides and seeks information while conversing using words, phrases, or sentences

D 2.1   Asks questions to obtain information

D 2.2   Describes objects, people, and events as part of social exchange

D 3.3   Responds to topic initiations from others

D 3.4   Alternates between speaker and listener roles during conversations with others

D 3.5   Responds to contingent questions from others

Embedded Learning Opportunities

■ *Finds box of town blocks after hearing peer say they can't find them*

■ *Picks up only red blocks and puts them on shelf after adult instructs child to do so*

■ *Talks about blocks, playing with blocks at home, or taking trip on airplane and playing with blocks during flight*

■ *Asks "Where my blocks?" "Who take my car?" "Why I need big block?"*

■ *Answers "I am building a castle" after adult asks "What are you building?"*

COGNITIVE Growing Skills

B 1   Imitates novel coordinated motor actions

B 2   Imitates novel words

B 3.1 Relates recent events without contextual cues

B 3.2 Relates recent events with contextual cues

B 3.3 Relates events immediately after they occur

C 1.1 Locates object in second of two hiding places

C 2   Recognizes symbols

C 2.1 Uses object to represent another object

C 3.1 Classifies according to function

C 3.2 Classifies according to physical attribute

C 3.3 Discriminates between objects or people using common attributes

C 4   Uses early conceptual comparisons

C 4.1 Identifies common concepts

C 4.2 Identifies concrete concepts

D 1.1 Uses part of an object or support to obtain another object

D 3.1 Evaluates common solutions to solve problems or reach goals

D 4.1 Draws conclusions about causes of events based on personal experience

E 3   Investigates to test hypotheses

E 3.1 Draws on prior knowledge to guide investigations

E 3.2 Manipulates materials to cause change

Embedded Learning Opportunities

■ *Repeats "more please" after hearing adult say "I want more blocks, please"; repeats "big trucks" after hearing peer say "You have big trucks!"; repeats "tower" after hearing adult say "Let's build a tower!"*

■ *Says "My tower too big" after tall tower falls down*

■ *Organizes blocks by shape and color, cars by size and color, toy people by gender or family role*

■ *Observes, "I have two red cars!" after looking in hand to check what cars are there*

■ *Notices that putting one more block on top of tower causes it to fall*

LITERACY Growing Skills

A 3.2 Recognizes common signs and logos

B 1.2 Participates in repetitive verbal play

Embedded Learning Opportunities

■ *Recognizes toy traffic signs for stop, yield, crosswalk in blocks area*

■ *Recognizes three ABC blocks with letters in own first name*

■ *Creates three letters using big blocks*

■ *Identifies letters posted on wall in blocks area*

MATH Growing Skills

A 1 Counts out 3 items

A 1.1 Counts 3 items to determine "How many?"

B 1 Compares items in sets to 5 by counting

B 1.1 Compares items in sets to 5 by matching

B 1.2 Creates equivalent sets of 5 items

B 1.3 Uses quantity comparison words

Embedded Learning Opportunities

- *Counts 3 blocks, 3 cars, or 3 friends in blocks area*

- *Counts out 5 blocks each for three different friends (three sets of 5 blocks)*

- *Counts blocks used in building block creation when adult asks, "How many blocks did you use?"; after counting, responds, "10!"*

TIER 1

■ UNIVERSAL STRATEGIES

These are best practices for ALL young children, with attention to meeting learning outcomes within daily routines and activities of family life and early childhood classrooms while promoting positive adult–child relationships and peer interactions.

As children's skills increase at the Growing level, they can participate in block play independently, with adults, and with peers. Their increased motor skills allow them to walk or cruise to the blocks area, assemble toys that need to be put together (Lincoln Logs, Legos, other linking/building materials), and align objects such as blocks on the rug. Cognitively, children continue to imitate new movements and words, with increased ability to transfer knowledge from past events, make investigations, and draw conclusions about causes of events. They can identify common shapes, colors, and sizes of blocks and use conversational rules when communicating this information to others. With their increasingly complex social and communication skills, children can answer *who, what, why, how, when,* and *where* questions while maintaining cooperative play with others. They can express their likes and dislikes, follow rules, and report those who are not following the rules or are using inappropriate behavior or actions. In the areas of mathematics and literacy, children can count blocks, use comparison words, and recognize letters from their own first names on the blocks.

Interactions

At the Growing level, adults can support block play by providing opportunities throughout the day to play with blocks independently, with adults, and with peers. Adults and peers can model stacking blocks and knocking them over using their hands, feet, or another object such as a toy car or ball. During block play, positive interactions should occur among adults and children. Following are some suggestions for the Growing level:

▲ Give choices by asking children questions about their preferences and allowing them to answer.

▲ Refrain from asking yes-or-no questions to give children an opportunity to expand their language skills by giving more complex responses.

▲ Give immediate and specific feedback ("Look at the tall tower you built! Nice job!").

▲ Introduce new vocabulary and concepts, such as numbers, letters, colors, aligning objects, and building more complex structures with blocks.

▲ Teach the expectations of block play and keep rules consistent ("Use nice hands," "Use your walking feet," "Be nice to friends and teachers").

▲ Display the do and don't rules of block play using picture charts so children can look at pictures for a reminder.

▲ Role-play what would happen if a child knocked down a peer's creation without asking the peer first or if a child took a block from a peer's creation without asking first.

▲ Use the "forgetting" teaching strategy:

△ Start building a tower or other structure, then stop and tell the child you forgot how to do it. This allows the child the opportunity to show you how to do something and also encourages them to tell you verbally what they are doing.

▲ Incorporate math into block play:

△ Count 1, 2, 3, and then crash a toy car into the blocks.

△ Count blocks and compare quantities of blocks using comparison words such as *more* and *less*.

▲ Apply literacy concepts:

△ Use blocks with letters on them to help develop letter recognition.

△ Give children blocks with letters in their first names.

Environment and Materials

Block play can take place indoors or outdoors, at home, at child care, or at school. If block play takes place outside, adults must ensure that the area is safe for play. Following are some suggestions for environment and materials at the Growing level:

▲ Provide buckets of blocks of different shapes, sizes, and colors, made from different materials (wood, plastic, cardboard), with letters and numbers printed on them. Blocks may be store-bought or handmade.

▲ Ensure safety with materials used because young children like to put things in their mouths and chew on them:

△ Make sure the paint on handmade blocks is nontoxic.

△ Keep block size in mind.

△ Stay away from items not recommended for toddlers because they pose a choking hazard.

▲ Include a variety of other items to complement block play—the possibilities are endless:

△ Big and little toy cars, trains and train tracks, people and dollhouse furniture, toy animals, or town or city blocks.

△ Fine motor building materials such as Lincoln Logs, Legos, puzzles, ABC stackable blocks, and other linking/building materials.

TIER 2

■ FOCUSED STRATEGIES

These strategies are for teaching SOME children who are struggling with a component of a skill or whose development is stalled and who need extra help to catch up or keep up. The strategies include a variety of minor adaptations or modifications to daily routines, activities, and environments to meet targeted outcomes at home and in classrooms.

▲ Follow children's lead:

△ If the child shows signs of needing to take a break from blocks (seems easily angered or upset, keeps knocking down peers' creations, throws objects), engage the child in a different activity for a while and revisit blocks later.

△   If the child is experiencing sensory overload (as when the room is too loud for them), take the child and some blocks to another area or room that is quieter, or take a break from blocks.

▲   Simplify activities during block play. Show children one activity to do with the blocks, such as building a tower, and limit the number of blocks provided to avoid overstimulation.

▲   Allow children to knock over an adult's tower, while the adult models and verbally talks about their feelings ("This is fun!" "You can knock over your tower now"). Never knock over a child's tower without their permission.

▲   Provide verbal prompts to encourage children to build a tower or play with peers.

▲   Use a verbal prompt ("Five minutes until clean up!") and visual timer (holding up five fingers) to help with transitions.

▲   Use a visual timer (sand timer) to help children take turns playing with a popular set of blocks in a group. Let the child whose turn it is help set the timer, and have them tell you when the time is up so you can help with the exchange.

▲   Ask children probing questions about their block creations and let them think of the answers on their own. If they are unable to come up with answers, offer prompts:

△   Use scaffolding by asking questions that offer possible answers ("Are you building a house?" "Are you building a barn?").

△   Ask children what they can do after they have finished building their tower.

▲   Use consistent language when talking with children about the routine, as when talking about

△   Characteristics of the blocks

△   Actions to do with blocks

△   Rules for using blocks

▲   Vary the environments where children engage in block play (indoors, outdoors, tabletops, floor), using settings children find interesting (to provide additional opportunities to practice skills):

△   Take a bag of blocks to the park or playground.

△   Put Legos in a tub of water.

△   Provide building materials during tabletop play in small-group settings.

▲   Use verbal prompts and adult–peer models to provide specific, consistent instructions to help children understand what they should be doing during block play.

▲   Learn to recognize children's cues and preferences.

▲   Teach children who cannot speak to use simple signs (MORE, ALL DONE) so they can communicate their preferences.

▲   Pair sign language with spoken words for children who are nonverbal or who have a hearing impairment.

▲   Make sure children with physical disabilities are positioned appropriately (hips flexed, feet on floor, chest supported) so they can use their arms and hands more effectively.

▲   Learn to recognize children's cues and preferences.

▲   Pair sign language with spoken words for children who are nonverbal or who have hearing impairments.

■ SPECIALIZED STRATEGIES

These strategies for teaching the FEW children who need intensive supports include a variety of specialized, individualized, precise evidence-based strategies to meet children's unique goals/outcomes:

▲ Adapt the routine for children who cannot walk or crawl to the block area:

△ Provide extra support by having peers or adults help them walk.

△ Provide a wheelchair or other mobility device to allow the child to access the blocks area.

△ Carry the child if necessary.

△ Bring blocks to the child.

▲ Teach sign language or use picture cards or technology apps to help children who cannot speak communicate their likes, dislikes, wants, and needs while playing.

▲ Provide adaptable materials to make it possible for children to participate:

△ Use a toddler seat or highchair for a child who cannot sit upright on the floor, or place pillows around their sides and back.

△ Put a knit or felt glove on a child who cannot hold onto blocks, use blocks with Velcro on them, or let the child use a "grabber" tool for reaching.

▲ Use system of least prompts (see Chapter 4) for teaching children how to reach for, grasp, and release blocks:

△ Give the child an opportunity to perform each action independently, allowing time for the child to respond.

△ Provide increased support until the child performs the action (model, then offer a physical prompt).

△ Reinforce each behavior the child does (both independently and with assistance).

▲ Use first-then boards to show children what they need to do (first you build a tower, then you knock it down with your toy car or ball).

AEPS-3 Curriculum Resources (Appendix A)

Appendix A in this volume contains numerous additional resources to supplement the AEPS-3 Curriculum. The first part of the appendix presents a list of general curriculum resources, and the second part provides lists of supplementary resources for each individual routine and activity.

AEPS-3 Skills Matrix (Appendix B)

The AEPS-3 Skills Matrix in Appendix B of this volume spotlights individual skills by showing functional application across all routines and activities. Each skills matrix (there are eight total, one for each of the test's eight developmental areas) allows you to select individual AEPS-3 items for children who require an intensive focus on a few skills across routines and activities. For children who have difficulty learning new skills at the level of individual AEPS-3 items, the Foundation Steps (FS) provide an even more granular breakdown of component subskills that are either a sequence of developmental precursors or steps in task analyses.

11

Circle Time

Circle Time incorporates many skills and activities, including storytime (looking at and reading books), singing with others, rhyming, identifying letters, reading a class schedule, and choosing activities, among numerous others. This routine changes over time as children's social-communication, social-emotional, cognitive, and literacy skills become more advanced. Circle time occurs most commonly in a classroom or child care setting, and storytime may occur in any setting with an adult or other person with whom a child can share books. Depending on the environment and the schedule, this routine may occur up to three times a day. The AEPS-3 Growing level of Circle Time includes skills from eight developmental areas.

Concurrent Skills

The following concurrent skills are AEPS-3 skills that can be easily embedded and taught during regular occurrences of Circle Time.

FINE MOTOR Growing Skills

B 2 Rotates wrist to manipulate object
D 1 Uses fingers to interact with electronic device

Embedded Learning Opportunities

- *Uses wrist to turn page in book or flip book from front cover to back cover*

- *Uses fingers to tap "next page" button on tablet to read story, "yes" or "no" buttons to answer questions during circle time*

GROSS MOTOR Growing Skills

B 3 Walks avoiding people, furniture, or objects
B 3.1 Walks without support
B 4.3 Gets up and down from low structure

Embedded Learning Opportunities

- *Walks with and without support to circle time area or location of story reading*

- *Gets up and down from floor or stool when finished or starting to listen to story*

ADAPTIVE Growing Skills

D 1   Takes independent action to alleviate distress, discomfort, and pain

D 1.1   Communicates internal distress, discomfort, or pain to adult

Embedded Learning Opportunities

■ *Gets up to go to bathroom during circle time, telling adult they do not feel well*

■ *Asks for new book because current story is scary or sad*

SOCIAL-EMOTIONAL Growing Skills

A 3.1   Initiates next step of familiar social routine

A 3.2   Follows familiar social routines with familiar adults

B 1   Responds appropriately to others' emotions

B 1.1   Identifies/labels emotions in others

B 1.2   Identifies/labels own emotions

B 3   Makes positive statements about self or accomplishments

B 3.1   Explains or shows others how to do tasks mastered

B 3.2   Shares accomplishment with familiar caregiver

D 1   Interacts appropriately with others during small-group activities

D 1.1   Interacts appropriately with materials during small-group activities

D 1.2   Responds appropriately to directions during small-group activities

D 1.3   Remains with group during small-group activity

D 2   Interacts appropriately with others during large-group activities

D 2.1   Interacts appropriately with materials during large-group activities

D 2.2   Responds appropriately to directions during large-group activities

D 2.3   Remains with group during large-group activities

D 3.2   Responds to request to begin activity

E 2.1   Meets behavioral expectations in familiar environments

E 2.2   Adjusts behavior based on feedback from others or environment

E 3.2   Follows established social rules in familiar environments

E 4.2   States age

E 4.3   Provides given name or nickname of self and others

Embedded Learning Opportunities

■ *Walks to library area when teacher says "It's circle time," chooses book, and hands it to teacher to read*

■ *Responds "He crying. He sad," when teacher points out crying peer and asks how peer feels*

■ *Says "I did it!" when lifting flap in a book during shared book reading*

■ *Follows directions, answers questions, follows along with book with eyes and ears, asks questions during small- and large-group circle time*

■ *Stays in designated location and follows classroom rules during circle time*

■ *Gets up quietly to go to bathroom, interrupts teacher if bleeding, quietly walks to new preferred activity*

■ *Answers "I 2!" when teacher says "This little boy is 2. How many of my friends are 2?"*

SOCIAL-COMMUNICATION Growing Skills

B 2   Locates common objects, people, or events

B 3   Follows multistep directions without contextual cues

B 3.1 Follows multistep directions with contextual cues

B 3.2 Follows one-step direction without contextual cues

B 3.3 Follows one-step direction with contextual cues

B 4.1 Answers *who*, *what*, and *where* questions

C 1   Produces multiple-word sentences to communicate

C 1.1 Uses two-word utterances

C 1.2 Uses 50 single words, signs, or symbols

C 2   Uses plural form of pronouns to indicate subjects, objects, and possession in multiple-word sentences

C 2.1 Uses irregular plural nouns in multiple-word sentences

C 2.2 Uses regular plural nouns

C 3   Uses helping verbs

C 3.2 Uses regular past tense of common verbs

C 3.3 Uses *to be* verbs

C 4   Asks questions using inverted auxiliary

C 4.1 Asks *wh-* questions

D 1   Uses language to initiate and sustain social interaction

D 2   Provides and seeks information while conversing using words, phrases, or sentences

D 2.1 Asks questions to obtain information

D 2.2 Describes objects, people, and events as part of social exchange

D 3.3 Responds to topic initiations from others

D 3.4 Alternates between speaker and listener roles during conversations with others

D 3.5 Responds to contingent questions from others

Embedded Learning Opportunities

■ *Finds familiar things in books (food, family members, birthday party)*

■ *Goes to circle time rug and sits down after teacher holds up picture of little boy sitting in circle and says "Time to walk to the circle time rug and sit down with your legs crossed!"*

■ *Answers questions adult asks ("Why is the boy sad?" "What do you think will happen next?")*

■ *Uses irregular plural nouns, plural nouns, helping verbs, regular past tense of common verbs, to be verbs in conversation*

■ *Asks "What happened?" during circle time story*

■ *Looks at teacher when teacher talks*

■ *Takes turns speaking and listening during conversations with peers and adults*

COGNITIVE Growing Skills

B 1   Imitates novel coordinated motor actions

B 2   Imitates novel words

B 3.1 Relates recent events without contextual cues

B 3.2 Relates recent events with contextual cues

B 3.3 Relates events immediately after they occur

C 2.1 Uses object to represent another object

C 3.1 Classifies according to function

C 3.2 Classifies according to physical attribute

C 3.3 Discriminates between objects or people using common attributes

C 4   Uses early conceptual comparisons

C 4.1 Identifies common concepts

C 4.2 Identifies concrete concepts

D 3.1 Evaluates common solutions to solve problems or reach goals

D 4.1 Draws conclusions about causes of events based on personal experience

E 1   Expands simple observations and explorations into further inquiry

E 2.2 Demonstrates knowledge about natural happenings

Embedded Learning Opportunities

■ *Imitates adult crisscrossing legs*

■ *Repeats "green ball" when adult says "Ronnie rolled the green ball down the hill"*

■ *Raises hand and answers "Farley found a bone!" when teacher shows picture of dog holding bone and asks if children remember what happened in yesterday's story*

■ *Separates books according to size, color (black and white, or color), or type (books about animals, families, trees)*

■ *Sees book page with gray clouds and asks "It going to rain?" after noticing gray clouds and rain on previous day's drive to school*

■ *Says names of people, animals, colors, or numbers in a book*

LITERACY Growing Skills

A 1   Participates in shared group reading

A 2   Demonstrates understanding that text is read in one direction and from top to bottom of page

A 2.1   Turns pages of book from beginning toward end

A 2.2   Holds book or other printed material with pictures correctly oriented

A 3.1   Recognizes own first name in print

A 3.2   Recognizes common signs and logos

B 1.2   Participates in repetitive verbal play

D 1   Demonstrates understanding that pictures represent text

D 1.1   Labels familiar people, actions, objects, and events in picture books

D 1.2   Locates familiar objects, people, events, and actions in picture books

D 1.3   Matches pictures to actual objects, people, or actions

D 2   Retells simple story

D 2.1   Makes predictions about what will happen next in story

D 2.2   Answers and asks questions related to story

D 2.3   Tells story associated with series of pictures

D 3   Demonstrates understanding of abstract story vocabulary

D 3.1   Demonstrates understanding of key vocabulary in picture books

D 3.2   Demonstrates understanding of title, author, and illustrator

D 3.3   Demonstrates understanding of vocabulary associated with early literacy concepts

Embedded Learning Opportunities

■ *Sits down for shared group reading during circle time or sits with adult in library and looks at book*

■ *Uses pointer finger to follow along with words being read in story*

■ *Says "I see a cat!" when adult asks, while reading book during circle time, "Can you find a cat that looks just like this one?"*

■ *Says "Apple!" when seeing picture of apple in book*

■ *Says "That bear says hello!" after reading book about talking bear*

■ *Retells simple story from pictures during story time (Brown Bear, Brown Bear, What Do You See?, The Very Hungry Caterpillar, If You Give a Mouse a Cookie)*

■ *Says "Bat!" when adult asks "What word rhymes with cat?"*

MATH Growing Skills

A 1   Counts out 3 items

A 1.1   Counts 3 items to determine "How many?"

A 2.2   Recites numbers 1–10

B 1.3   Uses quantity comparison words

Embedded Learning Opportunities

■ *Counts out 3 books in library, 3 circle time mats, 3 friends sitting at circle time*

■ *Recites numbers 1 to 10 when reading counting book or singing counting song*

TIER
1

■ UNIVERSAL STRATEGIES

These are best practices for ALL young children, with attention to meeting learning outcomes within daily routines and activities of family life and early childhood classrooms while promoting positive adult–child relationships and peer interactions.

As children grow older, they have increased knowledge about circle time and new skills. They can rotate their wrists to hold a book and turn pages from front to back. They can recognize letters and numbers and can label events in picture books. With their increasingly complex social and communication skills, children can ask questions to get answers and can answer *who, what, where, when, why,* and *how* questions, as well as retell stories and make predictions about stories. They can count, compare, use quantity words to describe their observations, and classify objects by color, shape, and size. They can follow rules and report those who are not following rules. With their increased gross motor skills, children can walk and get up and down from low structures.

Interactions

As children's skills increase, they become more willing and able to participate independently in circle time, which continues to consist of music and movement for meet and greet and reading to increase vocabulary. However, children are still learning this routine and the skills they need for it, so adults must continue to model skills, offer prompts, and provide direction. Following are some suggestions for interactions at the Growing level:

▲ Point to words while reading books, singing songs, doing movements, and counting during calendar time.

▲ Incorporate a picture schedule into the routine to provide consistency and let children know what to expect for the day.

▲ Assign children jobs to do during circle time (counting helper, schedule reader) to help them engage more fully with the learning activities.

▲ Introduce new vocabulary and behaviors through reading and singing.

▲ Discuss what vocabulary words mean and let children ask questions.

▲ Read books that incorporate comparison words and concepts such as color, shape, and size.

▲ Give children a little time to answer questions (10–20 seconds for girls at this level, up to 30 seconds for boys); if they are unable to do so, encourage other children to help answer.

▲ Use the appropriate tone of voice for each activity (loud and boisterous with a smile when singing, calm when answering questions).

▲ Give children choices when possible:

△ Book for group to read

△ Song for group to sing

△ Whether to be your classroom or child care helper for the day (keep track of who has been helper so everyone gets a chance to choose the role if desired)

▲ Follow children's lead throughout the day as much as possible, whether at home, school, or child care (if they want to read a book, spend time reading and bonding with them).

Environment and Materials

Circle time most often takes place indoors in one location in a child care, school, or home setting. With appropriate materials and weather permitting, this routine can also occur outdoors. Many of the materials used for the Growing level are the same as those for the Beginning level (books on various topics that interest children, books of varying lengths). Some children still need short stories to sustain their attention, whereas others can sit through reading longer books. A rug to sit on is still a good visual prompt to show children where they need to be located for this routine. Following are some suggestions for environment and materials at the Growing level:

▲ Incorporate sensory (touch and feel) books, picture books, number books, and books that incorporate concepts such as shapes, sizes, colors, and quantity words.

▲ Continue using board books at this level because they are sturdy and can withstand young children's handling.

▲ Use a picture schedule to show children what they will be doing that day.

▲ Use a circle time rug that features shapes and colors, both to visually remind children where to sit and to give adults the opportunity to teach shapes and colors.

▲ Use child-size chairs and stuffed animals to set up a reading corner in the classroom, child care setting, or at home to make reading an appealing routine.

▲ Include a variety of materials such as songs, science materials, wooden rings, bean bags, and other items during circle time depending on the discussion topic.

TIER 2

■ FOCUSED STRATEGIES

These strategies are for teaching SOME children who are struggling with a component of a skill or whose development is stalled and who need extra help to catch up or keep up. The strategies include a variety of minor adaptations or modifications to daily routines, activities, and environments to meet targeted outcomes at home and in classrooms.

▲ Follow children's lead whenever possible:

△ Let them take a break from storytime and do a different activity for a while if they need to, revisiting the book at a later time.

▲ Give children their own copy of the book to see if they can follow along.

▲ Shorten or extend the time spent on this routine according to children's individual needs.

▲ Let children who become agitated, upset, or fidgety move to a different area of the classroom (quiet cube, library corner) with or without another adult, then continue the routine with the remaining children.

▲ Use first-then boards to show children what they need to do (first we do circle time, then we have snack).

▲ Simplify circle time activities:

△ Let children who cannot count and point to numbers at the same time do one or the other separately.

△ Break up circle time into shorter time increments (hold two shorter periods of different circle time activities during the day).

▲ Provide verbal prompts and cues to help children with classroom jobs.

▲ Use verbal prompts and a visual timer to help with transitions:

△ Use a visual timer to help children in a group take turns with a popular book or using a book corner.

△ Let children help set timers and tell adults when time is up so adults can help with exchanges of materials.

▲ Provide adaptive materials for children who have specific sensory needs (fidget toys, stuffed animals, vibrating snakes, spikey balls, light-up toys, squishy materials, soft chewy toys for oral stimulation).

▲ Use peer models to complete tasks when possible.

▲ Learn to recognize children's cues and preferences.

▲ Pair sign language with spoken words for children who are nonverbal or who have hearing impairments.

▲ Teach children who cannot speak to use sign language, picture cards, a technology app, or simple signs (MORE, ALL DONE) to communicate their likes and dislikes and help them participate in activities.

■ SPECIALIZED STRATEGIES

These strategies for teaching the FEW children who need intensive supports include a variety of specialized, individualized, precise evidence-based strategies to meet children's unique goals/outcomes:

▲ Provide adaptive materials as needed:

△ Make sure children are all seated at the same physical level so children who have disabilities feel included (if a child cannot sit on the floor and needs an adaptable stroller, have the other children sit in chairs).

△ Provide BackJack chairs, pillows for positioning, or weighted cushions and vests to help with body awareness and control.

▲ Implement graduated guidance and use hand-over-hand assistance as needed so children can perform hand movements during music or tasks.

▲ Provide adaptive switches for children with physical disabilities or who are nonverbal so that they can

△ Push a switch attached to a prerecorded song so the child can "sing" along with others.

△ Make choices about which book to read, with each choice programmed into two recordable switches.

▲ Provide options for children with autism and/or experience sensory overload:

△ Let children take a book to a quieter room to read if the room is too loud for them.

△ Give children who cannot focus on reading choices of other things to do.

▲ Offer options for students who have visual impairments:

△ Provide an extra copy of a book so they can hold it close to their face.

△ Provide tactile books for children who are blind, objects they can manipulate while listening to a story (stuffed animal that goes along with the book), or objects with defined textures.

△ Use hand-under-hand support to help children with visual impairments move instruments.

▲ Provide options for children who have hearing impairments:

△ Use sign language for key vocabulary words, and let children practice signing the words.

△ Teach new words by pointing to a picture in a book and then showing children the sign for the word.

△ Work with speech and occupational therapists to help make sure children can participate to their maximum potential.

AEPS-3 Curriculum Resources (Appendix A)

Appendix A in this volume contains numerous additional resources to supplement the AEPS-3 Curriculum. The first part of the appendix presents a list of general curriculum resources, and the second part provides lists of supplementary resources for each individual routine and activity.

AEPS-3 Skills Matrix (Appendix B)

The AEPS-3 Skills Matrix in Appendix B of this volume spotlights individual skills by showing functional application across all routines and activities. Each skills matrix (there are eight total, one for each of the test's eight developmental areas) allows you to select individual AEPS-3 items for children who require an intensive focus on a few skills across routines and activities. For children who have difficulty learning new skills at the level of individual AEPS-3 items, the Foundation Steps (*FS*) provide an even more granular breakdown of component subskills that are either a sequence of developmental precursors or steps in task analyses.

12

Diapering, Toileting, & Handwashing

At the Growing level of Diapering, Toileting, & Handwashing, most children should become able to perform most steps independently. This routine occurs several times a day and includes getting to and from the bathroom or changing location, getting on the toilet, and moving to the sink. It takes place at school, home, and child care and in community facilities. The AEPS-3 Growing level of this routine uses skills from eight developmental areas.

Concurrent Skills

The following concurrent skills are AEPS-3 skills that can be easily embedded and taught during regular occurrences of Diapering, Toileting, & Handwashing.

FINE MOTOR Growing Skills	
B 1	Activates object with finger
B 2	Rotates wrist to manipulate object
B 3	Manipulates object with two hands, each performing different action

Embedded Learning Opportunities

- *Pushes button on baby wipe dispenser to open box after adult asks them to get wipe*

- *Rotates wrist to twist sink knob from hot to cold water or flip diaper from front to back before putting it on*

- *Holds soap dispenser while pressing lever to get soap*

GROSS MOTOR Growing Skills

B 3   Walks avoiding people, furniture, or objects

B 3.1 Walks without support

B 4.2 Moves up and down stairs

B 4.3 Gets up and down from low structure

B 5.2 Walks fast

Embedded Learning Opportunities

■ *Walks quickly or slowly to go to toilet, changing table, or sink, with or without support*

■ *Moves up and down steps to access toilet or sink (step stool, set of two or three stairs)*

■ *Gets up and down from squatting to sit on toilet, lying on floor for diaper change, or using step stool to reach sink*

ADAPTIVE Growing Skills

B 1.1 Indicates need to use toilet

B 1.2 Has bowel and bladder control

B 1.3 Indicates awareness of soiled and wet pants or diapers

B 2.2 Washes and dries hands

C 1.4 Takes off pants

C 2.4 Puts on pull-up clothing

D 1.1 Communicates internal distress, discomfort, or pain to adult

D 3.1 Responds appropriately to warnings of dangerous conditions or substances

Embedded Learning Opportunities

■ *Says "I need go potty!" then walks to bathroom, pulls down own pants, sits on toilet, wipes and flushes, pulls up pants, and washes hands*

■ *Answers "My diaper dry" or "I wet, I pee," when adult asks "Is your diaper wet or dry?"*

■ *Washes and dries hands after using toilet or having diaper changed*

■ *Reports another child yelling in bathroom, splashing water from sink onto walls, or flushing toilet multiple times when not necessary*

SOCIAL-EMOTIONAL Growing Skills

A 3.1   Initiates next step of familiar social routine

A 3.2   Follows familiar social routines with familiar adults

B 1.2   Identifies/labels own emotions

B 2   Uses appropriate strategies to manage emotional states

B 3   Makes positive statements about self or accomplishments

B 3.1   Explains or shows others how to do tasks mastered

B 3.2   Shares accomplishment with familiar caregiver

D 3   Initiates and completes independent activities

D 3.1   Responds to request to finish activity

D 3.2   Responds to request to begin activity

D 4   Resolves conflicts using negotiation

D 4.1   Uses strategies to resolve conflicts

E 1   Meets observable physical needs in socially appropriate ways

E 2.1   Meets behavioral expectations in familiar environments

E 2.2   Adjusts behavior based on feedback from others or environment

E 3.1   Seeks adult permission when appropriate

E 3.2   Follows established social rules in familiar environments

Embedded Learning Opportunities

■ *Initiates next step in handwashing by squirting soap on hands, then turning on water and washing hands*

■ *Labels own emotions (cries after peeing pants; responds to adult's question "How are you feeling right now?" with "I sad. I pee my pants")*

■ *Meets observable physical needs in socially appropriate ways (pees into toilet in public, washes hands using appropriate steps, throws paper towel away in correct location)*

■ *Asks adult's permission when in community, "I go potty?"; asks adult at school, "Can I wash my hands?"*

■ *Communicates likes and dislikes (says "That's cold! I don't like it!" after being wiped by adult during diaper change; says "Potty too big! I don't like it!" while using public toilet)*

SOCIAL-COMMUNICATION Growing Skills

B 2   Locates common objects, people, or events

B 3   Follows multistep directions without contextual cues

B 3.1   Follows multistep directions with contextual cues

B 3.2   Follows one-step direction without contextual cues

B 3.3   Follows one-step direction with contextual cues

B 4.1   Answers *who*, *what*, and *where* questions

C 1   Produces multiple-word sentences to communicate

C 1.1   Uses two-word utterances

C 1.2   Uses 50 single words, signs, or symbols

C 2   Uses plural pronouns to indicate subjects, objects, and possession in multiple-word sentences

C 2.1   Uses irregular plural nouns in multiple-word sentences

C 2.2   Uses regular plural nouns

C 3   Uses helping verbs

C 3.2   Uses regular past tense of common verbs

C 3.3   Uses *to be* verbs

C 4   Asks questions using inverted auxiliary

C 4.1   Asks *wh-* questions

D 1   Uses language to initiate and sustain social interaction

D 1.1   Follows social conventions of language

D 2   Provides and seeks information while conversing using words, phrases, or sentences

D 2.2   Describes objects, people, and events as part of social exchange

D 3.4   Alternates between speaker and listener roles during conversations with others

D 3.5   Responds to contingent questions from others

Embedded Learning Opportunities

■ *Locates diapers or wipes, bathroom, or adult*

■ *Follows multistep directions when adult says "Pull up your pants, flush the toilet, and go wash your hands"*

■ *Responds "After art" when adult asks "When did you wash your hands?"*

■ *Uses single words, signs, or symbols* (potty, wash, pee, bathroom)

COGNITIVE Growing Skills

B 1   Imitates novel coordinated motor actions

B 2   Imitates novel words

B 3.1   Relates recent events without contextual cues

B 3.2   Relates recent events with contextual cues

B 3.3   Relates events immediately after they occur

C 2.1   Uses object to represent another object

C 4   Uses early conceptual comparisons

D 3.1   Evaluates common solutions to solve problems or reach goals

D 4.1   Draws conclusions about causes of events based on personal experience

Embedded Learning Opportunities

■ *Sits on toilet and goes potty after seeing peer's mother sit on toilet to use bathroom*

■ *Imitates new words while using bathroom, washing hands, or getting diaper changed (diaper, potty, poop, dirty, wash)*

■ *Answers "Pee go down!" when adult asks "What will happen if I flush the toilet like we did yesterday?"*

■ *Reaches for toilet paper and, when unable to get it, turns own body to get it without asking for help*

■ *Says "If I pee, I get my dress wet" or "If I wipe, I be all clean!"*

LITERACY Growing Skills

A 3.2   Recognizes common signs and logos

B 1.2   Participates in repetitive verbal play

Embedded Learning Opportunities

■ *Recognizes figure of woman on bathroom sign, caution sign indicating wet floor, red X on stall door indicating toilet out of order*

■ *Sings "Row, Row, Row Your Boat" with adult while washing hands or "Twinkle, Twinkle, Little Star" with peer while waiting to use toilet*

MATH Growing Skills

A 2.2   Recites numbers 1-10

Embedded Learning Opportunities

■ *Counts with adult while washing hands or using the toilet*

TIER 1

■ UNIVERSAL STRATEGIES

These are best practices for ALL young children, with attention to meeting learning outcomes within daily routines and activities of family life and early childhood classrooms while promoting positive adult–child relationships and peer interactions.

As children's adaptive skills increase, they gain bowel and bladder control, communicate their need to use the toilet, independently pull their pants up and down to use the toilet, and wash and dry their hands after using the bathroom. Their increased motor skills allow them to walk to and from the bathroom with and without support while avoiding people and furniture or other objects.

Socially, children are able to use conversational rules when answering *who, what, why, how,* and *when* questions and can initiate the next step in a familiar activity. They can communicate to adults their accomplishments ("I went potty!") as well as their likes and dislikes ("Warm water nice!" when washing hands; "That baby wipe too cold!" during a diaper change). Cognitively, they continue to imitate new movements and words, and they are increasingly able to transfer knowledge from past events, relate events immediately after they occur, and recognize some symbols related to the routine (bathroom signs, caution signs). Children can incorporate math into this routine by counting while they are washing their hands or using the toilet.

Interactions

At the Growing level, some children may begin to potty train in accordance with cultural beliefs or adults' opinions that it is time for them to do so. When children begin to potty train, make sure the child is physically and cognitively able to do so and is interested in potty training. The key to successful potty training is constant communication between the home caregiver and the classroom teacher. Typical best practice is for the home caregiver to spend 2 continuous weeks potty training the child at home. When the child is successfully potty trained at home, the teacher tries it at school.

Adults can support diapering, toileting, and handwashing by giving children multiple opportunities throughout the day to complete these routines as independently as possible before offering help. Following are some suggestions for interactions at the Growing level:

▲ Use a verbal prompt to let children know it is time to use the bathroom ("It's your turn to get your diaper changed. Let's go to the bathroom").

▲ Expand on children's vocabulary by using descriptive language during the routine, singing songs, or having a conversation with the child (if the child says "Potty!" you could say "You have to go potty?").

▲ Continue to enforce the expectations of the routine (washing hands after going potty).

▲ Incorporate mathematics into the routine by counting whenever possible (have the child count with you during the handwashing, diapering, or toileting process).

▲ Give the child immediate, consistent feedback about the routine they are learning ("You washed your hands in the sink. I'm proud of you!").

▲ Use a calm, uplifting voice and keep a smile on your face when interacting with children, whether you are giving feedback, teaching, or having a conversation.

▲ Follow the child's lead (if they say they need to wash their hands or use the bathroom, encourage them to do so!).

▲ Read books and stories and sing songs about potty training before starting the process, both at home and in the classroom.

▲ Use consistent "potty" language across home and classroom environments (if the home caregiver says "go potty" to refer to going to the bathroom, then the classroom teacher should do so too).

▲ Make sure children who are potty training have opportunities to try to "go pee" at regular intervals throughout the day.

▲ Start decreasing the number of prompts given throughout the day as children become capable of independently initiating the bathroom routine when they need it.

▲ Dress children (or ask that they be dressed) in easy-to-remove pants to decrease struggles when using the toilet.

▲ Use training pants when possible instead of pull-ups or diapers. Training pants are easier for children to remove and less absorbent than diapers, which may encourage children to use the toilet rather than soil their clothing.

▲ Consider teaching male children to start learning to urinate in the toilet while sitting down rather than standing up. They can stand once they have learned how to distinguish between urination and a bowel movement. (Many adults have their own preferences and opinions around this practice, so this is only a suggestion.)

▲ Make the bathroom a relaxing and interesting place (hang wall posters about the bathroom routine, hang a mobile over the changing table).

Environment and Materials

Toileting and handwashing routines usually take place indoors in a bathroom at home, child care, and school. Diapering may take place in the bathroom but often occurs wherever the adult prefers, such as in a nursery or on the bedroom floor with a changing mat under the child. Sometimes children use outdoor restrooms with adults' help.

Materials needed at the Growing level are the same as those for the Beginning stage (soap, water, diapers, baby wipes, toilet paper, and any other hygiene products adults wish to use for the routine). However, at the Growing level, children can manipulate these materials more independently. Following are some suggestions for environment and materials at the Growing level:

▲ Mount a mobile, wind chime, or kite over the diapering area for visual interest during diapering.

▲ Provide a soft changing pad to lay children on for diaper changes (you may not need to purchase a pad made specifically for this purpose if you have a soft pad on hand that can be disinfected easily).

▲ Teach children to notice sensory cues that tell them when they have peed or pooped, so they can learn to identify when they need a diaper change:

△ Direct the child's attention to the wet or dirty diaper before you change it.

△ Talk about what the dirty diaper looks like, what it feels like, or what it smells like.

△ Point out color-changing strips or dots on the diaper that indicate when it is wet or soiled (these are a feature on some disposable diapers).

▲ Keep children occupied during diapering by talking with them or singing to them.

▲ Provide a step stool for the changing table, a potty chair, or a small toilet seat that fits on the full-size seat for the toileting portion of the routine.

■ FOCUSED STRATEGIES

These strategies are for teaching SOME children who are struggling with a component of a skill or whose development is stalled and who need extra help to catch up or keep up. The strategies include a variety of minor adaptations or modifications to daily routines, activities, and environments to meet targeted outcomes at home and in classrooms.

Diapering

▲ Make available a sturdy stool for the child to stand on if the diaper changing area is too high for the child to reach.

▲ Use specific, consistent words to label clean and dirty diapers when changing diapers. Use these words in other parts of the day to help the child learn new vocabulary words.

▲ Take diaper garbage outside often to keep the area smelling fresh, as some children are sensitive to strong odors.

Toileting

▲ To help children transition to the bathroom routine,

△ Provide a basket or shelf near the bathroom where children can deposit toys they want to keep playing with after using the bathroom or getting their diaper changed. This encourages them to stop playing and use the bathroom and also reduces their anxiety about another child taking their toy while they are gone.

△ Use a visual timer and verbal prompts to help transition out of the current activity.

▲ Have children who struggle with toileting work on learning only one or two important aspects of the routine at a time (pulling pants down and sitting on the toilet independently) before working on the whole sequence.

▲ If the toilet seat is too big for the child, use a potty chair or a smaller toilet seat that fits on the larger one.

▲ Turn male children around to face the back of the toilet when sitting to urinate, as this helps if they struggle to keep their urine in the toilet. This position rests their legs on the widest part of the toilet seat, which helps keep urine in the toilet by spreading their legs more widely and angling their hips downward.

▲ Provide reinforcement (hugs, high fives, stickers) for successfully urinating into the toilet.

▲ Consult the families of children who are struggling with potty training to see if the problem occurs at home too, or if children use the potty successfully there because the family does things differently (children who are used to using a toilet seat at home may not want to sit on a child-size toilet at school).

▲ Try a system of least prompts if toilet training seems to be stressful, reinforcing after each learned step and fading when necessary. For example, give only as much help as children need to pull down pants, sit on toilet, go to the bathroom, wipe, and pull pants up. Give verbal cues and wait to see what they will do on their own before helping.

Handwashing

▲ Provide a sturdy stool for the child to stand on if the area with the soap, sink, and towel is too high for the child to reach.

▲ Say "What do we do to clean our hands?" when children need to wash their hands, and wait for a response.

▲ Give children verbal cues about what they need to do for this routine:

△ "Turn on the water."

△ "Use the soap."

△ "Dry your hands."

△ "Put away [throw away] the towel."

▲ Provide a contextual cue by having an adult wash and dry their hands at the same time children do.

▲ Use a visual schedule to show children the steps in completing a task (handwashing).

▲ Provide multiple opportunities throughout the day for children to practice the skills used in washing and drying hands:

△ Let a child wash and dry dishes, dolls, or toys and then wash and dry their hands afterward.

△ Let a child practice the rubbing skills involved in handwashing by applying hand lotion or baby powder to their clean hands and telling them to rub it over their hands to "get all the spots." (This is usually a pleasant treat as well as a helpful visual cue.)

▲ Teach children who cannot speak to use simple signs (MORE, ALL DONE) so they can communicate their preferences.

▲ Learn to recognize children's cues and preferences.

▲ Pair sign language with spoken words for children who are nonverbal or who have hearing impairments.

■ SPECIALIZED STRATEGIES

These strategies for teaching the FEW children who need intensive supports include a variety of specialized, individualized, precise evidence-based strategies to meet children's unique goals/outcomes:

▲ Consult with the physicians of children diagnosed with a disability to determine the extent to which they can participate in toileting.

▲ Adapt the routine on the basis of children's physical and cognitive abilities:

  △ Let a child who cannot crawl or walk to the diapering area, toilet, or sink use a walker, stroller, or other adaptive device.

  △ Position a child who has physical disabilities correctly to facilitate elimination (hips and knees secured at a 90-degree angle, feet flat on the floor or on a stool).

▲ Make available a potty chair specially designed for children who have physical disabilities.

  △ Teach a child who cannot speak sign language for this routine, or use picture cards to help them communicate their need to go to the bathroom.

▲ Change diapers on the ground, floor, or other low surface if children are afraid of being changed on a raised platform.

▲ Play calming music or sounds during diaper changes to encourage calm and provide a soothing distraction.

▲ Place a piece of toilet paper over the sensor in self-flushing restrooms to keep the toilet from flushing while children are sitting on the seat (children who have autism may be upset by the noise of toilet flushing or the overstimulation of the bathroom process).

AEPS-3 Curriculum Resources (Appendix A)

Appendix A in this volume contains numerous additional resources to supplement the AEPS-3 Curriculum. The first part of the appendix presents a list of general curriculum resources, and the second part provides lists of supplementary resources for each individual routine and activity.

AEPS-3 Skills Matrix (Appendix B)

The AEPS-3 Skills Matrix in Appendix B of this volume spotlights individual skills by showing functional application across all routines and activities. Each skills matrix (there are eight total, one for each of the test's eight developmental areas) allows you to select individual AEPS-3 items for children who require an intensive focus on a few skills across routines and activities. For children who have difficulty learning new skills at the level of individual AEPS-3 items, the Foundation Steps (*FS*) provide an even more granular breakdown of component subskills that are either a sequence of developmental precursors or steps in task analyses.

13

Dramatic Play

In Dramatic Play, children and others act out character parts (store clerk, farmer, doctor) by using imitation and imagination, often dressing up in clothes to act out their role. This type of play is often child led and can occur several times a day in any familiar setting. The activity changes over time as children's communication, cognitive, motor, and adaptive skills increase. The AEPS-3 Growing level of Dramatic Play uses skills from eight developmental areas.

Concurrent Skills

The following concurrent skills are AEPS-3 skills that can be easily embedded and taught during regular occurrences of Dramatic Play.

FINE MOTOR Growing Skills

B 1   Activates object with finger
B 2   Rotates wrist to manipulate object
C 1.1 Writes or draws using mixed strokes
C 1.2 Writes or draws using curved lines
C 1.3 Writes or draws using straight lines
C 1.4 Scribbles

Embedded Learning Opportunities

■ *Uses one finger to push buttons on toy telephone, open and close toy cash register, or take picture with toy camera*

■ *Holds dress with one hand and lowers it to ground with other hand to get foot through top*

■ *Uses various types of lines to write or draw (writes pretend prescriptions while playing doctor, writes orders while playing restaurant, writes flight names and draws locations at airport)*

GROSS MOTOR Growing Skills

B 3   Walks avoiding people, furniture, or objects

B 3.1   Walks without support

C 3.3   Pushes riding toy with feet while steering

Embedded Learning Opportunities

■ *Walks to dramatic play area or dress-up center with or without support*

ADAPTIVE Growing Skills

C 1.2   Takes off pullover clothing over head

C 1.3   Takes off front-opening coat, jacket, or shirt

C 1.4   Takes off pants

C 2.2   Puts on front-opening clothing

C 2.3   Puts on pullover clothing

C 2.4   Puts on pull-up clothing

C 2.5   Puts on socks

C 2.6   Puts on shoes

D 1   Takes independent action to alleviate distress, discomfort, and pain

D 1.1   Communicates internal distress, discomfort, or pain to adult

Embedded Learning Opportunities

■ *Unfastens garments (dress up doctor's coat with buttons, shoes with Velcro closures, dress with zipper)*

■ *Puts on and takes off variety of clothes (pretend doctor's coat, princess dress, flip-flops, overalls, superhero cape, tiara, firefighter jacket, Hawaiian shirt)*

■ *Leaves peer playing doctor to tell adult they truly are not feeling well*

SOCIAL-EMOTIONAL Growing Skills

B 1   Responds appropriately to others' emotions

B 1.1   Identifies/labels emotions in others

B 1.2   Identifies/labels own emotions

B 2   Uses appropriate strategies to manage emotional states

B 2.1   Responds appropriately to soothing by peer

B 3   Makes positive statements about self or accomplishments

B 3.1   Explains or shows others how to do tasks mastered

B 3.2   Shares accomplishment with familiar caregiver

C 1   Maintains interaction with peer

C 1.1   Initiates social behavior toward peer

C 1.2   Responds appropriately to peer social behavior

C 3.1   Initiates cooperative activity

C 3.2   Joins others in cooperative activity

C 3.3   Shares or exchanges objects

D 1   Interacts appropriately with others during small-group activities

D 1.1   Interacts appropriately with materials during small-group activities

D 1.2   Responds appropriately to directions during small-group activities

D 1.3   Remains with group during small-group activities

D 3.1   Responds to request to finish activity

D 3.2   Responds to request to begin activity

D 3.3   Entertains self by playing with toys

D 4   Resolves conflicts using negotiation

D 4.1   Uses strategies to resolve conflicts

D 4.2   Claims and defends possessions

E 1.1   Meets internal physical needs of hunger and thirst

E 2.1   Meets behavioral expectations in familiar environments

E 2.2   Adjusts behavior based on feedback from others or environment

E 3.1   Seeks adult permission when appropriate

E 3.2   Follows established social rules in familiar environments

E 4.2   States age

E 4.3   Provides given name or nickname of self and others

Embedded Learning Opportunities

■ *Gives toy phone back to crying child to make them happy again*

■ *Says, while playing doctor, "Me and Anna sick," or while playing kitchen, "Abby is happy; she makes spaghetti"*

■ *Says "I did it!" after cooking spaghetti, putting on dress, or fastening shoe*

■ *Pretends to be firefighter, princess, or chef*

■ *Starts cleaning up play clothes when adult says "Please clean up the clothes"*

■ *Follows all rules and remains engaged while playing puppy game during dramatic play*

■ *Says "That's my phone!" after peer takes it away*

■ *Asks adult's permission to join dramatic play, put on dress, or take off shoes*

■ *Gives name and age when playing doctor with peer and doctor asks for information*

SOCIAL-COMMUNICATION Growing Skills

B 2 Locates common objects, people, or events

B 3 Follows multistep directions without contextual cues

B 3.1 Follows multistep directions with contextual cues

B 3.2 Follows one-step direction without contextual cues

B 3.3 Follows one-step direction with contextual cues

B 4.1 Answers *who*, *what*, and *where* questions

C 1 Produces multiple-word sentences to communicate

C 1.1 Uses two-word utterances

C 1.2 Uses 50 single words, signs, or symbols

C 2 Uses plural pronouns to indicate subjects, objects, and possession in multiple-word sentences

C 2.1 Uses irregular plural nouns in multiple-word sentences

C 2.2 Uses regular plural nouns

C 3 Uses helping verbs

C 3.2 Uses regular past tense of common verbs

C 3.3 Uses *to be* verbs

C 4 Asks questions using inverted auxiliary

C 4.1 Asks *wh-* questions

D 1 Uses language to initiate and sustain social interaction

D 1.1 Follows social conventions of language

D 2 Provides and seeks information while conversing using words, phrases, or sentences

D 2.1 Asks questions to obtain information

D 2.2 Describes objects, people, and events as part of social exchange

D 3.3 Responds to topic initiations from others

D 3.4 Alternates between speaker and listener roles during conversations with others

D 3.5 Responds to contingent questions from others

Embedded Learning Opportunities

■ *Answers question from peer looking for another child (points to other child and says "She's in the kitchen" when peer asks "Where's Lily?")*

■ *Follows all directions when adult says "Take off the play clothes, hang them up, and get your coat so we can leave"*

■ *Answers with two words ("Annie did") when adult asks "Who left the princess dress on the floor?"*

■ *Says "I am tired" during play and pretends to nap*

■ *Asks wh- questions ("Where is Abby?" "Why I have no soup?" "When can I play?")*

■ *Waits until peer is finished talking before starting to speak*

■ *Answers adult's question "What did you play today?" by saying "I was an ice cream guy"*

COGNITIVE Growing Skills

B 1 Imitates novel coordinated motor actions

B 2 Imitates novel words

B 3.1 Relates recent events without contextual cues

B 3.2 Relates recent events with contextual cues

B 3.3 Relates events immediately after they occur

C 1.1 Locates object in second of two hiding places

C 2 Recognizes symbols

C 2.1 Uses object to represent another object

C 3.1 Classifies according to function

C 3.2 Classifies according to physical attribute

C 3.3 Discriminates between objects or people using common attributes

C 4 Uses early conceptual comparisons

C 4.1 Identifies common concepts

C 4.2 Identifies concrete concepts

D 1.1 Uses part of an object or support to obtain another object

D 3.1 Evaluates common solutions to solve problems or reach goals

D 4.1 Draws conclusions about causes of events based on personal experience

Embedded Learning Opportunities

- *Says "I played with the Superman cape yesterday!"*
- *Pairs real cup with picture of cup on shelf when putting items away*
- *Uses chair to reach whiteboard markers when playing teacher*

LITERACY Growing Skills

A 2 Demonstrates understanding that text is read in one direction and from top to bottom of page

A 2.1 Turns pages of book from beginning toward end

A 2.2 Holds book or other printed material with pictures correctly oriented

A 3.1 Recognizes own first name in print

A 3.2 Recognizes common signs and logos

B 1.2 Participates in repetitive verbal play

D 1 Demonstrates understanding that pictures represent text

D 3 Demonstrates understanding of abstract story vocabulary

E 2.1 Makes representational drawings

Embedded Learning Opportunities

- *Moves finger left to right while "reading" cookbook in play kitchen*
- *Flips through atlas from front to back while looking at different maps*
- *Reads own first name off of shirt in dramatic play*
- *Pauses and does not enter area with stop sign posted in front of it during dramatic play*
- *Opens cookbook, sees picture of two eggs, and says "I need two eggs"*

MATH Growing Skills

A 1   Counts out 3 items

A 1.1   Counts 3 items to determine "How many?"

A 2.2   Recites numbers 1–10

B 1   Compares items in sets to 5 by counting

B 1.1   Compares items in sets to 5 by matching

B 1.2   Creates equivalent sets of 5 items

B 1.3   Uses quantity comparison words

Embedded Learning Opportunities

■ *Counts 3 shoes, 3 hats, 3 friends in dramatic play*

■ *Recites numbers 1 to 10 by singing number song when pretending to work in shop or counting aloud to tell peer how long to wait during Hide and Seek*

■ *Counts out number of items when adult asks "How many?"*

■ *Counts out 3 "dollars" to give as change at play restaurant*

■ *Says to peer, "I only have one hat and you have two; you have more"*

TIER 1

■ UNIVERSAL STRATEGIES

These are best practices for ALL young children, with attention to meeting learning outcomes within daily routines and activities of family life and early childhood classrooms while promoting positive adult–child relationships and peer interactions. As children learn and grow, they gain skills they can use for dramatic play:

▲ Walking and climbing to explore different environments

▲ Using their hands to manipulate objects and hold writing implements to write or scribble

▲ Dressing more independently (fastening garments, putting on and taking off clothing)

▲ Using cognitive skills to let objects represent other objects, recognize symbols (McDonald's arch), and classify objects by shape, color, and size

▲ Communicating by using more complex language to ask and answer questions, using joint attention, and following conversational rules

▲ Maintaining cooperative play with others socially (acting out roles with props during imaginary play)

▲ Following rules and reporting others who are not following them

▲ Using their increasing knowledge of books to follow along during dramatic play

▲ Role-playing with menus, store catalogs, and maps during pretend play (restaurant, shop, airport)

▲ Using their expanding knowledge of numbers to count cups at a dinner table, sort spoons and forks, match pairs of shoes by color, and count to 10 while waiting for their turn

Interactions

Following are some suggestions for interactions at the Growing level of this routine:

▲ Keep interactions positive:

△ Use a calm voice, and smile.

△ Base interactions on children's interests.

▲ Teach the expectations of play ("When using play clothes, put them on over your own clothes").

▲ Wait for a child to try a task (dressing) before you offer help.

▲ Let children come to you to engage in conversation if they need help.

▲ Use children's questions about how to use an item as an opportunity to expand their vocabulary while you model the item's use.

▲ Give immediate, specific praise when you witness children doing things they are supposed to do (picking up toys already used before starting to play with other toys).

▲ Encourage children to play with peers rather than adults.

Environment and Materials

Dramatic play can occur both indoors and outdoors, in environments including home, child care, schools, parks, and playgrounds. Following are some suggestions for environment and materials at the Growing level of this routine:

▲ When choosing materials, consider items such as the following:

△ Kitchen sets (refrigerator, stove, sink, microwave, counters, dishwasher, dish racks, dishes, food, coffee maker)

△ Dolls of various ethnicities and genders and doll accessories (blankets, shoes, clothes, bottles, diapers, pretend baby food)

△ Riding toys (tricycles, cardboard box cars)

△ Old or new items (clothing, cell phones, cardboard box houses, tools and tool belts, jewelry, hats, shoes, writing utensils, paper)

▲ Consider a variety of sources for dramatic play items:

△ New items purchased specifically for dramatic play

△ Old items from around the house

△ Inexpensive items from garage sales and thrift stores

△ Pretend items fashioned from cardboard, wood, or PVC pipe

▲ Use your imagination when finding items for dramatic play, and consider children's interests.

▲ Create themed dramatic play areas (airport, grocery store, baby nursery, house, ice skating rink, florist, shoe store, bakery).

■ FOCUSED STRATEGIES

TIER 2

These strategies are for teaching SOME children who are struggling with a component of a skill or whose development is stalled and who need extra help to catch up or keep up. The strategies include a variety of minor adaptations or modifications to daily routines, activities, and environments to meet targeted outcomes at home and in classrooms.

▲ Offer multiple opportunities throughout the day to engage in dramatic play both indoors and outdoors.

▲ Keep dramatic play areas at home, child care, or school set up for at least a week before changing them (repetition allows children to practice old skills and learn new ones).

▲ Vary the environment where dramatic play occurs, using settings of interest to children so they can practice their skills (provide playhouse, dishes, baby dolls, and dress-up clothes outdoors on the playground).

▲ Use first-then boards ("First you must take off your shoes, then you can put on the play shoes.")

▲ Use pictures to give choices if children become overwhelmed and do not know what or whom to play with (picture of kitchen table with dishes, cash register with play money).

▲ Use a verbal prompt and visual timer to alert children when it is time to transition from one activity to another.

▲ Use adaptable materials:

 △ Adaptive device

 △ Pencil with a grip to hold while playing school

 △ Easy-to-use fasteners on clothing (Velcro instead of buttons)

▲ Encourage peer modeling by matching children who have more competent play skills with those whose skills are less sophisticated.

▲ Teach children who are unable to speak to use simple signs (MORE, ALL DONE) so they can communicate their preferences.

▲ Learn to recognize children's cues and preferences.

▲ Pair sign language with spoken words for children who are nonverbal or who have hearing impairments.

■ SPECIALIZED STRATEGIES

These strategies for teaching the FEW children who need intensive supports include a variety of specialized, individualized, precise evidence-based strategies to meet children's unique goals/outcomes:

▲ Make sure the dramatic play area is accessible for all children:

 △ Provide appropriate positioning equipment for children who are immobile (floor sitter).

 △ Adapt the environment so children can maneuver through it to participate.

 △ Teach children who are unable to speak to use sign language, picture cards, or technology apps so they can participate and communicate their preferences.

 △ Use adapted switches so children who have physical disabilities can access dramatic play materials (battery-operated blender, lamp, cash register).

 △ Provide clothing of different types and fabrics for children who have sensory concerns to help avoid struggles and irritability.

▲ Provide differential reinforcement for children who exhibit concerning behaviors (if a child continuously hits a peer during dramatic play, reinforce other children who are interacting appropriately with their friends).

▲ Use backward or forward chaining to teach dressing skills to children who have disabilities:

 △ Teach either the first or last step of a dressing skill (taking off pretend doctor's jacket).

 △ Then teach subsequent steps as the child masters each step.

AEPS-3 Curriculum Resources (Appendix A)

Appendix A in this volume contains numerous additional resources to supplement the AEPS-3 Curriculum. The first part of the appendix presents a list of general curriculum resources, and the second part provides lists of supplementary resources for each individual routine and activity.

AEPS-3 Skills Matrix (Appendix B)

The AEPS-3 Skills Matrix in Appendix B of this volume spotlights individual skills by showing functional application across all routines and activities. Each skills matrix (there are eight total, one for each of the test's eight developmental areas) allows you to select individual AEPS-3 items for children who require an intensive focus on a few skills across routines and activities. For children who have difficulty learning new skills at the level of individual AEPS-3 items, the Foundation Steps (*FS*) provide an even more granular breakdown of component subskills that are either a sequence of developmental precursors or steps in task analyses.

14

Dressing

The Growing level of the Dressing routine (which also includes undressing) changes over time as children start taking more interest in their appearance and develop preferences. Children's developing fine motor, gross motor, adaptive, and cognitive skills also promote greater independence. This routine often occurs several times a day for young children, as when their soiled clothes need changing or schedules and activities call for more appropriate clothing (outdoors, bedtime, after bath, visiting friends, attending community activities). The AEPS-3 Growing level of Dressing uses skills from eight developmental areas.

Concurrent Skills

The following concurrent skills are AEPS-3 skills that can be easily embedded and taught during regular occurrences of Dressing.

FINE MOTOR Growing Skills

B 2   Rotates wrist to manipulate object

B 3   Manipulates object with two hands, each performing different action

Embedded Learning Opportunities

- ■ *Rotates wrist to maneuver button through loop*

- ■ *Holds one side of jacket with one hand while putting other hand through sleeve*

GROSS MOTOR Growing Skills

B 3   Walks avoiding people, furniture, or objects

B 3.1 Walks without support

Embedded Learning Opportunities

- ■ *Walks with or without support to dressing area (closet, dresser, store dressing room)*

ADAPTIVE Growing Skills

C 1.2   Takes off pullover clothing over head

C 1.3   Takes off front-opening coat, jacket, or shirt

C 1.4   Takes off pants

C 2.2   Puts on front-opening clothing

C 2.3   Puts on pullover clothing

C 2.4   Puts on pull-up clothing

C 2.5   Puts on socks

C 2.6   Puts on shoes

D 1   Takes independent action to alleviate distress, discomfort, and pain

D 1.1   Communicates internal distress, discomfort, or pain to adult

Embedded Learning Opportunities

■ *Undresses self by removing all clothing (kicks off shoes, pulls down pants using two hands and steps out, removes shirt with two hands)*

■ *Dresses self appropriately for weather (grabs jacket after looking out window and seeing snow falling, puts on rain boots after hearing rain, puts on shorts after adult says day will be hot)*

■ *Takes off shoes that are too tight or tells adult "I too hot"*

SOCIAL-EMOTIONAL Growing Skills

A 3.1   Initiates next step of familiar social routine

A 3.2   Follows familiar social routines with familiar adults

B 3.1   Explains or shows others how to do tasks mastered

B 3.2   Shares accomplishment with familiar caregiver

C 3.1   Initiates cooperative activity

C 3.2   Joins others in cooperative activity

D 3   Initiates and completes independent activities

D 3.1   Responds to request to finish activity

D 3.2   Responds to request to begin activity

E 3.1   Seeks adult permission when appropriate

Embedded Learning Opportunities

■ *Starts picking out clothes when adult says "It's time to get dressed"*

■ *Shows peer how to button jacket when peer says they need help*

■ *Tells adult "I did it!" after zipping up coat*

■ *Uses imaginary props in play (prince or princess outfit; police uniform, hat, and badge; chef's apron, hat, and cooking utensils)*

■ *Starts putting clothes in closet after adult says "Clean up your dress up clothes, please"*

■ *Puts on jacket after adult says "Put on your coat, and I will zip it for you"*

■ *Communicates likes and dislikes (throws itchy shirt on floor and says "I no like it!" after trying on at store; sees dress during dramatic play and says "So pretty!")*

SOCIAL-COMMUNICATION Growing Skills

B 2   Locates common objects, people, or events

B 3   Follows multistep directions without contextual cues

B 3.1   Follows multistep directions with contextual cues

B 3.2   Follows one-step direction without contextual cues

B 3.3   Follows one-step direction with contextual cues

B 4.1   Answers *who*, *what*, and *where* questions

C 1   Produces multiple-word sentences to communicate

C 1.1   Uses two-word utterances

C 1.2   Uses 50 single words, signs, or symbols

C 2   Uses plural pronouns to indicate subjects, objects, and possession in multiple-word sentences

C 2.1   Uses irregular plural nouns in multiple-word sentences

C 2.2   Uses regular plural nouns

C 3   Uses helping verbs

C 3.2   Uses regular past tense of common verbs

C 3.3   Uses *to be* verbs

C 4   Asks questions using inverted auxiliary

C 4.1   Asks *wh-* questions

D 1   Uses language to initiate and sustain social interaction

D 1.1   Follows social conventions of language

D 2   Provides and seeks information while conversing using words, phrases, or sentences

D 2.1   Asks questions to obtain information

D 2.2   Describes objects, people, and events as part of social exchange

D 3.3   Responds to topic initiations from others

D 3.4   Alternates between speaker and listener roles during conversations with others

D 3.5   Responds to contingent questions from others

Embedded Learning Opportunities

- *Follows all directions when adult says "Go to your bedroom, take off your clothes, and put on your pajamas"*

- *Uses two-word utterances when talking about dressing ("Shirt on," "Boots please," "Too tight")*

- *Asks wh- questions ("Where my boots?" "Who take my shirt?" "Why I need socks?")*

- *Uses nouns (says "My feet are cold; I need socks")*

- *Alternates between speaking and listening during conversations about dressing (responds "I wear my new shirt!" when adult asks "What are you going to wear tomorrow?")*

COGNITIVE Growing Skills

B 1 Imitates novel coordinated motor actions

B 2 Imitates novel words

B 3.1 Relates recent events without contextual clues

C 2.1 Uses object to represent another object

C 3.1 Classifies according to function

C 3.2 Classifies according to physical attribute

C 4.1 Identifies common concepts

C 4.2 Identifies concrete concepts

D 1.1 Uses part of object or support to obtain another object

D 3.1 Evaluates common solutions to solve problems or reach goals

Embedded Learning Opportunities

■ Buttons shirt after seeing adult do so; puts on one shoe after seeing peer do so

■ Imitates new words (says "Shoe on" after adult says "Let's put your shoe on!" or "Shirt please" after adult asks "Do you want your T-shirt?"

■ Organizes all family rain boots in living room, gets own jacket and puts it with siblings' jackets, puts five pairs of shorts in suitcase for beach vacation

■ Puts all dress shoes in closet, chooses among five blue shirts to wear to school, finds all soft pants and puts them on bed

■ Climbs in chair to reach shirt in closet, uses stool to reach top dresser drawer

LITERACY Growing Skills

B 1.2 Participates in repetitive verbal play

Embedded Learning Opportunities

■ Sings song with adult about clothing item ("If you're cold and you know it, get a jacket" to tune of "If You're Happy and You Know It")

MATH Growing Skills

A 1 Counts out 3 items

A 1.1 Counts 3 items to determine "How many?"

A 2.2 Recites numbers 1–10

B 1.3 Uses quantity comparison words

Embedded Learning Opportunities

■ Counts out 3 items (3 buttons on a jacket; 3 shirts or 3 pairs of shoes to choose from to wear to school)

■ Recites numbers 1 to 10 when counting how many shirts in closet, how many shoes on floor, how many jackets hanging in cubbies

■ Counts number of buttons on own jacket and peer's jacket and says "I have less buttons!"

TIER 1

■ UNIVERSAL STRATEGIES

These are best practices for ALL young children, with attention to meeting learning outcomes within daily routines and activities of family life and early childhood classrooms while promoting positive adult–child relationships and peer interactions.

The toddler years are often characterized by increased independence and a do-it-myself mindset. Children at the Growing level generally have basic motor, communication, and cognitive skills that allow them not only to undress more independently but also to begin dressing themselves as well. Toddlers may exert their autonomy over clothing choices, developing favorite choices and becoming more insistent upon what they want to wear each day. They can ask questions, follow directions, and use new words to describe their clothes and make their preferences known. Adults often find themselves striking a balance between timely completion of dressing routines and letting toddlers exercise their developing skills. However, adults should always maintain positive social interactions during what can be a daunting and difficult task not only for themselves but for the toddlers as well. Some general strategies include the following:

▲ Give children opportunities to learn how to dress and undress themselves.

▲ Allow autonomy in children's clothing choices while still maintaining a weather-appropriate mindset.

▲ Give children ample time to choose favorite clothing.

Interactions

Adult–child interactions remain an important element of dressing for toddlers, as children are becoming able to do, see, and feel increasingly complex things. Being intentional about letting children do more for themselves in the routine allows them to practice new skills, but be prepared to spend more time on dressing routines to minimize conflicts. Following are some suggested interactions for the Growing level of Dressing:

▲ Point out and label characteristics of clothing and actions to help children build vocabulary and understand basic concepts of color, size, and texture.

▲ Use language to help children understand how clothing choices are associated with weather and activities to help them accept choices more readily:

△ "You don't need to get socks on today because it's sunny and you can wear your sandals."

△ "You need your best pants because we're going to Nana's birthday party."

△ "It's cold out today, so which long-sleeved shirt would you like to wear?"

▲ Support children's growing independence by letting children participate in the steps of dressing they can initiate:

△ Position the child's arms or feet in the openings of shirts or pants and let them push their own limbs through.

△ Let the child pull a shirt over their head, then help them guide their arms into the sleeves.

▲ Respect the wishes of families whose cultures dictate that adults dress children well into their preschool or kindergarten years (home visitors and other professionals should modify strategies and support accordingly; such cultural differences do not affect children's ability to learn to dress independently).

Environment and Materials

Dressing can be a frustrating task for some toddlers, so it is important to arrange dressing routines in ways that minimize frustrations and allow children to focus on the skills involved in dressing. Following are some suggestions for environment and materials for the Growing level of this routine:

▲ Make sure the dressing area has enough room for children to maneuver.

▲ Store children's clothing in accessible bins or lower drawers to allow both freedom of movement and independence in choosing clothing.

▲ Use the dressing routine as an opportunity to support toddlers' developing independence and awareness of their own preferences:

△ Provide loose-fitting clothing that either has no obvious buttons or snaps or that has hook-and-loop closures to make it easy for toddlers to begin dressing themselves.

△ Let toddlers choose the colors and styles of clothing they prefer when getting new clothes or selecting hand-me-downs.

▲ Reinforce concepts of clean/dirty and sorting/matching by letting children help sort laundry, load washing machines and dryers, and fold and put away their own clothing.

TIER 2

■ FOCUSED STRATEGIES

These strategies are for teaching SOME children who are struggling with a component of a skill or whose development is stalled and who need extra help to catch up or keep up. The strategies include a variety of minor adaptations or modifications to daily routines, activities, and environments to meet targeted outcomes at home and in classrooms.

▲ Use peer modeling by having children who struggle with dressing skills get dressed with a sibling who can dress independently.

▲ Accommodate the needs of children who are sensitive to certain textures by buying clothing types they prefer (soft fleece clothing, items without seams or strings, items without stiff decals or tags).

▲ Limit options for children who struggle with clothing choices (offer a choice between two items: "Would you like to wear the green shirt or the orange shirt?").

▲ Point out tags on the backs of shirts and pants or other visual cues to help children learn to distinguish between top and bottom, front and back.

▲ Let children who struggle with coordination or body position get dressed or undressed in front of a mirror so they can see the process from different angles.

▲ Dress and undress children whose attention spans present consistent problems during the routine in a quiet area free from distractions.

▲ Allow children to make choices while undressing (deciding which item of clothing to remove first).

▲ Let children watch or participate while a doll is being undressed to help them understand how clothes come off.

▲ Choose loose-fitting clothing with room for children to maneuver and room for adults to reach into when helping children undress.

▲ Play Peekaboo when dressing or undressing children:

△ Pull the child's T-shirt to about the level of the child's nose, then let the child pull the shirt the rest of the way off (or pull it the rest of the way on), and finally say "Peekaboo!"

△ Gradually let the child take off (or put on) more of the garment before saying "Peekaboo."

▲ Use the dressing routine to teach foundational skills such as standing, grasping, responding to adult interactions, and imitating sounds or words.

▲ Teach children who cannot speak to use simple signs (MORE, ALL DONE) so they can communicate their preferences.

▲ Learn to recognize children's cues and preferences.

▲ Pair sign language with spoken words for children who are nonverbal or who have hearing impairments.

▪ SPECIALIZED STRATEGIES

These strategies for teaching the FEW children who need intensive supports include a variety of specialized, individualized, precise evidence-based strategies to meet children's unique goals/outcomes:

▲ Position children for maximum stability while dressing and undressing:

△ Have the child lie down or sit on the floor with their back against the wall.

△ Provide a child-size chair with a supportive back that allows the child's feet to be flat on the ground.

▲ Use graduated guidance when undressing to help the child focus on removing one piece of clothing at a time:

△ Begin by giving the child whatever help they need to undress, and leave on one easy-to-remove item of clothing (shoes, socks) for them to take off.

△ Systematically leave on additional items of clothing for the child to remove as they become able to remove easier items independently.

▲ Help children who have motor conditions that affect specific body parts take the affected part out of their clothing last to increase mobility while undressing.

▲ Allow extra time when prompting a child for a motor or language response.

▲ For children who have sensory impairments, combine simple verbal cues with touch cues at each step in the routine (touch child's foot and say "Lift your foot and I will help you put your shoe on"; touch child's forearm and say "Straighten your arm and I will help you get on your coat).

▲ Support increased independence in undressing:

△ Adapt clothing with hook-and-loop closures, snaps, or other easier-to-use fasteners.

△ Buy clothing and accessories that are easy to take off (slip-on shoes, pants with elastic waists, short pants and short-sleeved shirts for warmer weather).

▲ Use system of least prompts for teaching children how to button or unbutton, snap or unsnap, or zip and unzip.

△ Provide a task direction for the child to perform the task ("Zip your coat").

△ Wait a predetermined number of seconds for the child to respond independently.

△ If the child performs the task independently, then provide specific praise ("You zipped your coat by yourself!").

△ If the child does not perform the step of the task (engage zipper), give a specific verbal prompt ("Put one part of the zipper in the other part") and wait for the child to follow the specific verbal prompt.

△ If the child still does not perform the task, model how to engage the zipper and wait for the child to try it.

△ If the child still does not respond, provide hand-over-hand physical prompting.

△ Provide specific praise regardless of the prompt used.

▲ Help children who have visual impairments by using hand-under-hand from behind so they can feel the natural movements of the task.

▲ Use picture cards that show the sequence of dressing to teach children the correct order in which to put on clothing, starting with underwear and progressing to outerwear.

▲ Offer positive reinforcement when children master difficult tasks or achieve short- and long-term goals.

▲ Use backward chaining to help build skills by helping children with all but the last step of taking off an item of clothing:

△ The first time, take off one of the child's socks completely, then take off the other sock almost all the way but let the child pull it off their toes.

△ Next time, leave the last sock on to the middle of the child's foot.

△ The time after that, leave the sock on all the way to the child's heel.

▲ Fade prompts and supports with each item of clothing as soon as children begin to learn to undress themselves.

▲ Consult a qualified motor specialist to design activities that include children who have sensory or motor impairments.

▲ Consider clothing adaptations that will help children achieve as much functional independence in dressing as possible, such as modifications that make fasteners easier to manipulate.

AEPS-3 Curriculum Resources (Appendix A)

Appendix A in this volume contains numerous additional resources to supplement the AEPS-3 Curriculum. The first part of the appendix presents a list of general curriculum resources, and the second part provides lists of supplementary resources for each individual routine and activity.

AEPS-3 Skills Matrix (Appendix B)

The AEPS-3 Skills Matrix in Appendix B of this volume spotlights individual skills by showing functional application across all routines and activities. Each skills matrix (there are eight total, one for each of the test's eight developmental areas) allows you to select individual AEPS-3 items for children who require an intensive focus on a few skills across routines and activities. For children who have difficulty learning new skills at the level of individual AEPS-3 items, the Foundation Steps (*FS*) provide an even more granular breakdown of component subskills that are either a sequence of developmental precursors or steps in task analyses.

15

Field Trips

The Field Trips activity offers opportunities for children and adults to explore and learn about their community and society together. During field trips and outings, children discover new experiences and environments they may not have access to in their usual daily routines. At the Growing level, this routine may involve riding in a stroller, walking, biking, or riding in vehicles with adults. It may mean going to a library, park, playground, recreational area, or museum. Depending on the adult and child, a field trip may take place several times a week. Types of outings taken evolve over time as children become more aware of their environment and develop cognitive, social-communication, and social-emotional skills that allow them to participate more actively in the activity. The AEPS-3 Growing level of this Field Trips uses skills from eight developmental areas.

Concurrent Skills

The following concurrent skills are AEPS-3 skills that can be easily embedded and taught during regular occurrences of Field Trips. Many of the concurrent goals and objectives in this range are foundational skills for specific field trip concepts and activities and later related play goals.

FINE MOTOR Growing Skills

B 1   Activates object with finger

B 2   Rotates wrist to manipulate object

B 3   Manipulates object with two hands, each performing different action

B 3.1   Assembles toy

B 3.2   Aligns objects

Embedded Learning Opportunities

- *Pushes button on elevator door*
- *Tries to twist bottle cap off water to get drink at park*
- *Puts together Legos at science museum*
- *Takes off shoes and lines them up against wall before getting in pool*
- *Grasps crayon with three fingers while drawing picture of favorite part of field trip*

GROSS MOTOR Growing Skills

B 3   Walks avoiding people, furniture, or objects

B 3.1   Walks without support

B 4   Alternates feet going up and down stairs

B 4.1   Walks up and down stairs using support

B 4.2   Moves up and down stairs

B 4.3   Gets up and down from low structure

B 5   Runs while avoiding people, furniture, or other objects

B 5.1   Runs

B 5.2   Walks fast

B 6   Jumps forward

B 6.1   Jumps up and down in place

B 6.2   Jumps down from low structure

C 1.2   Bounces ball with two hands

C 1.3   Catches ball

C 1.4   Kicks ball

C 1.5   Throws ball overhand at target with one hand

C 1.6   Throws or rolls ball at target with two hands

C 2.2   Climbs play equipment

C 2.3   Goes down small slide

C 3.1   Pedals and steers bicycle with training wheels

C 3.2   Pedals and steers tricycle

C 3.3   Pushes riding toy with feet while steering

Embedded Learning Opportunities

■ *Walks during field trip with and without support*

■ *Uses gross motor skills during trip to park (runs, jumps, plays with balls, plays on playground equipment)*

ADAPTIVE Growing Skills

A 2   Eats foods from variety of food groups with variety of textures

A 2.1 Eats hard and chewy foods

A 3   Eats with eating utensils

A 3.1 Brings food to mouth with eating utensil

A 4   Drinks from open-mouth container

A 5.1 Puts appropriate amount of food in mouth, chews, and swallows before taking another bite

A 5.2 Takes in appropriate amount of liquid and returns cup to surface

A 6.1 Pours liquid into variety of containers

A 6.2 Serves food with utensil

B 1.1 Indicates need to use toilet

B 1.2 Has bowel and bladder control

B 1.3 Indicates awareness of soiled and wet pants or diapers

D 1   Takes independent action to alleviate distress, discomfort, and pain

D 1.1 Communicates internal distress, discomfort, or pain to adult

D 3.1 Responds appropriately to warnings of dangerous conditions or substances

Embedded Learning Opportunities

■ *Eats crackers and cheese, raisins, and apple slices in field trip lunch*

■ *Drinks juice or water from cup and uses spoon to eat applesauce*

■ *Tells adult of need to use toilet or toileting accident on field trip*

■ *Washes hands after touching animals in petting zoo, climbing on play structure at park, playing with bubbles at science museum*

■ *Listens to adults' warnings when out in community*

■ *Talks about traffic signs seen in community*

■ *Follows safety rules when arriving at and departing from home or school (holds adult's hand when crossing street, tells another child to put on seat belt), reports others not following rules*

SOCIAL-EMOTIONAL Growing Skills

A 3.2 Follows familiar social routines with familiar adults

B 1 Responds appropriately to others' emotions

B 1.1 Identifies/labels emotions in others

B 1.2 Identifies/labels own emotions

B 2 Uses appropriate strategies to manage emotional states

B 2.1 Responds appropriately to soothing by peer

B 3 Makes positive statements about self or accomplishments

B 3.1 Explains or shows others how to do tasks mastered

B 3.2 Shares accomplishment with familiar caregiver

C 1 Maintains interaction with peer

C 1.1 Initiates social behavior toward peer

C 1.2 Responds appropriately to peer social behavior

C 3.1 Initiates cooperative activity

C 3.2 Joins others in cooperative activity

C 3.3 Shares or exchanges objects

D 1 Interacts appropriately with others during small-group activities

D 1.1 Interacts appropriately with materials during small-group activities

D 1.2 Responds appropriately to directions during small-group activities

D 1.3 Remains with group during small-group activities

D 2 Interacts appropriately with others during large-group activities

D 2.1 Interacts appropriately with materials during large-group activities

D 2.2 Responds appropriately to directions during large-group activities

D 2.3 Remains with group during large-group activities

D 3 Initiates and completes independent activities

D 3.1 Responds to request to finish activity

D 3.2 Responds to request to begin activity

D 3.3 Entertains self by playing with toys

D 4 Resolves conflicts using negotiation

D 4.1 Uses strategies to resolve conflicts

D 4.2 Claims and defends possessions

E 1.1 Meets internal physical needs of hunger and thirst

E 2.2 Adjusts behavior based on feedback from others or environment

E 3.1 Seeks adult permission when appropriate

Embedded Learning Opportunities

■ *Hugs peer who is scared about being in new place*

■ *Shows peer how to put on jacket, pet goat gently, climb on ladder at park*

■ *Pretends to be firefighter sliding down pole after visiting fire station*

■ *Reenacts storyline from read-aloud time at library*

■ *Follows and knows game rules while on field trip*

■ *Resolves conflict during field trip by asking to pet same animal peer is petting when peer is finished*

■ *Tells peer to stop pushing while waiting to go down slide*

■ *Stays with group while on field trip*

■ *Gets drink of water independently when walking past water fountain at park*

■ *Uses quiet voice in library after hearing peers use quiet voices*

■ *Gives own name and age to adult making name tags for field trip*

SOCIAL-COMMUNICATION Growing Skills

B 2   Locates common objects, people, or events

B 3   Follows multistep directions without contextual cues

B 3.1   Follows multistep directions with contextual cues

B 3.2   Follows one-step direction without contextual cues

B 3.3   Follows one-step direction with contextual cues

B 4.1   Answers *who*, *what*, and *where* questions

C 1   Produces multiple word sentences to communicate

C 1.1   Uses two-word utterances

C 1.2   Uses 50 single words, signs, or symbols

C 2   Uses plural pronouns to indicate subjects, objects, and possession in multiple-word sentences

C 2.1   Uses irregular plural nouns in multiple-word sentences

C 2.2   Uses regular plural nouns

C 3   Uses helping verbs

C 3.2   Uses regular past tense of common verbs

C 3.3   Uses *to be* verbs

C 4   Asks questions using inverted auxiliary

C 4.1   Asks *wh-* questions

D 1   Uses language to initiate and sustain social interaction

D 1.1   Follows social conventions of language

D 2   Provides and seeks information while conversing using words, phrases, or sentences

D 2.1   Asks questions to obtain information

D 2.2   Describes objects, people, and events as part of social exchange

D 3.3   Responds to topic initiations from others

D 3.4   Alternates between speaker and listener roles during conversations with others

D 3.5   Responds to contingent questions from others

Embedded Learning Opportunities

- *Follows multistep directions ("Get your backpack, put it on your back, and line up at the door")*

- *Tells adult about field trip using details and correct pronouns and tenses ("We flew kites at the park! Mine was blue.")*

- *Asks questions to get new information during read-aloud*

- *Listens to librarian and asks questions when appropriate*

COGNITIVE Growing Skills

B 1   Imitates novel coordinated motor actions

B 2   Imitates novel words

B 3.1   Relates recent events without contextual cues

B 3.2   Relates recent events with contextual cues

B 3.3   Relates events immediately after they occur

C 2   Recognizes symbols

C 2.1   Uses object to represent another object

C 3.1   Classifies according to function

C 3.2   Classifies according to physical attribute

C 3.3   Discriminates between objects or people using common attributes

C 4   Uses early conceptual comparisons

C 4.1   Identifies common concepts

C 4.2   Identifies concrete concepts

D 4.1   Draws conclusions about causes of events based on personal experience

E 1   Expands simple observations and explorations into further inquiry

E 1.1   Uses simple tools to gather information

E 2   Anticipates outcome of investigation

E 2.1   Generates specific questions for investigation

E 2.2   Demonstrates knowledge about natural happenings

E 3   Investigates to test hypotheses

E 3.1   Draws on prior knowledge to guide investigations

E 3.2   Manipulates materials to cause change

Embedded Learning Opportunities

■ *Imitates kicking ball during field trip to park after seeing adult kick it*

■ *Sees horse on field trip to farm and says "I rode a pony at my granny's!"*

■ *Points out pink pigs, small and large horses, barn, and farm house during trip to farm*

■ *Runs sand through sifter at science museum and asks "Why doesn't the sand go through?"*

■ *Observes leaves falling from trees while walking around community*

LITERACY Growing Skills

A 1   Participates in shared group reading

A 2   Demonstrates understanding that text is read in one direction and from top to bottom of page

A 2.1 Turns pages of book from beginning toward end

A 2.2 Holds book or other printed material with pictures correctly oriented

A 3.1 Recognizes own first name in print

A 3.2 Recognizes common signs and logos

B 1.2 Participates in repetitive verbal play

D 1   Demonstrates understanding that pictures represent text

D 1.1 Labels familiar people, actions, objects, and events in picture books

D 1.2 Locates familiar objects, people, events, and actions in picture books

D 2   Retells simple story

D 2.1 Makes predictions about what will happen next in story

D 2.2 Answers and asks questions related to story

D 3.1 Demonstrates understanding of key vocabulary in picture books

D 3.2 Demonstrates understanding of title, author, and illustrator

D 3.3 Demonstrates understanding of vocabulary associated with early literacy concepts

E 1.1 Dictates description of drawing

E 1.2 Verbally labels representational drawings

E 1.3 Verbally labels nonrepresentational drawings

Embedded Learning Opportunities

■ *Follows along during storytime at library*

■ *Recognizes letters and reads words on signs and posters in community and in books and magazines (words on poster at science museum)*

■ *Identifies familiar people in book after community helpers field trip (firefighters, police officers, mail carriers)*

■ *Answers questions about book during read-aloud at library*

■ *Dictates description of drawing of favorite part of field trip*

MATH Growing Skills

A 1   Counts out 3 items

A 1.1 Counts 3 items to determine "How many?"

B 1   Compares items in sets to 5 by counting

B 1.1 Compares items in sets to 5 by matching

B 1.2 Creates equivalent sets of 5 items

B 1.3 Uses quantity comparison words

Embedded Learning Opportunities

■ *Counts 3 fossils at science museum*

■ *Says "Janine has more fossils than me"*

■ *Counts from 1 to 10 while waiting to see animals come out at zoo*

TIER 1

■ UNIVERSAL STRATEGIES

These are best practices for ALL young children, with attention to meeting learning outcomes within daily routines and activities of family life and early childhood classrooms while promoting positive adult–child relationships and peer interactions.

At the Growing level, children now find it easier to walk or operate riding toys to go places in new environments. Children can verbalize where they want to go and what materials they want to take along. They now have the gross and fine motor skills to access play equipment and explore the world around them with little help. Their increased social-communication skills allow them to ask *wh-* questions that promote discovery during new experiences. At this level, children are acquiring early literacy skills and can participate more actively during library story times. They can explore museums actively thanks to their growing cognitive skills, such as anticipating outcomes, guiding investigations using prior knowledge, and telling caregivers about events that occurred at the museum.

▲ Ensure safety by keeping expectations and rules consistent and clear on all outings.

▲ Schedule trips for times of the day when children are most likely to handle them successfully, such as after meal or rest times.

Interactions

As with the Beginning level of this routine, familiar adults may have the most success introducing new environments and experiences. Following are some suggested interactions for the Growing level:

▲ Remain easily accessible to children during field trips to answer questions and provide support.

▲ Embed practice with developmental skills in field trip activities.

▲ Embed knowledge learned during field trips in other daily activities (during storytime, say "At the library, we learned what an author does. Who remembers what they do?").

▲ Keep field trips meaningful and interesting to children by letting them choose the location if possible; or choose locations based on children's interests.

▲ Build social-emotional, social-communication, fine motor, and gross motor skills into field trips (use simple games at a park to encourage children to interact and cooperate).

▲ Build literacy, math, cognitive, and social-communication skills with trips to the library, museum, zoo, or farm or a walk around the community.

▲ Debrief children on what they learned during the outing by summarizing main points and leaving time for children to ask questions and get answers.

Environments and Materials

Following are some suggestions for environments and materials at the Growing level:

▲ Choose field trips that are safe and ensure ample supervision.

▲ Vary field trip settings to provide a well-rounded set of experiences (indoors and outdoors). Age-appropriate experiences include

△ Visiting zoos, farms, and museums

△ Taking a walk through the community

△ Going to a park

△ Walking through a nearby college campus

△ Visiting a fire station, police station, or post office

△ Attending a play or other live event

▲ Invest time in preparing and organizing before field trips (making necessary arrangements or reservations, gathering emergency contact information, arranging ample supervision).

■ FOCUSED STRATEGIES

These strategies are for teaching SOME children who are struggling with a component of a skill or whose development is stalled and who need extra help to catch up or keep up. The strategies include a variety of minor adaptations or modifications to daily routines, activities, and environments to meet targeted outcomes at home and in classrooms.

▲ Give children who struggle with specific skills and concepts used during field trips (such as following directions) additional opportunities to practice:

△ Embed those concepts and skills in several different routines.

△ Incorporate repetition by finding activities and games that let children practice particular skills.

△ Have children practice skills at home or school in advance of an outing (following simple directions such as "Come here" and "Stop").

▲ Pair children whose social-emotional and social-communication skills are advanced with growing learners during outings so they can serve as role models.

▲ Let children choose field trip destinations and materials to take along whenever possible (ask children if they would rather go to the park or the swimming pool).

▲ Take along materials children are comfortable using in their natural environment and incorporate ways to use them in the new environment to help children become comfortable there.

▲ Support children who become overwhelmed easily in new places or have short attention spans by limiting the amount of time they spend in outings outside their natural environment.

▲ Teach children who cannot speak to use simple signs (MORE, ALL DONE) so they can communicate their preferences.

▲ Learn to recognize children's cues and preferences.

▲ Pair sign language with spoken words for children who are nonverbal or who have hearing impairments.

■ SPECIALIZED STRATEGIES

These strategies for teaching the FEW children who need intensive supports include a variety of specialized, individualized, precise evidence-based strategies to meet children's unique goals/outcomes:

▲ Identify priority skills and focus learning goals on one or two specific skills (following one-step directions during outings).

▲ Let children direct the pace of the activity:

△ Pay attention to children's cues.

△ Allow time for children to absorb and process information.

△ Look for signs that children are ready to move to the next step or to have an adult or peer direct their attention.

▲ Check in advance to make sure new environments are accessible (playgrounds with raised sand tables, ramped slides for children in wheelchairs).

▲ Accommodate special positioning needs:

△ Seat the child with a secure base and stabilize their arms and wrists during table activities (at museums, libraries).

△ Try different positions to find one that works (let the child listen to a story while lying on the floor, with their chest supported by a foam wedge, rather than while seated in a chair).

▲ Provide mobility devices (scooters or wheelchairs) for children who have mobility issues.

▲ Give children who have sensory or physical disabilities an opportunity to experience all parts of the activity (how the bubbles in the bubble room at the science museum feel, smell, look):

△ Use hand-under-hand guidance to help children who have visual impairments point to or manipulate small objects discovered during the field trip (pebbles, toy animals, fossils).

△ Use most-to-least prompts to fade hand-under-hand guidance and prepare children to explore objects independently.

▲ Offer children who have behavior concerns positive reinforcement ("I like the way you are petting the animals gently!") and provide differential reinforcement to other children who are displaying appropriate behavior.

▲ Use time delay when asking questions to give children time to think and respond (at the library, wait predetermined number of seconds between asking a child to label pictures in a book and saying the name of the picture).

▲ Use mand modeling for children who do not express their wants and needs (if a child kicks their feet when the swing stops, ask if they want to swing more, wait 3 seconds for the child to respond, then model "more" for the child).

▲ Bring any adaptive materials children will need to participate (frequency modulation [FM] system; adapted eating or writing utensils; communication system for children who have hearing impairments, physical disabilities, or communication delays).

AEPS-3 Curriculum Resources (Appendix A)

Appendix A in this volume contains numerous additional resources to supplement the AEPS-3 Curriculum. The first part of the appendix presents a list of general curriculum resources, and the second part provides lists of supplementary resources for each individual routine and activity.

AEPS-3 Skills Matrix (Appendix B)

The AEPS-3 Skills Matrix in Appendix B of this volume spotlights individual skills by showing functional application across all routines and activities. Each skills matrix (there are eight total, one for each of the test's eight developmental areas) allows you to select individual AEPS-3 items for children who require an intensive focus on a few skills across routines and activities. For children who have difficulty learning new skills at the level of individual AEPS-3 items, the Foundation Steps (*FS*) provide an even more granular breakdown of component subskills that are either a sequence of developmental precursors or steps in task analyses.

16

Math

Math is an important element in many children's daily routines and activities and at the Growing level includes counting and comparing small quantities using sets. Acquiring early math skills is essential in building a strong foundation for school readiness. Math can be embedded in any routine, at any time, in any environment, multiple times a day. Peer and adult guidance and modeling may be needed to help children relate their daily experiences to math. This routine changes over time as children develop cognitive, fine motor, and social-communication skills. The AEPS-3 Growing level of Math uses skills from eight developmental areas.

Concurrent Skills

The following concurrent skills are AEPS-3 skills that can be easily embedded and taught during regular occurrences of Math.

FINE MOTOR Growing Skills

B 1 Activates object with finger

B 2 Rotates wrist to manipulate object

B 3 Manipulates object with two hands, each performing different action

B 3.1 Assembles toy

B 3.2 Aligns objects

B 3.3 Fits variety of shapes into corresponding spaces

C 1.1 Writes or draws using mixed strokes

C 1.2 Writes or draws using curved lines

C 1.3 Writes or draws using straight lines

C 1.4 Scribbles

D 1 Uses finger to interact with electronic device

D 1.1 Uses finger to interact with simple electronic game

> **Embedded Learning Opportunities**
>
> - *Attempts to write numbers and draw shapes*
> - *Puts pieces of a puzzle back together*
> - *Lines up objects to count*
> - *Plays interactive math game on tablet*

GROSS MOTOR Growing Skills

B 4   Alternates feet going up and down stairs

B 4.1   Walks up and down stairs using support

B 4.2   Moves up and down stairs

B 6.1   Jumps up and down in place

C 1.2   Bounces ball with two hands

C 1.3   Catches ball

C 1.5   Throws ball overhand at target with one hand

C 1.6   Throws or rolls ball at target with two hands

C 2.3   Goes down small slide

Embedded Learning Opportunities

■ *Counts while walking up and down stairs, hopping, and bouncing and throwing a ball*

■ *Counts to 3 before going down slide*

■ *Counts how many times they swing back and forth*

ADAPTIVE Growing Skills

D 1   Takes independent action to alleviate distress, discomfort, and pain

Embedded Learning Opportunities

■ *Counts to 3 to relax when frustrated*

■ *Keeps manipulatives on table instead of throwing them*

SOCIAL-EMOTIONAL Growing Skills

B 3.1   Explains or shows others how to do tasks mastered

B 3.2   Shares accomplishment with familiar caregiver

C 1.1   Initiates social behavior toward peer

C 1.2   Responds appropriately to peer social behavior

C 3.3   Shares or exchanges objects

D 1   Interacts appropriately with others during small-group activities

D 1.1   Interacts appropriately with materials during small-group activities

D 1.2   Responds appropriately to directions during small-group activities

D 1.3   Remains with group during small-group activities

D 2   Interacts appropriately with others during large-group activities

D 2.1   Interacts appropriately with materials during large-group activities

D 2.2   Responds appropriately to directions during large-group activities

D 2.3   Remains with group during large-group activities

D 3   Initiates and completes independent activities

D 3.1   Responds to request to finish activity

D 3.2   Responds to request to begin activity

D 3.3   Entertains self by playing with toys

D 4.1   Uses strategies to resolve conflicts

D 4.2   Claims and defends possessions

E 2.1   Meets behavioral expectations in familiar environments

E 2.2   Adjusts behavior based on feedback from others or environment

E 3.2   Follows established social rules in familiar environments

Embedded Learning Opportunities

■ *Says "I counted to 10 while I washed my hands!"*

■ *Shows peer how to count, sort, or match objects*

■ *Says they want to do math activity once peer is finished, then says they are finished and it is next peer's turn*

■ *Tells peer to stop because it is their turn with activity and says peer can have another turn when they are done*

■ *Remains with group during circle time and keeps materials from counting songs (frogs, monkeys, ducks) in lap while still singing*

SOCIAL-COMMUNICATION Growing Skills

B 2   Locates common objects, people, or events

B 3   Follows multistep directions without contextual cues

B 3.1   Follows multistep directions with contextual cues

B 3.2   Follows one-step direction without contextual cues

B 3.3   Follows one-step direction with contextual cues

B 4.1   Answers *who*, *what*, and *where* questions

C 1   Produces multiple-word sentences to communicate

C 1.1   Uses two-word utterances

C 1.2   Uses 50 single words, signs, or symbols

C 2   Uses plural pronouns to indicate subjects, objects, and possession in multiple-word sentences

C 2.1   Uses irregular plural nouns in multiple-word sentences

C 2.2   Uses regular plural nouns

C 3.2   Uses regular past tense of common verbs

C 3.3   Uses *to be* verbs

C 4   Asks questions using inverted auxiliary

C 4.1   Asks *wh-* questions

D 1   Uses language to initiate and sustain social interaction

D 1.1   Follows social conventions of language

D 2   Provides and seeks information while conversing using words, phrases, or sentences

D 2.2   Describes objects, people, and events as part of social exchange

D 3.3   Responds to topic initiations from others

D 3.4   Alternates between speaker and listener roles during conversations with others

D 3.5   Responds to contingent questions from others

Embedded Learning Opportunities

- *Gets two blocks and returns to table activity after adult directs*

- *Works and converses with peer or adult on math activity (counting, sorting, matching)*

- *Asks adult "What is this?" while holding up calculator*

- *Talks with peer about number of food items they have on napkin*

- *Looks at adult after adult calls child's name*

COGNITIVE Growing Skills

B 1   Imitates novel coordinated motor actions

B 2   Imitates novel words

C 3.1 Classifies according to function

C 3.2 Classifies according to physical attribute

C 3.3 Discriminates between objects or people using common attributes

C 4   Uses early conceptual comparisons

C 4.1 Identifies common concepts

C 4.2 Identifies concrete concepts

D 3.1 Evaluates common solutions to solve problems or reach goals

E 3.2 Manipulates materials to cause change

Embedded Learning Opportunities

■ *Uses new words involving math concepts (more, less)*

■ *Sorts objects or manipulatives into proper containers*

■ *Makes observations and communicates to say which object has more or is taller*

LITERACY Growing Skills

A 2   Demonstrates understanding that text is read in one direction and from top to bottom of page

A 2.1 Turns pages of book from beginning toward end

A 2.2 Holds book or other printed material with pictures correctly oriented

A 3.1 Recognizes own first name in print

B 1.2 Participates in repetitive verbal play

D 1.3 Matches pictures to actual objects, people, or actions

Embedded Learning Opportunities

■ *Follows along during read-aloud children's book with math concepts (Pete the Cat and His Four Groovy Buttons, Ten Wriggly Wiggly Caterpillars)*

■ *Sings along to songs with math concepts ("5 Green and Speckled Frogs," "5 Little Ducks," "5 Little Monkeys")*

■ *Matches shapes in shape sorter, animal patterns to animal, animal objects to pictures*

MATH Growing Skills

A 1   Counts out 3 items

A 1.1   Counts 3 items to determine "How many?"

B 1   Compares items in sets to 5 by counting

B 1.1   Compares items in sets to 5 by matching

B 1.2   Creates equivalent sets of 5 items

B 1.3   Uses quantity comparison words

Embedded Learning Opportunities

- *Counts out blocks while handing to peers*

- *Counts crackers and says "Tyrone has more crackers than I do!"*

- *Counts out trains to determine how many*

- *Counts out 10 animal crackers for peers during snack time*

TIER 1

■ UNIVERSAL STRATEGIES

These are best practices for ALL young children, with attention to meeting learning outcomes within daily routines and activities of family life and early childhood classrooms while promoting positive adult–child relationships and peer interactions.

Children advance from perceptual exploration and begin to learn conceptual math skills such as ordering, matching familiar items, and understanding common concepts such as big and little. More precise fine motor control allows them to become increasingly adept at exploring and manipulating the world around them. Children at the Growing level often are interested in and able to engage with puzzles, stacking and sorting toys, shape sorters, and similar games. Rapidly expanding communication skills during the toddler years support math learning by enabling children to imitate others, follow simple directions, share their interests and preferences, and ask questions. This period of growth is often characterized by the active nature of play and general engagement. Embedding math concepts in social-communication activities (counting objects around them, talking about different ages), fine motor activities (using tongs to count, doing a number puzzle), and gross motor activities (counting steps, hopping three times, stretching for 10 seconds) is an effective way to capture children's interest and engage them in learning.

Interactions

Embedding math learning into existing classroom music and movement activities provides many opportunities that are likely to motivate children to participate. As toddlers begin to learn conceptual math skills (such as counting to 3), it is important that adults continue to build a foundational base of math experiences. For younger children, the best way to make math meaningful is to use important, familiar aspects of their lives (such as family photos) as the vehicle for teaching. Math learning is also easily embedded in both gross motor play and music. For example, many songs combine actions used to follow directions with basic math concepts such as counting, colors, and size, by directing children to do various things ("Reach up high and reach down low," "Put your hand on your head," "Turn around two times," "Clap, clap, clap"). Such activities teach opposites (up and down), positioning and spatial relationships (on top of, under, to the side of), and quantity (clap, clap, clap = 3 claps). Music also builds children's knowledge of rhythm, which is a pattern.

Following are some suggested interactions for the Growing level of Math:

▲ Incorporate math learning into each routine and activity throughout the day by using math talk, elaborating and extending naturally occurring math opportunities, and providing a math-rich environment:

△ During cleanup, say "I like how you are lining up those trucks so neatly. Here's one more; now there are 1, 2, 3, 4 trucks."

▲ Embed math in various types of play and routines by incorporating opportunities to count and use quantity words (counting children at circle time, setting a limit on the number of children who can use a particular center at one time).

▲ Develop and use intentional planned activities to give children a range of experiences with different math concepts.

▲ Use family photos to talk about how many people are in each child's family or to make a large class calendar to display birthdays. (Toddlers may not yet fully grasp the sequential format or general idea of the calendar, but exposure to such functional uses of numbers can help them build connections and become ready to learn more complex concepts.)

▲ Embed math activities in gross motor play:

△ Include math learning in simple movement games involving numbers, such as modified Hopscotch, Follow the Leader, and Simon Says. (Typically, these games focus on using motor movements to follow directions, but the games are easily modified to include math.)

△ Draw a number line from 1 to 10 on the ground with chalk, and encourage children to jump to specific numbers down the number line or to see how fast they can run from 1 to 10 compared with running from 1 to a lower number. (This activity can help children understand the sequence of numbers, introduces the concept of cardinality, and shows concretely how numbers can be used to organize the world.)

▲ Embed math learning in music.

Environments and Materials

Following are some suggestions for environment and materials at the Growing level of this activity:

▲ Provide a dedicated math center or offer a math table activity each day to highlight math as an important element of the classroom and incorporate math talk and activities throughout the day:

△ Include items that are already in the environment, such as puzzles, sorting toys, or lacing beads (which support not only fine motor skills but also early math learning, such as sequencing).

△ Provide collections of objects that have patterns or many pieces to count, number lines, art collages, sorting bins, or other such materials.

▲ Place number-rich items in the dramatic play area (telephones, toy clocks, play money, cash registers, menus, calendars). Include books with counting, numbers, and other math concepts in the library center.

▲ Encourage children to use functional numbers in the classroom by labeling cubbies and bins with numbers as well as names.

▲ Provide fewer high-preference toys so children have to count and compare them.

▲ Offer many different representations of mathematical concepts, both verbally and in print:

△ Include a number puzzle, a poster of written and drawn number concepts, and a physical number display in the room where children count items.

△ Say numbers while counting objects during a small group activity.

▲ Include a variety of scooping and pouring devices of different sizes and shapes (such as measuring cups and spoons) in the sensory table to begin building children's understanding of quantity.

◼ FOCUSED STRATEGIES

TIER
2

These strategies are for teaching SOME children who are struggling with a component of a skill or whose development is stalled and who need extra help to catch up or keep up. The strategies include a variety of minor adaptations or modifications to daily routines, activities, and environments to meet targeted outcomes at home and in classrooms.

▲ Give children numerous opportunities to engage with math concepts:

△ Find multiple routines in which to embed math activities.

△ Repeat activities and games to help make sure children have many chances to try them.

△ Incorporate opportunities throughout the day for children to hear and see numbers, count, and use quantitative language.

▲ Select manipulatives and other materials children enjoy:

△ Let a child choose which counting set they like.

△ Let a child use a favorite cracker to count and eat at snack time.

▲ Modify math outcomes to limit the number of concepts children learn at one time (make sure a child can count reliably to 4 before adding 5).

▲ Give children jobs in the classroom to incorporate math learning into functional parts of the day (if children are learning to count, assign the job of counting cups for snack time).

▲ Engage children who do not spontaneously express interest in mathematical play by modifying a favorite activity:

△ Bury large plastic numbers in a sensory bin for toddlers to explore.

△ Write numbers on a ball to roll back and forth, and talk about the number each person catches.

▲ Let children who are struggling with a concept work in a quiet space free of distractions:

△ Arrange for the child to work in the library corner.

△ Wait until outdoor time and bring a small group of children into the empty classroom for a quiet learning opportunity.

△ Create individual workspaces using box lids or trays to define workspaces and reduce the need to share materials with other children.

▲ Use different grouping strategies to facilitate learning:

△ Group children by skill level and create activities that target a specific skill.

△ Group children with more proficient peers to encourage peer modeling and shared learning.

▲ Schedule learning new math concepts for times of the day when children are most likely to be successful (such as after snack or naptime).

▲ Teach children who cannot speak to use simple signs (MORE, ALL DONE) so they can communicate their preferences.

▲ Learn to recognize children's cues and preferences.

▲ Pair sign language with spoken words for children who are nonverbal or who have hearing impairments.

■ SPECIALIZED STRATEGIES

These strategies for teaching the FEW children who need intensive supports include a variety of specialized, individualized, precise evidence-based strategies to meet children's unique goals/outcomes:

▲ Identify priority skills and focus children's learning goals on one or two specific skills (for a child who needs individual attention and intervention to support learning AEPS-3 Math objective MA.B1.3, Uses quantity comparison words, a priority skill might be using one quantity comparison word, such as *more,* to request additional items during the day).

▲ Let children direct the pace of the activity:

△ Pay attention to the child's cues and give them time to absorb and process information.

△ Look for signs the child is ready to move to the next step or to have an adult or peer direct their attention.

△ Let the child work through each step or part of the activity at their own pace.

▲ For children who have specific positioning and mobility needs,

△ Seat the child with a secure base, and stabilize their arms and wrists when working at table activities.

△ Try different positions for play (playing with a puzzle while lying on the floor, with a foam wedge supporting the chest, rather than while sitting at a table).

▲ For children who have fine motor challenges,

△ Provide manipulatives designed for easier grasping (larger or smaller size than usual, with a built-up handle).

△ Modify toys to make them easier to grasp and manipulate (attach magnets, felt, or hook-and-loop fasteners to help children maneuver pieces successfully without accidentally knocking them off a table or other surface).

▲ Use a sticky mat to help keep things from sliding around.

△ Let the child use a technology app to sort and match objects.

▲ For children who have visual impairments,

△ Start by counting familiar objects so the child can focus on the counting rather than on the new object.

△ Place math materials on a light table.

AEPS-3 Curriculum Resources (Appendix A)

Appendix A in this volume contains numerous additional resources to supplement the AEPS-3 Curriculum. The first part of the appendix presents a list of general curriculum resources, and the second part provides lists of supplementary resources for each individual routine and activity.

AEPS-3 Skills Matrix (Appendix B)

The AEPS-3 Skills Matrix in Appendix B of this volume spotlights individual skills by showing functional application across all routines and activities. Each skills matrix (there are eight total, one for each of the test's eight developmental areas) allows you to select individual AEPS-3 items for children who require an intensive focus on a few skills across routines and activities. For children who have difficulty learning new skills at the level of individual AEPS-3 items, the Foundation Steps (*FS*) provide an even more granular breakdown of component subskills that are either a sequence of developmental precursors or steps in task analyses.

Meals & Snacks

Meals & Snacks can incorporate a variety of skills along with eating and provides opportunities to build intimate adult–child and peer relationships. This routine occurs frequently throughout the day, depending on individual child and family schedules. Meals & Snacks evolves over time, with infants depending completely on adults, toddlers being able to feed themselves independently, and preschoolers helping prepare meals and snacks. Through frequent repetition and growth, children acquire complex adaptive, social-communication, and fine motor skills in this routine. The AEPS-3 Growing level of Meals & Snacks uses skills from eight developmental areas.

Concurrent Skills

The following concurrent skills are AEPS-3 skills that can be easily embedded and taught during regular occurrences of Meals & Snacks.

FINE MOTOR Growing Skills

B 1   Activates object with finger

B 2   Rotates wrist to manipulate object

B 3   Manipulates object with two hands, each performing different action

B 3.2   Aligns objects

Embedded Learning Opportunities

- *Uses one finger to touch picture of apple on tablet*

- *Rotates wrist to turn water bottle around to see front, tears package open from back*

- *Aligns objects on napkin (goldfish, pretzels, gummy bears)*

GROSS MOTOR Growing Skills

B 3   Walks avoiding people, furniture, or objects

B 3.1   Walks without support

B 4.3   Gets up and down from low structure

Embedded Learning Opportunities

- *Walks without support to table to eat*

- *Gets up and down from child-size table and chair*

ADAPTIVE Growing Skills

A 2   Eats foods from variety of food groups with variety of textures

A 2.1 Eats hard and chewy foods

A 3   Eats with eating utensils

A 3.1 Brings food to mouth with eating utensil

A 4   Drinks from open-mouth container

A 5.1 Puts appropriate amount of food in mouth, chews, and swallows before taking another bite

A 5.2 Takes in appropriate amount of liquid and returns cup to surface

A 6.1 Pours liquid into variety of containers

A 6.2 Serves food with utensil

B 2.1 Washes and dries face

B 2.2 Washes and dries hands

B 3.1 Completes some steps to brush teeth, comb hair, and wipe nose

C 1.2 Takes off pullover clothing over head

D 1   Takes independent action to alleviate distress, discomfort, and pain

D 1.1 Communicates internal distress, discomfort, or pain to adult

D 3.1 Responds appropriately to warnings of dangerous conditions or substances

Embedded Learning Opportunities

■ *Eats foods with different textures (granola, chips, mashed potatoes, pudding, yogurt, cottage cheese)*

■ *Eats variety of foods (meat, dairy, fruits, vegetables)*

■ *Eats with spoon and fork with minimal spilling*

■ *Puts small amount of food in mouth at one time to chew and swallow*

■ *Pours liquid (juice, water, milk) into cup and bowl*

■ *Serves food with tongs, large spoon, or spatula*

■ *Completes all steps to wash hands and face after meal*

■ *Pulls bib over own head to take it off*

■ *Gets up during meal to throw away "gross" food, get napkin when spill occurs, or go to bathroom*

■ *Blows on food when adult says it is hot*

SOCIAL-EMOTIONAL Growing Skills

A 3   Participates in familiar social routines with caregivers

A 3.1   Initiates next step of familiar social routine

A 3.2   Follows familiar social routines with familiar adults

B 1   Responds appropriately to others' emotions

B 2   Uses appropriate strategies to manage emotional states

B 3.1   Explains or shows others how to do tasks mastered

B 3.2   Shares accomplishment with familiar caregiver

C 1   Maintains interaction with peer

C 1.1   Initiates social behavior toward peer

C 1.2   Responds appropriately to peer social behavior

D 1   Interacts appropriately with others during small-group activities

D 1.1   Interacts appropriately with materials during small-group activities

D 1.2   Responds appropriately to directions during small-group activities

D 1.3   Remains with group during small-group activities

D 3   Initiates and completes independent activities

D 3.1   Responds to request to finish activity

D 3.2   Responds to request to begin activity

D 4   Resolves conflicts using negotiation

D 4.1   Uses strategies to resolve conflicts

D 4.2   Claims and defends possessions

E 1.1   Meets internal physical needs of hunger and thirst

E 2.1   Meets behavioral expectations in familiar environments

E 2.2   Adjusts behavior based on feedback from others or environment

E 3.2   Follows established social rules in familiar environments

Embedded Learning Opportunities

■ *Washes hands before helping set table*

■ *Throws away disliked food instead of crying*

■ *Shows peer how to set table, peel banana, or pour milk into cup*

■ *Defends favorite snack when peer or sibling reaches for it*

■ *Initiates setting table when adult says it is time for snack*

■ *Tells peer who takes wrong cup at snack time "This one yours, this one mine"*

■ *Stays in family dining space until told okay to leave*

SOCIAL-COMMUNICATION Growing Skills

B 2   Locates common objects, people, or events

B 3   Follows multistep directions without contextual cues

B 3.1   Follows multistep directions with contextual cues

B 3.2   Follows one-step direction without contextual cues

B 3.3   Follows one-step direction with contextual cues

B 4.1   Answers *who*, *what*, and *where* questions

C 1   Produces multiple-word sentences to communicate

C 1.1   Uses two-word utterances

C 1.2   Uses 50 single words, signs, or symbols

C 2   Uses plural pronouns to indicate subjects, objects, and possession in multiple-word sentences

C 2.1   Uses irregular plural nouns in multiple-word sentences

C 2.2   Uses regular plural nouns

C 3.2   Uses regular past tense of common verbs

C 3.3   Uses *to be* verbs

C 4   Asks questions using inverted auxiliary

C 4.1   Asks *wh-* questions

D 1   Uses language to initiate and sustain social interaction

D 1.1   Follows social conventions of language

D 2   Provides and seeks information while conversing using words, phrases, or sentences

D 2.2   Describes objects, people, and events as part of social exchange

D 3.3   Responds to topic initiations from others

D 3.4   Alternates between speaker and listener roles during conversations with others

D 3.5   Responds to contingent questions from others

Embedded Learning Opportunities

■ *Follows multistep directions ("Pick up your napkin, throw it away, and go wash your hands")*

■ *Tells peer at snack time "Give them some crackers"*

■ *Says "We ate this snack yesterday"*

■ *Waits while peer talks, then says "Let's eat all our bananas"*

COGNITIVE Growing Skills

B 1   Imitates novel coordinated motor actions

B 2   Imitates novel words

B 3.1   Relates recent events without contextual cues

C 3.1   Classifies according to function

C 3.2   Classifies according to physical attribute

C 3.3   Discriminates between objects or people using common attributes

C 4   Uses early conceptual comparisons

C 4.1   Identifies common concepts

C 4.2   Identifies concrete concepts

D 1.1   Uses part of object or support to obtain another object

D 3.1   Evaluates common solutions to solve problems or reach goals

E 2.2   Demonstrates knowledge about natural happenings

Embedded Learning Opportunities

■ *Says "napkin" and puts napkin on table after adult says "Let's put out some napkins"*

■ *Classifies fruits by color, vegetables by size, utensils by function*

■ *Identifies favorite food textures or temperatures ("Me want cold juice!")*

■ *Uses spoon to reach cereal bowl across table*

■ *Looks at snack table items and says "No raisins"*

LITERACY Growing Skills

A 3.1   Recognizes own first name in print

A 3.2   Recognizes common signs and logos

B 1.2   Participates in repetitive verbal play

Embedded Learning Opportunities

■ *Sits at placemat with own name written on it*

■ *Participates in singing repetitive song about eating food ("This is the way we eat our food, eat our food, eat our food")*

MATH Growing Skills

A 1   Counts out 3 items

A 1.1   Counts 3 items to determine "How many?"

B 1   Compares items in sets to 5 by counting

B 1.2   Creates equivalent sets of 5 items

Embedded Learning Opportunities

■ *Counts out 3 crackers when handing them to others*

■ *Counts "1, 2, 3!" while pouring milk*

■ *Says "Fadia got more crackers than me"*

TIER 1

■ UNIVERSAL STRATEGIES

These are best practices for ALL young children, with attention to meeting learning outcomes within daily routines and activities of family life and early childhood classrooms while promoting positive adult-child relationships and peer interactions.

Meals & Snacks offers children many opportunities to learn new skills by helping cook, set up, or clean up:

▲ Give children short, specific jobs (handing out cups at snack time) to help them practice adaptive and social-communication skills during this routine.

▲ Avoid power struggles around food by setting and enforcing clear mealtime rules and making sure expectations are developmentally appropriate:

△ Have toddlers taste each item of food on their plate, but do not force them to finish all of it.

△ Learn and use appropriate portion sizes for children as they grow. (Adult portions look very different from children's. Adults tend to overfeed children with adult-size portions and worry when they don't eat it all.)

△ Set a reasonable length of time for staying seated during meals (15 instead of 30 minutes).

Interactions

This routine presents many valuable opportunities for interactions between adults and children, so it is important for them to sit together while eating. Following are some suggested interactions for the Growing level:

▲ For home visitors,

△ Teach skills that will improve children's participation in the family's existing eating routines and schedules.

▲ In the classroom,

△ Get to know the family's mealtime routines to support young children who are learning different ways of doing things at home and school. (Mealtime routines vary greatly from family to family, and this can be confusing for toddlers who are becoming more independent and responsible at the table.)

△ Avoid judgment about family mealtime habits that differ from those at school, as long as children's nutritional requirements are being met.

△ Become aware of your own cultural and personal values and preferences around eating, and take care with messages you may be sending children.

▲ In general,

△ Encourage children to communicate with peers and siblings with minimal adult involvement.

△ Converse with children about interesting things related to the meal.

△ Use food to introduce new concepts (colors, textures, sizes).

△ Use mealtime to review or preview events from the day.

△ Let adults and more skilled peers model socially appropriate eating behaviors, utensil use, and willingness to try new foods.

△ Encourage young children's growing awareness of their body's natural cycles of satiety and hunger, and do not force them to eat if they are not hungry. (Forcing them to eat not only may teach them to ignore their body's internal cues but also may create power struggles).

△ Prepare for children to be more resistant to new foods when they are tired or very hungry, and be patient with them.

Environment and Materials

A relaxed, unhurried mealtime environment prevents many problems at the Growing level. Following are some suggestions for environment and materials:

▲ Keep meal schedules flexible because some children eat quickly, and others need more time.

▲ Observe children's needs and preferences, and adapt daily meals to their needs.

▲ Offer regular meals and snacks that include a variety of healthful, enjoyable food options.

▲ Avoid using food (especially sweets and desserts) as rewards. Making dessert a reward can lead children to overeat at meals and ignore internal hunger cues. It can also lead to power struggles.

▲ Offer multiple opportunities (15 or more) for children to become familiar with new flavors and textures.

▲ Offer new or less preferred foods along with acceptable alternatives to give children an opportunity to try new foods while making sure they do not go hungry.

▲ Promote willingness to try new foods by letting children spit out foods they do not like without having to swallow things that taste unpleasant.

▲ Teach children ways to spit out food that the family finds acceptable (spit it into a napkin, set out a separate dish for rejected food).

▲ Offer a variety of food options to encourage children who are considered picky eaters:

　△ Keep in mind that children's food dislikes are not always consistent. They may eat a particular food one day and refuse it the next.

　△ Offer several food options (apple, banana, orange with lunch) so children can choose among them rather than accepting or rejecting a single option.

■ FOCUSED STRATEGIES

These strategies are for teaching SOME children who are struggling with a component of a skill or whose development is stalled and who need extra help to catch up or keep up. The strategies include a variety of minor adaptations or modifications to daily routines, activities, and environments to meet targeted outcomes at home and in classrooms.

▲ Give children plenty of alerts about transitions to mealtime, especially if they are engaged in an activity that is difficult for them to leave.

▲ Assign table buddies by pairing children who have slightly more advanced mealtime skills and more varied food preferences with children who are more cautious and have less advanced skills.

▲ Thin or thicken new foods to encourage young children who are sensitive to new textures to try them.

▲ Pay attention to children's cues for when they are getting hungry, and make sure mealtime occurs before they get too sleepy to participate.

▲ Remove children who become distressed at the table for a minute or two to let them calm down, and reseat them afterward if they want to come back to the table.

▲ Position children for comfort and stability during mealtimes:

　△ Seat a young child who is learning independent eating skills in a child-size chair or highchair if possible.

　△ Provide seating with foot and arm support and a comfortable seat with a back, so the child can focus on eating rather than maintaining their sitting posture.

▲ For children who struggle with participating in family or classroom mealtimes,

  △ Encourage practice with the social routines and expectations of mealtime by providing a pretend food or kitchen set to play with.

  △ Teach the child to use culturally accepted table manners and language they may need to be successful at the table.

▲ For children who are picky eaters,

  △ Start with foods the child likes or tolerates, and introduce new foods gradually. A picky eater may have a sensitive gag reflex, sensitive taste buds, or increased sensitivity to smells. Uncomfortable or otherwise unpleasant sensory experiences can make it difficult to enjoy the experience of trying new foods.

  △ Pay attention to food preferences (keep a food journal) to see if any patterns emerge. Typically, a child will show a preference for either strong tastes (spicy, sour, salty) or bland tastes.

  △ Keep close track of food consistencies, tastes, and textures the child will eat.

  △ Offer small amounts of new foods many times.

▲ Address concerns about extreme eating habits and resistance to change by having a specialist do an oral-motor examination to rule out physical causes for eating issues.

▲ Teach children who cannot speak to use simple signs (MORE, ALL DONE) so they can communicate their preferences.

▲ Learn to recognize children's cues and preferences.

▲ Pair sign language with spoken words for children who are nonverbal or who have hearing impairments.

■ SPECIALIZED STRATEGIES

TIER 3

These strategies for teaching the FEW children who need intensive supports include a variety of specialized, individualized, precise evidence-based strategies to meet children's unique goals/outcomes:

▲ Provide hand-over-hand graduated guidance (physical prompts) for skills that children find difficult (bringing one hand to the mouth to eat, scooping food from a bowl, drinking from a cup). As the child begins to perform the specific skill or step with full support, fade help gradually from hands, to wrists, to elbows.

▲ Encourage teamwork among parents, teachers, and any specialists to help ensure proper nutrition and the best possible mealtime experiences for children who have autism. Children who have autism are often hypersensitive to food tastes and textures and may have a higher rate of food refusal, and some will eat only a limited variety of foods. Teamwork is essential.

▲ Encourage children who have significant eating needs to accept new foods by introducing them gradually:

  △ Begin by offering the child new foods side by side with accepted foods.

  △ Encourage the child to smell and touch the new food, with no pressure for them to eat it or put it in their mouth. Provide multiple opportunities for this.

  △ Encourage the child to touch the new food to their lips next, while showing them how to do this and talking about the food (what it might taste like, how it might feel). Again, provide multiple opportunities.

  △ Next, have the child take a bite of the new food, and allow them to spit it out if necessary.

△ Finally, have the child take a bite of the new food and swallow it.

△ Provide positive reinforcement for children who use appropriate mealtime behaviors, especially when trying new foods.

▲ For children who have specific positioning and mobility needs,

△ Ensure seating for mealtime and snack time that offers a secure base as well as arm and wrist fixation, if possible (adaptive chair with seat belt, tray, or cushions that can be repositioned to meet the child's needs).

△ Use a pillow to elevate and provide extra support to keep the child's head and neck positioned properly.

▲ For children who struggle to coordinate the suck-swallow-breathe cycle,

△ Use a semi-reclined (partly upright) position.

△ Try a side-lying position to support coordination.

▲ For children who have extraneous tongue movements,

△ Try placing a finger underneath the bony point of the jaw.

▲ For children who struggle to eat, have been tube fed, or have other eating-related issues that have made eating a negative experience, provide positive experiences:

△ Gently stroke the child's cheeks and mouth to provide oral stimulation.

△ Use a teething toy, pacifier, or parent's finger in the mouth.

▲ Use a prompt hierarchy to encourage children to feed themselves independently, employing only the prompts necessary for the child to complete the routine—for example, if using system of least prompts:

△ Start with a gesture prompt and point to the child's spoon.

△ Wait for the child to pick up the spoon.

△ Then provide a verbal prompt ("Take a bite") if the child does not pick up the spoon. Wait again.

△ Next, use a partial physical prompt to lift the child's arm if they do not pick up the spoon with the verbal prompt. Wait again.

△ Finally, provide a full physical prompt to help the child pick up the spoon.

△ Repeat the prompt hierarchy for each step of the routine.

AEPS-3 Curriculum Resources (Appendix A)

Appendix A in this volume contains numerous additional resources to supplement the AEPS-3 Curriculum. The first part of the appendix presents a list of general curriculum resources, and the second part provides lists of supplementary resources for each individual routine and activity.

AEPS-3 Skills Matrix (Appendix B)

The AEPS-3 Skills Matrix in Appendix B of this volume spotlights individual skills by showing functional application across all routines and activities. Each skills matrix (there are eight total, one for each of the test's eight developmental areas) allows you to select individual AEPS-3 items for children who require an intensive focus on a few skills across routines and activities. For children who have difficulty learning new skills at the level of individual AEPS-3 items, the Foundation Steps (FS) provide an even more granular breakdown of component subskills that are either a sequence of developmental precursors or steps in task analyses.

Music & Movement

The Music & Movement activity may include singing, dancing, taking part in fingerplays, playing musical instruments, and other activities, singly or in combination. These activities give children opportunities to learn a variety of skills in an active, social manner. They may take place one to one with individual children or in groups of any size.

Children at the Growing level enjoy music activities, benefit from language-rich experiences associated with music activities, and need many opportunities to move throughout the day, so the activities in this routine may support children's development in most areas. The AEPS-3 Growing level of Music & Movement uses skills from seven developmental areas.

Concurrent Skills

The following concurrent skills are AEPS-3 skills that can be easily embedded and taught during regular occurrences of Music & Movement.

FINE MOTOR Growing Skills

B 1   Activates object with finger
B 2   Rotates wrist to manipulate object
B 3   Manipulates object with two hands, each performing different action

Embedded Learning Opportunities

- Uses one finger to play toy piano
- Shakes tambourine by rotating wrist
- Holds guitar with one hand while strumming with other

GROSS MOTOR Growing Skills

B 3   Walks avoiding people, furniture, or objects
B 3.1   Walks without support
B 4.3   Gets up and down from low structure
B 5.2   Walks fast
B 6   Jumps forward
B 6.1   Jumps up and down in place

Embedded Learning Opportunities

- Produces variety of gross motor movements while dancing to song ("The Freeze," "If You're Happy and You Know It")

ADAPTIVE Growing Skills

D 1 Takes independent action to alleviate distress, discomfort, and pain

D 1.1 Communicates internal distress, discomfort, or pain to adult

Embedded Learning Opportunities

■ *Waits for adult to operate music player or radio when wanting to listen to music or dance*

SOCIAL-EMOTIONAL Growing Skills

A 3 Participates in familiar social routines with caregivers

A 3.1 Initiates next step of familiar social routine

A 3.2 Follows familiar social routines with familiar adults

B 2 Uses appropriate strategies to manage emotional states

B 2.1 Responds appropriately to soothing by peer

B 3.1 Explains or shows others how to do tasks mastered

B 3.2 Shares accomplishment with familiar caregiver

C 1 Maintains interaction with peer

C 1.1 Initiates social behavior toward peer

C 1.2 Responds appropriately to peer social behavior

C 3.3 Shares or exchanges objects

D 1 Interacts appropriately with others during small-group activities

D 1.1 Interacts appropriately with materials during small-group activities

D 1.2 Responds appropriately to directions during small-group activities

D 1.3 Remains with group during small-group activities

D 2 Interacts appropriately with others during large-group activities

D 2.1 Interacts appropriately with materials during large-group activities

D 2.2 Responds appropriately to directions during large-group activities

D 2.3 Remains with group during large-group activities

D 4 Resolves conflicts using negotiation

D 4.1 Uses strategies to resolve conflicts

D 4.2 Claims and defends possessions

E 2.1 Meets behavioral expectations in familiar environments

E 2.2 Adjusts behavior based on feedback from others or environment

E 3.1 Seeks adult permission when appropriate

E 3.2 Follows established social rules in familiar environments

Embedded Learning Opportunities

■ *Cleans up for circle time or for music and movement upon hearing cleanup song*

■ *Responds to peer or adult during greeting song*

■ *Stops banging drum when adult says "Freeze"*

■ *Covers ears if environment gets too loud*

■ *Remains with group and dances*

■ *Gets tissue if they sneeze during activity*

■ *Stops poking peer when peer says "Stop!"*

■ *Says "Mine!" when peer takes instrument from them*

■ *Asks "Can I do it?" when time to turn off music player at end of activity*

SOCIAL-COMMUNICATION Growing Skills

B 2   Locates common objects, people, or events

B 3   Follows multistep directions without contextual cues

B 3.1 Follows multistep directions with contextual cues

B 3.2 Follows one-step direction without contextual cues

B 3.3 Follows one-step direction with contextual cues

C 1   Produces multiple-word sentences to communicate

C 1.1 Uses two-word utterances

C 1.2 Uses 50 single words, signs, or symbols

C 2   Uses plural pronouns to indicate subjects, objects, and possession in multiple-word sentences

C 2.1 Uses irregular plural nouns in multiple-word sentences

C 2.2 Uses regular plural nouns

C 3.2 Uses regular past tense of common verbs

C 3.3 Uses *to be* verbs

D 2   Provides and seeks information while conversing using words, phrases, or sentences

Embedded Learning Opportunities

- *Finds instrument and sits down in spot when directed*
- *Returns greeting during welcome song*
- *Complies when adult directs "Come to circle and sit on your spot"*
- *Says "I want to dance to the Chicken Dance!"*
- *Asks adult to sing favorite song*

COGNITIVE Growing Skills

B 1   Imitates novel coordinated motor actions

B 2   Imitates novel words

B 3.1 Relates recent events without contextual cues

B 3.2 Relates recent events with contextual cues

B 3.3 Relates events immediately after they occur

C 2   Recognizes symbols

C 2.1 Uses object to represent another object

C 3.3 Discriminates between objects or people using common attributes

C 4   Uses early conceptual comparisons

C 4.1 Identifies common concepts

C 4.2 Identifies concrete concepts

D 3.1 Evaluates common solutions to solve problems or reach goals

E 3.2 Manipulates materials to cause change

Embedded Learning Opportunities

- *Imitates new motor actions while dancing (Chicken Dance, Hokey Pokey)*
- *Demonstrates song learned at child care to adult at home*
- *Recognizes stop sign when adult holds it up during "Stop and Go" song*
- *Hits drum hard and then softly to hear difference in sound*

LITERACY Growing Skills

B 1.2 Participates in repetitive verbal play

Embedded Learning Opportunities

- *Sings "Where is Thumbkin?" song with adult*

■ UNIVERSAL STRATEGIES

These are best practices for ALL young children, with attention to meeting learning outcomes within daily routines and activities of family life and early childhood classrooms while promoting positive adult–child relationships and peer interactions.

At the Growing level, children's increased cognitive, social-communication, and motor skills allow them to advance from being guided through music and movement opportunities to taking part in them more independently. However, children still need adult assistance to learn new songs, movements, and vocabulary. Increasingly precise fine motor control gives children more ability to explore and manipulate items associated with this activity. Children at the Growing level are often interested in engaging with peers and new materials, such as by using musical instruments and noisemakers or making noises with their mouths. Social-communication skills are expanding rapidly at this time, so in this routine, learning through imitation, following simple commands, sharing interests or preferences, and asking questions all play major roles in children's development.

Interactions

Following are some suggested interactions for the Growing level:

▲ Expand children's foundational music and movement skills by continuing to build on them.

▲ Incorporate music and movement activities throughout daily routines (transitions, math, literacy, rest time, arrival and departure).

▲ Embed music and movement activities into home routines (bath time, bedtime, playtime, travel time).

▲ Encourage children's creativity while making music time meaningful to them:

△ Invite them to dance freestyle to a variety of music.

△ Demonstrate different types of dances while encouraging them to create their own actions to songs.

▲ Promote participation and other skills by continuing to add actions to songs:

△ Teach rhythm and beat by modeling chanting while children clap along.

△ Add new movements (marching, waving arms, stomping feet, swaying) once children have mastered clapping to a beat.

Environment and Materials

Following are some suggestions for environment and materials at the Growing level, in addition to the suggestion to embed music and movement into ongoing routines and activities:

▲ Create a dedicated music area or music time that offers children opportunities to learn new instruments, new styles of music, and new vocabulary words associated with music and movement activities.

▲ Preteach how to sing new songs or use new instruments.

▲ Encourage children to experiment with instruments and movements (marching while beating a drum) to encourage them to explore and solve problems.

▲ Use movement and music activities that encourage listening and following directions ("Freeze Dance").

▲ Provide children with a variety of musical instruments and encourage them to use instruments to imitate the sound of a specific animal.

TIER 2

■ FOCUSED STRATEGIES

These strategies are for teaching SOME children who are struggling with a component of a skill or whose development is stalled and who need extra help to catch up or keep up. The strategies include a variety of minor adaptations or modifications to daily routines, activities, and environments to meet targeted outcomes at home and in classrooms.

▲ Allow children to participate in movement activities in a variety of different ways (do not expect them all to move in the same way):

△ Let a child observe as a way to remain involved if they are uncomfortable participating actively.

△ Let a child dance with an adult or hold hands with another child if this helps them feel more comfortable participating.

▲ Repeat music and movement activities to make sure children have many opportunities with a particular activity.

▲ Modify music and movement for children who have limited attention spans by choosing shorter activities and songs.

▲ Pair children who are developmentally more advanced with those who are developmentally younger so they can serve as peer models during movement activities.

▲ Incorporate children's preferences when selecting music or other materials:

△ Let the child choose the instrument they would like to play, song they would like to sing, or movement they would like to do.

△ Choose new songs that relate to child-directed themes.

▲ Teach children who cannot speak to use simple signs (MORE, ALL DONE) so they can communicate their preferences.

▲ Learn to recognize children's cues and preferences.

▲ Pair sign language with spoken words for children who are nonverbal or who have hearing impairments.

TIER 3

■ SPECIALIZED STRATEGIES

These strategies for teaching the FEW children who need intensive supports include a variety of specialized, individualized, precise evidence-based strategies to meet children's unique goals/outcomes:

▲ For children who become easily overwhelmed by external stimuli,

△ Choose instruments and music that are calm and quiet.

△ Move the child to a different area of the room if stimuli become too overwhelming.

△ Let the child wear noise-reducing headphones.

▲ For children who have specific positioning and mobility needs,

△ Provide seating with a secure base, hip support, and chest support so they can use their arms and hands to take part in movement activities and play musical instruments.

▲ For children who have fine motor challenges,

△ Provide instruments or materials that have been modified to make them easier to grasp and manipulate (smaller or larger size than usual, with a built-up handle).

▲ For children who have severe muscle spasticity,

△ Provide a technology device that allows them to participate (tablet with a touch screen app that makes it possible to "play an instrument").

▲ For children who have hearing impairments,

△ Pair music with visual cues (flashing lights, vibration).

▲ For children who have visual impairments,

△ Use tangible items that relate to the song being sung.

▲ Identify children's priority skills and focus their learning goals on one or two specific skills.

▲ Use hand-over-hand assistance to help children clap rhythm with music or learn a new musical instrument:

△ Use most to least prompting to fade hand-over-hand assistance.

△ Move physical prompting from hands, to wrists, to forearms.

AEPS-3 Curriculum Resources (Appendix A)

Appendix A in this volume contains numerous additional resources to supplement the AEPS-3 Curriculum. The first part of the appendix presents a list of general curriculum resources, and the second part provides lists of supplementary resources for each individual routine and activity.

AEPS-3 Skills Matrix (Appendix B)

The AEPS-3 Skills Matrix in Appendix B of this volume spotlights individual skills by showing functional application across all routines and activities. Each skills matrix (there are eight total, one for each of the test's eight developmental areas) allows you to select individual AEPS-3 items for children who require an intensive focus on a few skills across routines and activities. For children who have difficulty learning new skills at the level of individual AEPS-3 items, the Foundation Steps (*FS*) provide an even more granular breakdown of component subskills that are either a sequence of developmental precursors or steps in task analyses.

Nap & Sleep

Nap & Sleep can occur in any environment, and young children may sleep several times a day. The number of times children sleep daily and the number of hours needed generally decrease as the children grow. This routine changes over time as children's adaptive, cognitive, social-emotional, and motor skills develop.

Sleep is critical for children to stay healthy and regulated. Whereas infants depend completely on adults to support their need for rest and sleep, toddlers' need for help may involve being rocked or patted to sleep and extra time to accommodate increasing independence in preparing for sleep. The AEPS-3 Growing level of the Nap & Sleep routine uses skills from eight developmental areas.

Concurrent Skills

The following concurrent skills are AEPS-3 skills that can be easily embedded and taught during regular occurrences of Nap & Sleep.

FINE MOTOR Growing Skills

B 2   Rotates wrist to manipulate object

B 3   Manipulates object with two hands, each performing different action

B 3.2 Aligns objects

Embedded Learning Opportunities

- *Takes off own shoes and lines them up next to bed or cubby*
- *Participates in shared reading or looks at book before sleep*

GROSS MOTOR Growing Skills

B 3   Walks avoiding people, furniture, or objects

B 3.1 Walks without support

Embedded Learning Opportunities

- *Walks to own cot or bed*

ADAPTIVE Growing

B 1.1   Indicates need to use toilet

B 1.2   Has bowel and bladder control

B 1.3   Indicates awareness of soiled and wet pants
or diapers

B 2.2   Washes and dries hands

B 3.1   Completes some steps to brush teeth, comb hair,
and wipe nose

C 1.2   Takes off pullover clothing over head

C 1.4   Takes off pants

C 2.3   Puts on pullover clothing

C 2.4   Puts on pull-up clothing

C 2.5   Puts on socks

Embedded Learning Opportunities

■ *Uses bathroom before and after sleep*

■ *Brushes teeth while getting ready for bed and upon waking*

■ *Takes off clothes to get ready for bed*

■ *Puts on clothes for day after waking*

■ *Puts on pajamas before going to bed*

SOCIAL-EMOTIONAL Growing Skills

A 3   Participates in familiar social routines with caregivers

A 3.1   Initiates next step of familiar social routine

A 3.2   Follows familiar social routines with familiar adults

B 2   Uses appropriate strategies to manage
emotional states

B 3.1   Explains or shows others how to do tasks mastered

B 3.2   Shares accomplishment with familiar caregiver

D 3   Initiates and completes independent activities

D 4   Resolves conflicts using negotiation

D 4.1   Uses strategies to resolve conflicts

E 2.1   Meets behavioral expectations in familiar
environments

E 2.2   Adjusts behavior based on feedback from others
or environment

E 3.2   Follows established social rules in familiar
environments

Embedded Learning Opportunities

■ *Puts on pajamas after brushing teeth*

■ *Shows adult they took off own shoes without help*

■ *Shows peer where shoes go during naptime*

■ *Asks for blanket when cold*

■ *States preference not to have a blanket on when sleeping*

SOCIAL-COMMUNICATION Growing Skills

B 3	Follows multistep directions without contextual cues
B 3.1	Follows multistep directions with contextual cues
B 3.2	Follows one-step direction without contextual cues
B 3.3	Follows one-step direction with contextual cues
B 4.1	Answers *who*, *what*, and *where* questions
C 1	Produces multiple-word sentences to communicate
C 1.1	Uses two-word utterances
C 1.2	Uses 50 single words, signs, or symbols
C 2	Uses plural pronouns to indicate subjects, objects, and possession in multiple-word sentences
C 2.1	Uses irregular plural nouns in multiple-word sentences
C 2.2	Uses regular plural nouns
C 3	Uses helping verbs
C 3.2	Uses regular past tense of common verbs
C 3.3	Uses *to be* verbs
C 4	Asks questions using inverted auxiliary
C 4.1	Asks *wh-* questions
D 1	Uses language to initiate and sustain social interaction
D 1.1	Follows social conventions of language
D 2.2	Describes objects, people, and events as part of social exchange
D 3.4	Alternates between speaker and listener roles during conversations with others
D 3.5	Responds to contingent questions from others

Embedded Learning Opportunities

- *Gets bath toys, pajamas, favorite book from other room when asked*
- *Uses various forms of language to tell adult about day*
- *Asks and answers questions about day's events*
- *Requests bedtime story*
- *Says "I did it!" when asked if they brushed their teeth*
- *Asks "Is Daddy going to read to me?"*
- *Has conversation with adult about story before going to bed*

COGNITIVE Growing Skills

B 2	Imitates novel words
B 3.1	Relates recent events without contextual cues
B 3.2	Relates recent events with contextual cues
B 3.3	Relates events immediately after they occur
C 4	Uses early conceptual comparisons
C 4.1	Identifies common concepts
C 4.2	Identifies concrete concepts

Embedded Learning Opportunities

- *Discusses day's events with adult before going to sleep*
- *Describes clothing, bedding, stories using common concepts and comparisons*

LITERACY Growing Skills

A 2   Demonstrates understanding that text is read in one direction and from top to bottom of page

A 2.1   Turns pages of book from beginning toward end

A 2.2   Holds book or other printed material with pictures correctly oriented

A 3.2   Recognizes common signs and logos

D 1   Demonstrates understanding that pictures represent text

D 1.1   Labels familiar people, actions, objects, and events in picture books

D 1.2   Locates familiar objects, people, events, and actions in picture books

D 2   Retells simple story

D 2.1   Makes predictions about what will happen next in story

D 2.2   Answers and asks questions related to story

D 2.3   Tells story associated with series of pictures

D 3.3   Demonstrates understanding of vocabulary associated with early literacy concepts

Embedded Learning Opportunities

- *Finds book, holds it correctly, turns pages, labels pictures while reading book with adult before sleep*
- *Labels pictures during story before sleep*
- *Predicts what will happen during story*
- *Points out letters and logos in books with adult prompting*

MATH Growing Skills

A 1   Counts out 3 items

A 1.1   Counts 3 items to determine "How many?"

Embedded Learning Opportunities

- *Reads counting books and counts out items within book*
- *Counts fingers and toes during counting song before bed*

TIER 1

■ UNIVERSAL STRATEGIES

These are best practices for ALL young children, with attention to meeting learning outcomes within daily routines and activities of family life and early childhood classrooms while promoting positive adult–child relationships and peer interactions.

Children at the Growing level start to realize on their own when they are getting tired and may begin to initiate sleep without adult support. As children develop, they continue to learn adaptive behavior skills, start to help get themselves ready for rest (picking out their pajamas, getting into and out of bed, pulling up their pants, helping wash and dry their hands), and may become aware of their need to use the toilet. Naps will become less frequent during this time and will last longer. Quiet activities continue to be encouraged before rest times to help young children calm their bodies. These include reading books, listening to music, rocking, counting, and other ways of reviewing literacy, math, social-emotional, adaptive, and social-communication skills during quiet times.

Interactions

Concurrent with their developing more sophisticated adaptive, social, and motor skills, young children also may start experiencing a variety of sleeping difficulties associated with separation anxiety, growing needs for independence, and an increase in cognitive abilities. For example, night terrors may occur as children's imagination develops and their fears cause vivid dreams. Following are some suggested interactions for the Growing level:

▲ Maintain a consistent bedtime routine and daily sleep schedule, to help children feel comfortable and safe.

▲ Communicate and enforce rest and sleep time limits so children know both what to expect and what is expected of them and so sleeping routines remain consistent and predictable for children and adults alike.

▲ Balance adults' responses to children's needs for soothing and calming with limit setting.

▲ Follow toddlers' leads in adjusting the frequency and duration of naps and the timing of bedtime at night as children grow and develop.

Environment and Materials

Following are some suggestions for environment and materials at the Growing level:

▲ Maintain consistency over time with rest environments to help young children feel secure and safe.

▲ Keep rest environments quiet and free of items that may distract from sleep (noisy and active toys, televisions and other screens, disruptive noises and lights).

▲ Encourage children who experience regular night terrors to fall asleep with a security object (blanket, stuffed animal).

▲ Use night terrors as a time to help children identify their feelings and emotions and to promote child–adult bonding through physical contact and quiet singing.

▲ Allow children who need comfort during naptime at child care to have a favorite stuffed animal or blanket from home.

■ FOCUSED STRATEGIES

These strategies are for teaching SOME children who are struggling with a component of a skill or whose development is stalled and who need extra help to catch up or keep up. The strategies include a variety of minor adaptations or modifications to daily routines, activities, and environments to meet targeted outcomes at home and in classrooms.

▲ Alert children about transitions from active activities to quiet, calming activities, and allow sufficient time.

▲ Make sure children rest in acceptable environments with calming sounds or quiet surroundings.

▲ Read soothing books, sing calming songs, and rock or pat children who need help calming down and falling asleep.

▲ Use prompts to guide children through rest and sleep routines:

　△ Provide a visual schedule with pictures of the naptime or bedtime routine.

　△ Give step-by-step verbal reminders and instructions that include pointing gestures for the various parts of the routine (getting undressed, brushing teeth).

　△ Use a first-then board (first book, then rest).

▲ Select one part of the bedtime routine (such as getting undressed) that the child can do with relatively little help, and let the child do that part. Provide more physical assistance with other parts of the routine.

▲ Use a more desirable part of the routine to encourage less desirable steps (make sure the child is ready for sleep by having them lie down before rubbing their back, singing, or reading, then let the child choose a favorite book or song).

▲ Learn to recognize children's cues and preferences.

▲ Teach children who cannot speak to use simple signs (MORE, ALL DONE) so they can communicate their preferences.

▲ Pair sign language with spoken words for students who are nonverbal or who have impaired hearing.

▲ Start the routine earlier to preserve a consistent sleep or nap start time for children who become easily distracted or take longer to settle into nap and bedtime.

■ SPECIALIZED STRATEGIES

These strategies for teaching the FEW children who need intensive supports include a variety of specialized, individualized, precise evidence-based strategies to meet children's unique goals/outcomes:

▲ Accommodate specific physical or medical needs:

△ Provide adapted sleep equipment as necessary.

△ Make sure all adaptations have been written up and approved by a physician or physical therapist.

△ Reposition a child who has motor needs frequently to lower the risk of bed sores and skin breakdown.

▲ For children who have difficulty calming down for sleep,

△ Use positive reinforcement by letting the child choose a soft toy from a basket once they are lying appropriately on a cot.

△ Fade calming that relies on an adult's physical presence:

▷ Put the child in the crib or on the cot and walk away.

▷ Wait a specified amount of time. If the child has not calmed down to go to sleep by that point, only then go back to help.

▷ Gradually increase the amount of wait time before going back.

▷ Move from physical calming (rubbing, patting) to verbal calming (singing, soothing voice). Then fade verbal calming from using your voice next to the crib to using it at the bedroom door.

AEPS-3 Curriculum Resources (Appendix A)

Appendix A in this volume contains numerous additional resources to supplement the AEPS-3 Curriculum. The first part of the appendix presents a list of general curriculum resources, and the second part provides lists of supplementary resources for each individual routine and activity.

AEPS-3 Skills Matrix (Appendix B)

The AEPS-3 Skills Matrix in Appendix B of this volume spotlights individual skills by showing functional application across all routines and activities. Each skills matrix (there are eight total, one for each of the test's eight developmental areas) allows you to select individual AEPS-3 items for children who require an intensive focus on a few skills across routines and activities. For children who have difficulty learning new skills at the level of individual AEPS-3 items, the Foundation Steps (FS) provide an even more granular breakdown of component subskills that are either a sequence of developmental precursors or steps in task analyses.

20

Science

Science activities may vary vastly in the means used to help children explore their bodies and environments—materials, media, locations, participants, and use of children's own creativity and imagination. As children become increasingly aware of the environment around them, they start to ask questions and investigate possible solutions to problems. As they engage with and manipulate materials and phenomena found in their everyday settings and routines (pots and pans, eating utensils, foods, weather conditions, animals, plants), they "design" investigations and experiments to generate solutions. The AEPS-3 Growing level of Science uses skills from eight developmental areas.

Concurrent Skills

The following concurrent skills are AEPS-3 skills that can be easily embedded and taught during regular occurrences of Science.

FINE MOTOR Growing Skills

B 1	Activates object with finger
B 2	Rotates wrist to manipulate object
B 3	Manipulates object with two hands, each performing different action
B 3.1	Assembles toy
B 3.2	Aligns objects
B 3.3	Fits variety of shapes into corresponding spaces
C 1.1	Writes or draws using mixed strokes
C 1.2	Writes or draws using curved lines
C 1.3	Writes or draws using straight lines
C 1.4	Scribbles

Embedded Learning Opportunities

- *Rotates pinecone to look at ridges*
- *Holds bucket in one hand while pouring sand into bucket with other hand*
- *Lines up seashells*
- *"Writes" about different bugs seen outdoors*

SOCIAL-COMMUNICATION Growing Skills

B 2	Locates common objects, people, or events
B 3	Follows multistep directions without contextual cues
B 3.1	Follows multistep directions with contextual cues
B 3.2	Follows one-step direction without contextual cues
B 3.3	Follows one-step direction with contextual cues
B 4.1	Answers *who, what,* and *where* questions
C 1	Produces multiple-word sentences to communicate
C 1.1	Uses two-word utterances
C 1.2	Uses 50 single words, signs, or symbols
C 2	Uses plural pronouns to indicate subjects, objects, and possession in multiple-word sentences
C 2.1	Uses irregular plural nouns in multiple-word sentences
C 2.2	Uses regular plural nouns
C 3	Uses helping verbs
C 3.2	Uses regular past tense of common verbs
C 3.3	Uses *to be* verbs
C 4	Asks questions using inverted auxiliary
C 4.1	Asks *wh-* questions
D 1	Uses language to initiate and sustain social interaction
D 1.1	Follows social conventions of language
D 2	Provides and seeks information while conversing using words, phrases, or sentences
D 2.2	Describes objects, people, and events as part of social exchange
D 3.4	Alternates between speaker and listener roles during conversations with others
D 3.5	Responds to contingent questions from others

Embedded Learning Opportunities

- *Follows verbal directions to help water plants (gets cup, puts water in cup, then waters plant)*
- *Asks "Where do the snow and rain come from?"*
- *Asks "How did the sunflower get so tall?"*
- *Says "The caterpillar turned into a butterfly!"*
- *Asks "When do fish sleep?"*
- *Asks "Why did the pet hermit crab die?"*
- *Answers adult's questions about their scientific knowledge (says "The pet hermit crab died because it was too cold in the room")*

COGNITIVE Growing Skills

B 1   Imitates novel coordinated motor actions

B 2   Imitates novel words

B 3.1   Relates recent events without contextual cues

B 3.2   Relates recent events with contextual cues

B 3.3   Relates events immediately after they occur

C 1.1   Locates object in second of two hiding places

C 2   Recognizes symbols

C 2.1   Uses object to represent another object

C 3.1   Classifies according to function

C 3.2   Classifies according to physical attribute

C 3.3   Discriminates between objects or people using common attributes

C 4   Uses early conceptual comparisons

C 4.1   Identifies common concepts

C 4.2   Identifies concrete concepts

D 1.1   Uses part of an object or support to obtain another object

D 3.1   Evaluates common solutions to solve problems or reach goals

D 4.1   Draws conclusions about causes of events based on personal experience

E 1   Expands simple observations and explorations into further inquiry

E 1.1   Uses simple tools to gather information

E 2   Anticipates outcome of investigation

E 2.1   Generates specific questions for investigation

E 2.2   Demonstrates knowledge about natural happenings

E 3   Investigates to test hypotheses

E 3.1   Draws on prior knowledge to guide investigations

E 3.2   Manipulates materials to cause change

Embedded Learning Opportunities

- *Imitates new science words (hypothesis, investigation, observation, experiment)*

- *Shares information about animal they saw at zoo*

- *Sorts out rocks, shells, bugs*

- *Guesses what color water will become when mixing food colors, then watches water change colors when coloring is added*

- *Tells adult what happened during investigation and why (why water changed colors)*

- *Manipulates water with ice cubes to change temperature*

LITERACY Growing Skills

A 1   Participates in shared group reading

A 2   Demonstrates understanding that text is read in one direction and from top to bottom of page

A 2.1   Turns pages of book from beginning toward end

A 2.2   Holds book or other printed material with pictures correctly oriented

D 1   Demonstrates understanding that pictures represent text

D 1.1   Labels familiar people, actions, objects, and events in picture books

D 1.2   Locates familiar objects, people, events, and actions in picture books

D 2   Retells simple story

D 2.1   Makes predictions about what will happen next in story

D 2.2   Answers and asks questions related to story

D 2.3   Tells story associated with series of pictures

D 3.2   Demonstrates understanding of title, author, and illustrator

D 3.3   Demonstrates understanding of vocabulary associated with early literacy concepts

E 1.1   Dictates description of drawing

E 1.2   Verbally labels representational drawings

E 1.3   Verbally labels nonrepresentational drawings

E 2.1   Makes representational drawings

Embedded Learning Opportunities

■ *Reads or follows along with books about science activity or topics*

■ *Predicts what will happen to tree leaves in story when it rains or snows*

■ *Retells sequence of story about life cycle of tree*

■ *Draws picture and says "It's a bug!" (plant, something related to weather)*

■ *Lists order of events in book (seed cycle, butterfly life cycle)*

MATH Growing Skills

A 1   Counts out 3 items

A 1.1   Counts 3 items to determine "How many?"

B 1   Compares items in sets to 5 by counting

B 1.1   Compares items in sets to 5 by matching

B 1.2   Creates equivalent sets of 5 items

B 1.3   Uses quantity comparison words

Embedded Learning Opportunities

■ *Counts seeds before planting them in pot*

■ *Says "There's leaves on this tree and none on the other!"*

■ *Counts out 5 sets of 3 seeds each to put in 5 pots*

TIER 1

■ UNIVERSAL STRATEGIES

These are best practices for ALL young children, with attention to meeting learning outcomes within daily routines and activities of family life and early childhood classrooms while promoting positive adult–child relationships and peer interactions.

Children advance from using their five senses to play in and explore their environment to observing and experimenting with materials found in their environment. Children begin to learn common concepts such as *heavy* and *light*, *fast* and *slow*, and *soft* and *hard*, and more advanced fine motor control allows children to explore and manipulate items in their environment. Young children at the Growing level are interested and engaged in observing others, investigating and experimenting with a variety of materials, and communicating their results. Through rapidly expanding communication skills, children are able to share their interests and preferences, follow directions, and ask questions. Science activities can be embedded in any routine throughout a child's day, such as playground time, circle time, mealtime, and art.

Interactions

When science activities are embedded in play, young children learn about characteristics of materials and cause–effect relationship. Adults can help children build a foundational base for science concepts by guiding them through inquiry. Following are some suggested interactions for the Growing level of Science:

▲ Provide children with a variety of opportunities and materials they can observe, describe, ask questions about, and make predictions about.

▲ Use parallel talk to describe what the child is seeing, hearing, feeling, smelling, or tasting.

▲ Ask open-ended questions associated with the scientific inquiry process to promote higher level thinking ("What do you think will happen when these two colors are mixed together?").

Environment and Materials

Following are some suggestions for environment and materials at the Growing level:

▲ Create a dedicated science area or offer a science activity each day to show children that science is an important element of the classroom.

▲ Provide materials that are already in children's environments for science activities:

△ Natural items such as bugs, grass, leaves, water, and ice

△ Human-made objects such as magnifying glasses, sensory tubes, or magnets

▲ Place materials that promote scientific inquiry in the dramatic play area (flowers and empty pots of dirt to create a flower shop).

▲ Include books on topics that promote scientific thinking (weather, life cycles).

▲ Provide a variety of materials for the sensory table to give children opportunities to get acquainted with items they may not yet have had a chance to explore (dirt, sand, flowers, grass, pinecones, rocks, pumpkins).

TIER 2

■ FOCUSED STRATEGIES

These strategies are for teaching SOME children who are struggling with a component of a skill or whose development is stalled and who need extra help to catch up or keep up. The strategies include a variety of minor adaptations or modifications to daily routines, activities, and environments to meet targeted outcomes at home and in classrooms.

▲ Embed science activities or science-like thinking into multiple routines, to provide numerous opportunities for engagement.

▲ Repeat activities to give children many opportunities with a particular activity or game.

▲ Pay attention to children's preferences when selecting materials and other manipulatives (if children love to talk about snow, incorporate a winter theme or make "snow" as an activity).

▲ Teach children who cannot speak to use simple signs (MORE, ALL DONE) so they can communicate their preferences.

▲ Learn to recognize children's cues and preferences.

▲ Pair sign language with spoken words for children who are nonverbal or who have hearing impairments.

▲ Limit the number of science concepts children learn at one time (make sure children know the differences among a variety of textures before having them group textures accordingly).

▲ Create individual workspaces using box lids or trays to define workspaces and reduce the need to share materials.

▲ Let children direct the pace of the activity:

△ Pay attention to the child's cues and allow them time to absorb and process information.

△ Look for signs that the child is ready to move to the next step.

▲ Provide visuals that show the steps of how to conduct an experiment.

■ SPECIALIZED STRATEGIES

These strategies for teaching the FEW children who need intensive supports include a variety of specialized, individualized, precise evidence-based strategies to meet children's unique goals/outcomes:

▲ Identify children's priority skills and focus their learning goals on one or two specific skills (discriminations).

▲ Use sticky mats to keep items from moving around.

▲ Seat children who have specific positioning and mobility needs with a secure base, hips and knees flexed at a 90-degree angle, and chest secured so they can manipulate items more easily while working on table activities.

▲ Give children who have vision impairments a lighted magnifying glass, or let them use a light table to examine objects.

▲ Modify manipulatives and other items as needed for easier grasping, manipulating, and viewing:

△ Provide smaller or larger manipulatives for a child who has fine motor challenges, so they can grasp the pieces more easily.

▲ Provide an area and materials where children who have sensory delays or who are easily overstimulated can learn without distractions.

AEPS-3 Curriculum Resources (Appendix A)

Appendix A in this volume contains numerous additional resources to supplement the AEPS-3 Curriculum. The first part of the appendix presents a list of general curriculum resources, and the second part provides lists of supplementary resources for each individual routine and activity.

AEPS-3 Skills Matrix (Appendix B)

The AEPS-3 Skills Matrix in Appendix B of this volume spotlights individual skills by showing functional application across all routines and activities. Each skills matrix (there are eight total, one for each of the test's eight developmental areas) allows you to select individual AEPS-3 items for children who require an intensive focus on a few skills across routines and activities. For children who have difficulty learning new skills at the level of individual AEPS-3 items, the Foundation Steps (*FS*) provide an even more granular breakdown of component subskills that are either a sequence of developmental precursors or steps in task analyses.

21

Sensory

The Sensory activity offers opportunities for children to learn and explore a variety of materials through play, investigation, exploration, and sensory processes to develop touch, smell, taste, sight, and hearing skills. Sensory play encourages children to manipulate materials, lift, throw, roll, rotate, and pour, and it can take place in a variety of settings (sensory table, snack table, sandbox).

This routine evolves over time as children's cognitive, communication, social-emotional, and motor skills increase and as children shift from exploring common items (toys, blankets and fabrics, food containers, food) to more advanced materials (playdough, sand and dirt, chewable food items, dried beans). The AEPS-3 Growing level of Sensory uses skills from eight developmental areas.

Concurrent Skills

The following concurrent skills are AEPS-3 skills that can be easily embedded and taught during regular occurrences of Sensory.

FINE MOTOR Growing Skills

B 1   Activates object with finger

B 2   Rotates wrist to manipulate object

B 3   Manipulates object with two hands, each performing different action

Embedded Learning Opportunities

- *Rotates magnifier to look at bugs or flowers outdoors*
- *Holds sand bucket with one hand and scoops sand with other hand*

GROSS MOTOR Growing Skills

B 4   Alternates feet going up and down stairs

B 4.1   Walks up and down stairs using support

B 4.2   Moves up and down stairs

B 4.3   Gets up and down from low structure

C 1.2   Bounces ball with two hands

C 1.3   Catches ball

C 1.4   Kicks ball

C 1.5   Throws ball overhand at target with one hand

C 1.6   Throws or rolls ball at target with two hands

Embedded Learning Opportunities

- *Walks up and down steps to get to playground to play in sandbox*
- *Hears ball being kicked or bounced*
- *Bounces, catches, and kicks different textured balls*

ADAPTIVE Growing Skills

A 2   Eats foods from variety of food groups with variety of textures

A 2.1   Eats hard and chewy foods

A 3   Eats with eating utensils

A 3.1   Brings food to mouth with eating utensil

A 4   Drinks from open-mouth container

A 5.1   Puts appropriate amount of food in mouth, chews, and swallows before taking another bite

A 5.2   Takes in appropriate amount of liquid and returns cup to surface

A 6.1   Pours liquid into variety of containers

A 6.2   Serves food with utensil

B 2.1   Washes and dries face

B 2.2   Washes and dries hands

B 3.1   Completes some steps to brush teeth, comb hair, and wipe nose

C 1.2   Takes off pullover clothing over head

C 1.3   Takes off front-opening coat, jacket, or shirt

C 1.4   Takes off pants

C 2.2   Puts on front-opening clothing

C 2.3   Puts on pullover clothing

C 2.4   Puts on pull-up clothing

C 2.5   Puts on socks

C 2.6   Puts on shoes

D 1   Takes independent action to alleviate distress, discomfort, and pain

D 1.1   Communicates internal distress, discomfort, or pain to adult

D 3.1   Responds appropriately to warnings of dangerous conditions or substances

Embedded Learning Opportunities

■ *Feeds self foods with variety of textures (yogurt, cereal, fruit)*

■ *Pours water, sand, or other sensory material from cup to bowl while at water table*

■ *Reports to adult if material from sensory table is spilled or if child has paint on hands*

■ *Tolerates materials associated with personal routines (toothbrush bristles, toothpaste, water, towel)*

■ *Puts on clothes made from variety of textures (cotton, wool, flannel)*

■ *Tells adult about dislike for how texture feels on skin (clothes) or in mouth (crunchy food)*

■ *Says if bathwater is too cold or food too hot*

SOCIAL-EMOTIONAL Growing Skills

B 1.1   Identifies/labels emotions in others

B 1.2   Identifies/labels own emotions

B 2   Uses appropriate strategies to manage emotional states

B 2.1   Responds appropriately to soothing by peer

B 3.1   Explains or shows others how to do tasks mastered

B 3.2   Shares accomplishment with familiar caregiver

C 1   Maintains interaction with peer

C 1.1   Initiates social behavior toward peer

D 1   Interacts appropriately with others during small-group activities

D 1.1   Interacts appropriately with materials during small-group activities

D 1.2   Responds appropriately to directions during small-group activities

D 1.3   Remains with group during small-group activities

E 1   Meets observable physical needs in socially appropriate ways

E 2.1   Meets behavioral expectations in familiar environments

E 2.2   Adjusts behavior based on feedback from others or environment

E 3.2   Follows established social rules in familiar environments

Embedded Learning Opportunities

■ *Returns peer's favorite toy after taking it and hearing peer start to cry*

■ *Laughs when peer shows how to use musical instruments*

■ *Keeps sand in sandbox and water in water table*

■ *Washes hands to get bubbles or sand off after playing in sand or with bubbles in water table*

■ *States whether they like how slime feels*

■ *Selects type of food they like best when given two choices at snack*

SOCIAL-COMMUNICATION Growing Skills

B 2 Locates common objects, people, or events

B 3 Follows multistep directions without contextual cues

B 3.1 Follows multistep directions with contextual cues

B 3.2 Follows one-step direction without contextual cues

B 3.3 Follows one-step direction with contextual cues

B 4.1 Answers *who*, *what*, and *where* questions

C 1 Produces multiple-word sentences to communicate

C 1.1 Uses two-word utterances

C 1.2 Uses 50 single words, signs, or symbols

C 2 Uses plural pronouns to indicate subjects, objects, and possession in multiple-word sentences

D 2 Provides and seeks information while conversing using words, phrases, or sentences

D 2.2 Describes objects, people, and events as part of social exchange

D 3.4 Alternates between speaker and listener roles during conversations with others

D 3.5 Responds to contingent questions from others

Embedded Learning Opportunities

■ *Follows directions, "Roll your sleeves up, get a smock, and keep the water in the table"*

■ *Says loudly "I'm playing with the playdough!"*

■ *Says "We are getting dirty!" when playing in sensory table with dirt*

■ *Discusses bubbles and water temperature with peer while washing hands*

■ *Says "This slime is sticky!" when playing with slime*

COGNITIVE Growing Skills

B 1 Imitates novel coordinated motor actions

B 2 Imitates novel words

B 3.1 Relates recent events without contextual clues

C 1.1 Locates object in second of two hiding places

C 3.3 Discriminates between objects or people using common attributes

C 4 Uses early conceptual comparisons

C 4.1 Identifies common concepts

C 4.2 Identifies concrete concepts

E 1.1 Uses simple tools to gather information

E 3.2 Manipulates materials to cause change

Embedded Learning Opportunities

■ *Uses playdough cutter to cut slime after adult models it*

■ *Locates shells buried in sand in sensory table*

■ *Distinguishes among different textures (cold or hot, soft or hard, rough or smooth)*

■ *Looks through magnifying glass at objects in science center (pinecone, rock, plant)*

LITERACY Growing Skills

A 1 Participates in shared group reading

A 2 Demonstrates understanding that text is read in one direction and from top to bottom of page

A 2.2 Holds book or other printed material with pictures correctly oriented

D 1.1 Labels familiar people, actions, objects, and events in picture books

D 1.3 Matches pictures to actual objects, people, or actions

Embedded Learning Opportunities

■ *Reads touch-and-feel book*

■ *Listens for sounds in noise-making book (farm animals, construction trucks) and labels pictures in book*

MATH Growing Skills

A 1   Counts out 3 items

A 1.1   Counts 3 items to determine "How many?"

B 1   Compares items in sets to 5 by counting

B 1.1   Compares items in sets to 5 by matching

B 1.2   Creates equivalent sets of 5 items

B 1.3   Uses quantity comparison words

Embedded Learning Opportunities

■ *Counts items in sensory table*

■ *Counts number of times they stomp, clap, and whistle during movement activity*

TIER 1

■ UNIVERSAL STRATEGIES

These are best practices for ALL young children, with attention to meeting learning outcomes within daily routines and activities of family life and early childhood classrooms while promoting positive adult–child relationships and peer interactions.

At the Growing level, children advance from being guided through sensory opportunities to exploring them more independently thanks to their increased cognitive, social-communication, and motor skills. However, children still need adult assistance to access new sensory stimuli and learn new words. More precise fine motor control allows children to explore and manipulate more items and materials within their environments. Children at the Growing level are often interested in engaging with peers and new materials such as foam, slime, and moon sand. Their social-communication skills are expanding quickly, and they are learning by imitating others, following simple commands, sharing their interests and preferences, and asking questions.

Interactions

Embedding sensory materials and activities in other daily routines is an effective way to capture children's interests and engage them in learning. Following are some suggested interactions for the Growing level of this routine:

▲   Increase the intensity of auditory, visual, and tactile cues:

△   Use louder, more distinct sounds (drums, shouts, large bells) in addition to speech and music.

△   Use contoured, brightly colored, large, or quickly moving visual stimuli.

△   Offer items such as sand and soft feathers for increased tactile experiences.

▲   Pair auditory events with visual or tactile cues to help children organize sensory events (signal a transition by turning off the light while also ringing a bell).

▲   Guide children through inquiry by embedding sensory activities in a variety of their daily routines:

△   Incorporate a variety of textured food and smells into mealtimes.

△   Identify children's personal preferences around sensory experiences (preferred food textures, comfort level when eating food with hands, preferred water temperature when washing hands, preferred place to initiate outdoor play or participate in messy play).

Environment and Materials

Following are some suggested strategies for environment and materials at the Growing level:

▲   Make sensory materials accessible for all children by bringing materials to their level:

△   Put sensory materials in small bins or trays on the floor or table so all children can access them easily.

△ Accommodate different sensory preferences by giving children choices of materials.

△ Use transparent sensory tables, if possible, to give children the option of observing from a comfortable distance and looking underneath or through the table if they are not ready to put their hands in the materials.

▲ Select materials that appeal to all the senses.

▲ Consider how materials will look, smell, and sound when used together.

▲ Make sure all sensory materials are developmentally appropriate and safe for mouth exploration.

■ FOCUSED STRATEGIES

These strategies are for teaching SOME children who are struggling with a component of a skill or whose development is stalled and who need extra help to catch up or keep up. The strategies include a variety of minor adaptations or modifications to daily routines, activities, and environments to meet targeted outcomes at home and in classrooms.

▲ Incorporate opportunities to engage with sensory materials into multiple routines (playing outside, dressing, bath time, meals).

▲ Repeat activities with materials to give children many opportunities to try them.

▲ Select materials and other manipulatives made of textures children prefer.

▲ Create defined sensory exploration spaces while also reducing the need to share materials by using box lids or trays to make individual sensory spaces.

▲ Offer modified sensory experiences for children who you know are sensitive to certain stimuli.

▲ Give children choices of sensory activities ("Do you want to play with sand, or with water?"), and respond by labeling the child's choice ("You want to play with sand"). This helps children begin to understand that the two experiences will give different types of sensory input.

■ SPECIALIZED STRATEGIES

These strategies for teaching the FEW children who need intensive supports include a variety of specialized, individualized, precise evidence-based strategies to meet children's unique goals/outcomes:

▲ For children who are easily overwhelmed by external stimuli,

△ Choose materials and activities that remain relatively calm and quiet and that stay within the child's comfort levels.

▲ For children who have sensory integration issues and find certain stimuli overwhelming,

△ Create a separate space where the child can get away from overwhelming stimuli.

▲ For children who are blind or who have other visual impairments,

△ Offer multiple opportunities for tactile or auditory sensory experiences.

△ Use hand-<u>under</u>-hand prompting.

△ Label all sensory experiences verbally.

▲ For children who are deaf or who have other hearing impairments,

△ Offer multiple opportunities for visual or tactile sensory experiences.

△ Use total communication (verbal and signed) to label sensory stimuli.

▲ For children who have fine motor challenges,

△ Use materials that are easy to grasp (items with built-up handles).

△ Choose items sized to suit the child's needs (smaller or larger than usual).

▲ For children who have specific positioning and mobility needs,

△ Make sure seating has a secure base.

 ## AEPS-3 Curriculum Resources (Appendix A)

Appendix A in this volume contains numerous additional resources to supplement the AEPS-3 Curriculum. The first part of the appendix presents a list of general curriculum resources, and the second part provides lists of supplementary resources for each individual routine and activity.

 ## AEPS-3 Skills Matrix (Appendix B)

The AEPS-3 Skills Matrix in Appendix B of this volume spotlights individual skills by showing functional application across all routines and activities. Each skills matrix (there are eight total, one for each of the test's eight developmental areas) allows you to select individual AEPS-3 items for children who require an intensive focus on a few skills across routines and activities. For children who have difficulty learning new skills at the level of individual AEPS-3 items, the Foundation Steps (*FS*) provide an even more granular breakdown of component subskills that are either a sequence of developmental precursors or steps in task analyses.

Technology

At the Growing level of Technology, children are starting to transition from a world of tangible objects to digital ones. Technology provides a means for children to individualize and self-pace their learning. Children become able to use a variety of technologies and devices (computers, tablets, media players, interactive smart boards). Despite the importance of technology, the American Academy of Pediatrics (AAP; 2016) recommends no more than 1 hour of screen time a day for children older than the age of 2 years.

This routine can occur multiple times a day and in multiple locations (school, home, park) as long as AAP recommendations are followed. The AEPS-3 Growing level of Technology uses skills from seven developmental areas.

Concurrent Skills

The following concurrent skills are AEPS-3 skills that can be easily embedded and taught during regular occurrences of Technology.

FINE MOTOR Growing Skills

B 1 Activates object with finger

C 1.1 Writes or draws using mixed strokes

C 1.2 Writes or draws using curved lines

C 1.3 Writes or draws using straight lines

C 1.4 Scribbles

D 1 Uses finger to interact with electronic device

D 1.1 Uses finger to interact with simple electronic game

Embedded Learning Opportunities

- *Activates game or activities on tablet using one finger*
- *Writes or draws on tablet using curved and straight lines*

GROSS MOTOR Growing Skills

B 3.1 Walks without support

B 5.1 Runs

B 5.2 Walks fast

B 6 Jumps forward

B 6.1 Jumps up and down in place

Embedded Learning Opportunities

- *Follows along to movement or dance being shown on interactive smart board*

SOCIAL-EMOTIONAL Growing Skills

A 3   Participates in familiar social routines with caregivers

B 1.1   Identifies/labels emotions in others

B 1.2   Identifies/labels own emotions

B 3   Makes positive statements about self or accomplishments

B 3.1   Explains or shows others how to do tasks mastered

B 3.2   Shares accomplishment with familiar caregiver

C 3.1   Initiates cooperative activity

C 3.2   Joins others in cooperative activity

D 1.1   Interacts appropriately with materials during small-group activities

D 1.2   Responds appropriately to directions during small-group activities

D 1.3   Remains with group during small-group activities

D 2.1   Interacts appropriately with materials during large-group activities

D 2.2   Responds appropriately to directions during large-group activities

D 3   Initiates and completes independent activities

D 3.1   Responds to request to finish activity

D 3.2   Responds to request to begin activity

D 4   Resolves conflicts using negotiation

D 4.1   Uses strategies to resolve conflicts

E 2.1   Meets behavioral expectations in familiar environments

E 2.2   Adjusts behavior based on feedback from others or environment

E 3.1   Seeks adult permission when appropriate

E 3.2   Follows established social rules in familiar environments

Embedded Learning Opportunities

■ *Pushes button to advance page while parent reads book on tablet to child*

■ *Matches faces to emotions on tablet app illustrating emotions*

■ *Shows adult finished activity on tablet*

■ *Asks peer to look at book on tablet together*

■ *Shows peer how tablet works or how to complete activity on it*

■ *Figures out how peer and self can have a turn using tablet ("After you are done, it will be my turn")*

■ *Remains with large or small group and interacts appropriately while using interactive smart board*

■ *Asks adult's permission to use technology and stops after adult says "Time is up"*

■ *Says whether they like specific activities or music on device*

SOCIAL-COMMUNICATION Growing Skills

B 2   Locates common objects, people, or events

B 3   Follows multistep directions without contextual cues

B 3.1   Follows multistep directions with contextual cues

B 3.2   Follows one-step direction without contextual cues

B 3.3   Follows one-step direction with contextual cues

B 4.1   Answers *who*, *what*, and *where* questions

C 1.1   Uses two-word utterances

C 1.2   Uses 50 single words, signs, or symbols

C 2   Uses plural pronouns to indicate subjects, objects, and possession in multiple-word sentences

C 2.1   Uses irregular plural nouns in multiple-word sentences

C 2.2   Uses regular plural nouns

C 3   Uses helping verbs

C 3.2   Uses regular past tense of common verbs

C 3.3   Uses *to be* verbs

C 4   Asks questions using inverted auxiliary

C 4.1   Asks *wh-* questions

D 1   Uses language to initiate and sustain social interaction

D 1.1   Follows social conventions of language

D 2   Provides and seeks information while conversing using words, phrases, or sentences

D 2.1   Asks questions to obtain information

D 2.2   Describes objects, people, and events as part of social exchange

Embedded Learning Opportunities

- *Responds to questions generated by audiobook (audiobook asks "Where is the cat?"; child touches picture of cat)*

- *Turns off tablet and puts it away when asked to do so*

- *Uses two words to ask for help or say they are ready to start or finish with technology*

- *Asks questions to get information on how to work a device (tablet, music player)*

COGNITIVE Growing Skills

B 1   Imitates novel coordinated motor actions

B 2   Imitates novel words

B 3.3   Relates events immediately after they occur

C 1.1   Locates object in second of two hiding places

C 2.1   Uses object to represent another object

C 3.1   Classifies according to function

C 3.2   Classifies according to physical attribute

C 3.3   Discriminates between objects or people using common attributes

C 4   Uses early conceptual comparisons

Embedded Learning Opportunities

- *Imitates motor actions from interactive smart board during dance or movement activity*

- *Imitates words from story on tablet (tablet shows picture of cat while audio says "cat"; child repeats word)*

- *Classifies animals, vehicles, or foods on tablet game*

LITERACY Growing Skills

A 1   Participates in shared group reading

A 2   Demonstrates understanding that text is read in one direction and from top to bottom of page

A 2.1 Turns pages of book from beginning toward end

A 2.2 Holds book or other printed material with pictures correctly oriented

A 3.1 Recognizes own first name in print

D 1   Demonstrates understanding that pictures represent text

D 1.1 Labels familiar people, actions, objects, and events in picture books

D 1.3 Matches pictures to actual objects, people, or actions

D 2   Retells simple story

D 2.1 Makes predictions about what will happen next in story

D 2.2 Answers and asks questions related to story

D 2.3 Tells story associated with series of pictures

D 3.1 Demonstrates understanding of key vocabulary in picture books

D 3.2 Demonstrates understanding of title, author, and illustrator

D 3.3 Demonstrates understanding of vocabulary associated with early literacy concepts

E 2.1 Makes representational drawings

Embedded Learning Opportunities

- *Listens to audiobook on device either individually or in group*
- *Identifies name while playing letter game on tablet*
- *Matches pictures of common objects on matching game app*
- *Puts story in correct sequence on tablet to retell it*
- *Answers questions before, during, and after listening to audiobook on a device*

MATH Growing Skills

A 1   Counts out 3 items

A 1.1 Counts 3 items to determine "How many?"

B 1   Compares items in sets to 5 by counting

B 1.1 Compares items in sets to 5 by matching

B 1.2 Creates equivalent sets of 5 items

Embedded Learning Opportunities

- *Counts items in e-book on tablet*
- *Counts objects, compares sets of items, or creates equivalent sets using math app on tablet*

TIER 1

■ UNIVERSAL STRATEGIES

These are best practices for ALL young children, with attention to meeting learning outcomes within daily routines and activities of family life and early childhood classrooms while promoting positive adult–child relationships and peer interactions.

Socially, toddlers' and young preschoolers' developing language skills at the Growing level allow them to communicate effectively and functionally with others using conversational rules (looking away from a device when someone is speaking to them). Children are also beginning to learn how to express their likes and dislikes, provide and seek information, and ask for help. By the toddler years, children are becoming more independent and willing to learn new tasks, especially as technology advances. Follow AAP guidelines for using technology with young children (limit children to no more than 1 hour of screen time a day).

At the Growing level, interacting with technological devices can help young children develop various skills:

- ▲ Cognitive skills:
  - △ Classifying objects
  - △ Imitating novel motor actions and words
  - △ Recognizing symbols
- ▲ Fine motor skills:
  - △ Differentiating between straight and curved lines
  - △ Starting to use mixed strokes
  - △ Holding a tablet while using a finger to manipulate the screen
- ▲ Advanced math and literacy skills:
  - △ Playing number and letter recognition games
  - △ Playing matching and sorting games

Interactions

Positive interactions with adults are crucial for all children, including toddlers and early preschoolers. As children become more interested in technology, it is important for adults to set appropriate limits and provide role modeling. Following are some suggested interactions for the Growing level of this routine:

- ▲ Engage with children while they use technology.
- ▲ Set clear, precise rules around technology use, and enforce them:
  - △ Limit children at school to using a music player only during circle time or at the listening center.
  - △ Limit children at school to using a tablet for 10 minutes a day.
  - △ Limit shared storytime on a tablet or other device at home to 15 minutes a day.
- ▲ Remain patient, and answer questions with a calm voice and a smile.
- ▲ Implement a system to ensure that all children receive the appropriate amount of time with devices.
- ▲ Role model how to use technological devices appropriately (limit your own time using technology around children).

Environment and Materials

Materials needed for technology can include, but are not limited to, computers, tablets (iPad, Kindle, Leapfrog), interactive smart boards, CD or other music players, digital cameras, and cell phones. Teaching children to use these materials appropriately requires a lot of assistance from adults. For young children, the AAP (2016) recommends the following:

- ▲ Use nonviolent apps and those that are not fast paced.
- ▲ Keep bedrooms, mealtimes, and parent–child playtime screen-free.
- ▲ Allow no screen time within 1 hour of children's bedtime.

Following are some suggestions for environment and materials at the Growing level:

- ▲ Make sure all materials are safe and age-appropriate for toddlers.
- ▲ Make sure computers and tablets are free of wires and cords children could access.
- ▲ Set up the environment so all children can participate and interact with devices.

▲ Set up computers on child-size tables with child-size chairs.

▲ Set up computers as a center activity with a 10-minute time limit per child.

▲ Provide a cover or stop sign to prevent children from accessing materials at inappropriate times.

▲ Allow children to use tablets during free choice, table activities, or related services (speech or occupational therapy).

▲ Let children use music players during circle time, music and movement, and at the listening center.

▲ Allow children to use digital cameras to take pictures of peers in the classroom or during dramatic play.

▲ Use interactive smart boards during large group, small group, or circle time for reading books and doing music or movement activities.

▲ Make sure children use cell phones only at home with adult supervision or only for pretend during dramatic play.

◼ FOCUSED STRATEGIES

These strategies are for teaching SOME children who are struggling with a component of a skill or whose development is stalled and who need extra help to catch up or keep up. The strategies include a variety of minor adaptations or modifications to daily routines, activities, and environments to meet targeted outcomes at home and in classrooms.

▲ Provide multiple opportunities for toddlers and growing preschoolers to learn how to manipulate parts of a computer or tablet (mouse, keyboard, buttons).

▲ Limit the types of apps children can open during specific times to work on individualized skills (for children who need to increase their math skills, provide access only to apps that advance math skills).

▲ Use peer or adult models to teach children specific skills for how to use technology appropriately.

▲ Provide visual aids (sand timer, clock, sign-up sheet) to limit time on the computer if children struggle with time limits.

▲ Provide an if-then chart to limit time for children who spend a lot of time doing technology activities (if a child writes their name and paints a picture, then they can spend 5 minutes on the computer or tablet).

▲ Teach children who cannot speak to use simple signs (MORE, ALL DONE) so they can communicate their preferences.

▲ Learn to recognize children's cues and preferences.

▲ Pair sign language with spoken words for children who are nonverbal or who have hearing impairments.

◼ SPECIALIZED STRATEGIES

These strategies for teaching the FEW children who need intensive supports include a variety of specialized, individualized, precise evidence-based strategies to meet children's unique goals/outcomes:

▲ Provide adaptive equipment for children with specific disabilities:

△ Children who have visual impairments can use screen readers and screen enlargement applications to help them view the screen more easily. Enlarged words and pictures provide additional support.

△ Children who have hearing impairments can use hearing aids or adaptive headphones.

△ Children who have motor delays can use adaptive switches, keyboards, book holders, or automatic page turners.

△ Children who are unable to speak their preferences while playing can benefit from learning sign language or using an application to help them communicate (Proloquo2Go).

△ Children who cannot sit up straight on the floor or in a child-size chair may need adaptive seating (wheelchair, seat with tray, BackJack chair, pillows for back support) or a space with adequate room to lie on their stomach.

▲ Use specific, consistent instructions along with visual, verbal, and physical prompts (hand-over-hand prompting) to teach children specific skills.

▲ Use system of least prompts to teach children how to interact with technology—for example, when teaching a child to use a matching game on a tablet,

△ Give the child an opportunity to match pictures independently.

△ If the child cannot match the items independently, give an indirect verbal prompt ("Which other animal makes this sound: *Meow*?"). Wait for the child to respond.

△ If the child still doesn't match the items, provide physical prompts.

△ Acknowledge the correct response regardless of the prompt used.

AEPS-3 Curriculum Resources (Appendix A)

Appendix A in this volume contains numerous additional resources to supplement the AEPS-3 Curriculum. The first part of the appendix presents a list of general curriculum resources, and the second part provides lists of supplementary resources for each individual routine and activity.

AEPS-3 Skills Matrix (Appendix B)

The AEPS-3 Skills Matrix in Appendix B of this volume spotlights individual skills by showing functional application across all routines and activities. Each skills matrix (there are eight total, one for each of the test's eight developmental areas) allows you to select individual AEPS-3 items for children who require an intensive focus on a few skills across routines and activities. For children who have difficulty learning new skills at the level of individual AEPS-3 items, the Foundation Steps (*FS*) provide an even more granular breakdown of component subskills that are either a sequence of developmental precursors or steps in task analyses.

Writing

The Writing routine changes over time as children develop more refined skills related to the activity. The elements of writing vary and include materials, media, location (indoors and outdoors), participants, and use of children's creativity and imagination to create projects. Writing activities at the Growing level can take place in the classroom, at home, or at child care; in large or small groups; and individually. Writing implements are not limited to pencils but can also include crayons, chalk, markers, paintbrushes, and finger paints; and materials may include butcher paper, envelopes, and receipt books in addition to regular paper. Young children start writing by first making marks on a surface; then scribbling; then making horizontal, vertical, and diagonal lines; and finally transitioning to forming letters, numbers, and words. Children may have many opportunities throughout their day to practice writing skills, depending on the child, the adult, and the setting. The AEPS-3 Growing level of Writing uses skills from eight developmental areas.

Concurrent Skills

The following concurrent skills are AEPS-3 skills that can be easily embedded and taught during regular occurrences of Writing.

FINE MOTOR Growing Skills

B 3 Manipulates object with two hands, each performing different action

C 1.1 Writes or draws using mixed strokes

C 1.2 Writes or draws using curved lines

C 1.3 Writes or draws using straight lines

C 1.4 Scribbles

D 1 Uses finger to interact with electronic device

Embedded Learning Opportunities

- *Holds paper down while writing or drawing*

- *Draws and writes variety of strokes using crayon, colored pencil, marker, or any other writing implement*

- *Uses fingers to tap letters on an alphabet game on tablet*

GROSS MOTOR Growing Skills

B 3 Walks avoiding people, furniture, or objects

B 3.1 Walks without support

B 4 Alternates feet going up and down stairs

B 4.1 Walks up and down stairs using support

B 4.2 Moves up and down stairs

B 4.3 Gets up and down from low structure

Embedded Learning Opportunities

■ *Walks to table to engage in writing activities, avoiding obstacles*

■ *Walks up playset steps to write on chalkboard section of climber*

■ *Gets up from chair after writing own name*

ADAPTIVE Growing Skills

B 2.2 Washes and dries hands

C 1.2 Takes off pullover clothing over head

C 1.3 Takes off front-opening coat, jacket, or shirt

C 2.2 Puts on front-opening clothing

C 2.3 Puts on pullover clothing

Embedded Learning Opportunities

■ *Washes and dries hands after drawing with chalk or markers*

■ *Puts on or takes off appropriate clothing before or after using writing media outdoors*

SOCIAL-EMOTIONAL Growing Skills

A 3.1 Initiates next step of familiar social routine

A 3.2 Follows familiar social routines with familiar adults

B 1 Responds appropriately to others' emotions

B 1.1 Identifies/labels emotions in others

B 1.2 Identifies/labels own emotions

B 2 Uses appropriate strategies to manage emotional states

B 2.1 Responds appropriately to soothing by peer

B 3.1 Explains or shows others how to do tasks mastered

B 3.2 Shares accomplishment with familiar caregiver

C 1 Maintains interaction with peer

C 1.1 Initiates social behavior toward peer

C 1.2 Responds appropriately to peer social behavior

C 3.3 Shares or exchanges objects

D 1 Interacts appropriately with others during small-group activities

D 1.1 Interacts appropriately with materials during small-group activities

D 1.2 Responds appropriately to directions during small-group activities

D 1.3 Remains with group during small-group activities

D 2 Interacts appropriately with others during large-group activities

D 2.1 Interacts appropriately with materials during large-group activities

D 2.2 Responds appropriately to directions during large-group activities

D 2.3 Remains with group during large-group activities

D 3 Initiates and completes independent activities

D 3.1 Responds to request to finish activity

D 3.2 Responds to request to begin activity

D 3.3 Entertains self by playing with toys

D 4 Resolves conflicts using negotiation

D 4.1 Uses strategies to resolve conflicts

D 4.2 Claims and defends possessions

E 3.2 Follows established social rules in familiar environments

Embedded Learning Opportunities

■ *Looks at art table rules and follows directions to wash hands when finished painting*

■ *Draws pictures of faces with different emotions and describes emotions to peer or adult*

■ *Writes card to their parents and pretends to mail it*

■ *Asks peer to help them color poster*

■ *Entertains self while writing or drawing on Magna Doodle*

■ *Holds writing implement correctly and replaces it in proper location when finished*

■ *Completes picture independently and shows adult*

■ *Tells peer "You can have the red marker when I'm finished"*

SOCIAL-COMMUNICATION Growing Skills

B 2 Locates common objects, people, or events

B 3 Follows multistep directions without contextual cues

B 3.1 Follows multistep directions with contextual cues

B 3.2 Follows one-step direction without contextual cues

B 3.3 Follows one-step direction with contextual cues

B 4.1 Answers *who*, *what*, and *where* questions

C 1 Produces multiple-word sentences to communicate

C 1.1 Uses two-word utterances

C 1.2 Uses 50 single words, signs, or symbols

C 2 Uses plural pronouns to indicate subjects, objects, and possession in multiple-word sentences

C 2.1 Uses irregular plural nouns in multiple-word sentences

C 2.2 Uses regular plural nouns

C 3.2 Uses regular past tense of common verbs

C 3.3 Uses *to be* verbs

C 4 Asks questions using inverted auxiliary

C 4.1 Asks *wh-* questions

D 1 Uses language to initiate and sustain social interaction

D 1.1 Follows social conventions of language

D 2 Provides and seeks information while conversing using words, phrases, or sentences

D 2.1 Asks questions to obtain information

D 2.2 Describes objects, people, and events as part of social exchange

D 3.4 Alternates between speaker and listener roles during conversations with others

D 3.5 Responds to contingent questions from others

Embedded Learning Opportunities

■ *Follows adult's directions to take off smock, wash hands, and put piece of paper on drying rack*

■ *Asks what first letter of their name looks like*

■ *Describes what they are drawing to adult*

■ *Tells adult what they have written using correct grammar*

■ *Tells adult what their "writing" says when asked*

COGNITIVE Growing Skills

B 1   Imitates novel coordinated motor actions

B 2   Imitates novel words

B 3.1   Relates recent events without contextual cues

B 3.2   Relates recent events with contextual cues

B 3.3   Relates events immediately after they occur

C 4   Uses early conceptual comparisons

C 4.1   Identifies common concepts

C 4.2   Identifies concrete concepts

D 1.1   Uses part of an object or support to obtain another object

E 3.2   Manipulates materials to cause change

Embedded Learning Opportunities

■ *Copies mark (curved or straight line) after adult models*

■ *Draws event and communicates details about it to adult*

■ *Tells adult they wrote them a letter at school*

■ *Identifies colors of writing implements, shapes written, sizes of shapes*

■ *Uses marker to pull basket of markers closer to get different one*

■ *Puts dried-up marker in water so it will write again*

LITERACY Growing Skills

A 3.1   Recognizes own first name in print

A 3.2   Recognizes common signs and logos

D 1   Demonstrates understanding that pictures represent text

E 1.1   Dictates description of drawing

E 1.2   Verbally labels representational drawings

E 1.3   Verbally labels nonrepresentational drawings

E 2.1   Makes representational drawings

Embedded Learning Opportunities

■ *Finds piece of paper with their name on it, begins to write or draw*

■ *Recognizes stop sign and tries to draw one*

■ *Finishes drawing and tells adult the people in picture are mom, dad, and baby sister*

MATH Growing Skills

A 1   Counts out 3 items

A 1.1   Counts 3 items to determine "How many?"

B 1.3   Uses quantity comparison words

Embedded Learning Opportunities

■ *Counts number of different kinds of art materials laid out*

■ *Says there are more crayons than colored pencils on table*

UNIVERSAL STRATEGIES

These are best practices for ALL young children, with attention to meeting learning outcomes within daily routines and activities of family life and early childhood classrooms while promoting positive adult–child relationships and peer interactions.

At the Growing level, children advance from using a whole-hand grasp on a writing implement to using a three-finger grasp, which gives them more control over writing implements as their fine motor skills develop. Activities such as copying shapes, drawing lines and circles, and scribbling encourage greater control with writing implements such as crayons, pencils, and markers. These activities also help develop perceptual motor skills and hand-eye coordination and foster visual discrimination.

Spontaneous scribbling serves several important purposes. It gives children an opportunity to experience the relationship between the finger movements used to guide writing tools and visual feedback, and it provides children with a means of expression and an opportunity to be creative. Scribbling is also the beginning of writing for children, as lines and circles are the basic elements of numbers and letters. Reproducing simple shapes and line types (straight, curved, slanted) and learning basic concepts such as continuity, enclosure, and intersection are important precursors to writing and drawing representational pictures.

Interactions

Following are some suggested interactions for the Growing level of this routine:

▲ Model copying a shape, circle, or lines with a writing implement to teach young children how to form a variety of figures.

▲ Model and verbally encourage children to scribble on paper.

▲ Use gestures and verbal instruction ("Go around and around," "One line here, another here")

▲ Use hand-over-hand to help guide children as needed when writing or drawing shapes:

△ Gently guide the writing tool through the desired motion, pairing the action with a verbal cue ("Zoom!" "Zip!" "Around and around!").

△ As the child begins to gain more control over their strokes, gradually use less physical assistance to guide their hand in copying shapes.

Environment and Materials

Following are some suggestions for environment and materials at the Growing level:

▲ Provide materials that are developmentally appropriate, safe, washable, and nontoxic.

▲ Offer a variety of fine motor activities that provide opportunities to develop the physical skills needed to use writing implements:

△ Stacking blocks

△ Using finger paints

△ Writing in sand with fingers or paintbrushes

△ Playing with playdough

▲ Make sure early preschool classrooms have a writing center with a variety of materials:

△ Materials to write on (paper, envelopes, cards)

△ Writing implements (colored pencils, markers, crayons)

△ Props (alphabet letters, stencils, lined paper)

▲ Make sure children have free access to writing implements:

△ Keep crayons, markers, colored pencils, and other writing media within easy reach.

△ Leave materials out on an easel or at the writing center so children can come and go as they please.

△ Provide Magna Doodles during free play for children to write and draw on. (This is a great time to show the child how to write their name and letters.)

▲ Introduce children to their first name. Children's names take on a special meaning as they begin to realize that they are individuals. Letter awareness develops as children start to recognize letters in their name:

  △ Draw attention to the letters in children's names where they appear in their environment.

  △ Have children watch you write their name during art, and let them practice writing it themselves.

▲ Respond to the intended meaning of children's marks on paper.

▲ Instill a sense of pride by displaying children's work at eye level.

▲ Let children make lines and circles in clay or cookie dough so they can "feel" the configuration.

▲ Have children start by making large, exaggerated versions of the desired shape and gradually diminish the size.

▲ Engage the child's attention in writing activities by making dots on a writing surface using a tapping sound (the auditory component usually captures the child's attention).

▲ Draw dot-to-dot shapes for children to trace.

▲ Give children precut shapes to paste, and let them use a glue stick or glue bottle to trace the shape's outline.

■ FOCUSED STRATEGIES

These strategies are for teaching SOME children who are struggling with a component of a skill or whose development is stalled and who need extra help to catch up or keep up. The strategies include a variety of minor adaptations or modifications to daily routines, activities, and environments to meet targeted outcomes at home and in classrooms.

▲ Create individual sensory spaces using box lids or trays to define exploration space and reduce the need to share materials (meal tray for an activity involving writing in sand).

▲ Use writing implements children can manage easily (chunky crayons, markers).

▲ Create multiple opportunities for children to engage in writing activities:

  △ Have children "sign in" when they arrive in the classroom or enter a center.

  △ Let them write "orders" in a dramatic play restaurant or "receipts" in a dramatic play store.

▲ Follow children's preferences when selecting materials and implements for writing activities (sand or playdough for children who prefer sensory activities).

▲ Teach children who cannot speak to use simple signs (MORE, ALL DONE) so they can communicate their preferences.

▲ Learn to recognize children's cues and preferences.

▲ Pair sign language with spoken words for children who are nonverbal or who have hearing impairments.

■ SPECIALIZED STRATEGIES

These strategies for teaching the FEW children who need intensive supports include a variety of specialized, individualized, precise evidence-based strategies to meet children's unique goals/outcomes:

▲ For children who have visual impairments,

  △ Use hand-under-hand prompting when supporting children as they learn to write.

  △ Use visual contrast when presenting writing implements and paper (black marker on yellow paper).

▲ For children who have sensory impairments,

△ Use objects that provide cues (paper with textured or raised shapes).

▲ For children who have specific mobility needs,

△ Position the child appropriately, with feet flat on the floor and hips and chest stabilized to give better use of the hands.

△ Use adaptations made specifically for supporting children who have physical disabilities (hook-and-loop or elastic hand braces, weighted writing implements, grippers for writing implements).

▲ Identify priority skills that affect writing (tripod grasp), and teach that skill as a prerequisite to writing (clay exercise, clothes pin games, crumbling paper).

▲ For children who become easily overwhelmed by external stimuli,

△ Choose materials and activities that remain relatively calm and quiet and that are within the child's comfort level.

△ Let the child work at a writing table alone if that works best.

▲ Use system of least prompts to teach early writing skills:

△ Ask the child first to write a simple shape independently.

△ Wait a designated number of seconds for the child to write the shape.

△ Model the shape if the child does not write it.

△ Wait a designated number of seconds again.

△ Provide full hand-over-hand assistance if the child still does not write the shape.

△ Offer specific verbal praise when the child writes the shape ("Super, you wrote a circle!").

AEPS-3 Curriculum Resources (Appendix A)

Appendix A in this volume contains numerous additional resources to supplement the AEPS-3 Curriculum. The first part of the appendix presents a list of general curriculum resources, and the second part provides lists of supplementary resources for each individual routine and activity.

AEPS-3 Skills Matrix (Appendix B)

The AEPS-3 Skills Matrix in Appendix B of this volume spotlights individual skills by showing functional application across all routines and activities. Each skills matrix (there are eight total, one for each of the test's eight developmental areas) allows you to select individual AEPS-3 items for children who require an intensive focus on a few skills across routines and activities. For children who have difficulty learning new skills at the level of individual AEPS-3 items, the Foundation Steps (*FS*) provide an even more granular breakdown of component subskills that are either a sequence of developmental precursors or steps in task analyses.

References

American Academy of Pediatrics. (2016). Media and young minds. *Pediatrics, 138*(5), e20162591. https://doi.org/10.1542/peds.2016-2591

Bronfenbrenner, U. (1994). Ecological models of human development. In *International Encyclopedia of Education, Vol. 3* (2nd ed). Elsevier.

Carta, J. J., & Miller Young, R. (Eds). (2019). *Multi-tiered systems of support for young children: Driving change in early education.* Brookes Publishing Co.

Coleman, M. R., Buysse, V., & Neitzel, J. (2006). *Recognition and Response: An early intervening system for young children at-risk for learning disabilities. Executive summary.* University of North Carolina at Chapel Hill, FPG Child Development Institute.

Collins, B. C. (2022). *Systematic instruction for students with moderate and severe disabilities* (2nd ed.). Brookes Publishing Co.

Cook, B., & Odom, S. L. (2013). Evidence-based practices and implementation science in special education. *Exceptional Children, 79*(3), 135–144.

Copple, C., & Bredekamp, S. (2009). *Developmentally appropriate practice in early childhood programs serving children from birth through age 8* (3rd ed.). National Association for the Education of Young Children.

DEC/NAEYC. (2009). *Early childhood inclusion: A joint position statement of the Division for Early Childhood (DEC) and the National Association for the Education of Young Children (NAEYC).* http://www.dec-sped.org/papers

Division for Early Childhood. (2014). *DEC recommended practices in early intervention/early childhood special education 2014.* Retrieved from https://www.dec-sped.org/dec-recommended-practices

Grisham-Brown, J., & Hemmeter, M. L. (2017). *Blended practices for teaching young children in inclusive settings* (2nd ed.). Brookes Publishing Co.

Harms, T., Cryer, D., & Clifford, R. (2006). *Infant/Toddler Environment Rating Scale–Revised Edition (ITERS-R).* Teachers College Press.

Hemmeter, M. L., Snyder, P. A., Fox, L., & Algina, J. (2016). Evaluating the implementation of the Pyramid Model for promoting social emotional competence in early childhood classrooms. *Topics in Early Childhood Special Education, 36*(3), 133–146.

Johnson, J., Rahn, N., & Bricker, D. (2015). *An activity-based approach to early intervention* (4th ed.). Brookes Publishing Co.

Piaget, J. (1955). *The language and thought of the child.* Meridian Books.

Sandall, S. R., Schwartz, I. S., Joseph, G. E., & Gauvreau, A. (2019). *Building blocks for teaching preschoolers with special needs* (3rd ed.). Brookes Publishing Co.

Skinner, B. F. (1953). *Science and human behavior.* Macmillan.

Children's Books Listed

Carle, E. (1969). *The very hungry caterpillar.* Scholastic.

Dean, J. (2012). *Pete the cat and his four groovy buttons.* HarperCollins.

Martin, B. (1967). *Brown bear, brown bear, what do you see?* Henry Holt and Company.

Numeroff, L. (1985). *If you give a mouse a cookie.* HarperCollins.

Tarbett, D. (2015). *Ten wriggly wiggly caterpillars.* Tiger Tales.

Resources for AEPS®-3 Curriculum Routines and Activities

General Resources

Books

Barton, E. E., & Smith, B. J. (2015). *The preschool inclusion toolbox: How to build and lead a high-quality program.* Brookes Publishing Co.

Bower, E., & Finnie, N. R. (2009). *Finnie's handling the young child with cerebral palsy at home.* Butterworth-Heinemann.

Chen, D. (2008). *Early intervention in action.* Brookes Publishing Co.

Crawford, M., & Weber, B. (2013). *Early intervention every day! Embedding activities in daily routines for young children and their families.* Brookes Publishing Co.

Deiner, P. L. (2008). *Infants & toddlers: Development and curriculum planning* (2nd ed.). Cengage Learning.

Derman-Sparks, L., & Edwards, J. O. (2010). *Anti-bias education for young children and ourselves.* National Association for the Education of Young Children.

Ensher, G., & Clark, D. (2016). *The early years: Foundations for best practice with special children and their families.* ZERO TO THREE.

Grisham-Brown, J., & Hemmeter, M. L. (2017). *Blended practices for teaching young children in inclusive settings* (2nd ed.). Brookes Publishing Co.

Horn, E., Palmer, S. B., Butera, G. D., & Lieber, J. (2016). *Six steps to inclusive preschool curriculum: A UDL-based framework for children's school success.* Brookes Publishing Co.

Johnson, J., Rahn, N., & Bricker, D. (2015). *An activity-based approach to early intervention* (4th ed.). Brookes Publishing Co.

McWilliam, R. A., & Casey, A. M. (2008). *Engagement of every child in the preschool classroom.* Brookes Publishing Co.

Noonan, M. J., & McCormick, L. (2013). *Teaching young children with disabilities in natural environments* (2nd ed.). Brookes Publishing Co.

Richardson-Gibbs, A. M., & Klein, M. D. (2014). *Making preschool inclusion work: Strategies for supporting children, teachers, and programs.* Brookes Publishing Co.

Sandall, S., Schwartz, I., Joseph, G., & Gauvreau, A. (2019). *Building blocks for teaching preschoolers with special needs* (3rd ed.). Brookes Publishing Co.

Schwartz, I., Ashmun, J., McBride, B., Scott, C., & Sandall, S. (2017). *The DATA model for teaching preschoolers with autism: Blending approaches to meet individual needs.* Brookes Publishing Co.

Wittmer, D. S., & Petersen, S. (2017). *Infant and toddler development and responsive program planning: A relationship-based approach* (4th ed.). Pearson.

Journals

Teaching Young Children. https://www.naeyc.org/resources/pubs/tyc
Teaching Exceptional Children. https://journals.sagepub.com/home/tcx
Young Children. https://www.naeyc.org/resources/pubs/yc
Young Exceptional Children. https://journals.sagepub.com/home/yec

Web Sites

American Printing House for the Blind. https://www.aph.org

Discovery Education. https://www.discoveryeducation.com

Division for Early Childhood. https://www.dec-sped.org

Early Childhood Technical Assistance Center. https://ectacenter.org

National Association for the Education of Young Children. https://www.naeyc.org

Parents. http://www.parents.com

PBS Kids/PBS Learning Media. https://pbskids.org

Positive Parenting Connection. https://www.positiveparentingconnection.net

Results Matter Video Library. https://www.cde.state.co.us/resultsmatter/rmvideoseries

Starfall Education. https://www.starfall.com/h

The STEM Innovation for Inclusion in Early Education Center (STEMI²E²). https://stemie.fpg.unc.edu

ZERO TO THREE. https://www.zerotothree.org

Resources for Individual Routines and Activities

Active & Outdoor Play

Articles and Readings

Early Childhood Today Editorial Staff. (n.d.). Infants & toddlers/activities: Exploring the great outdoors! *Early Childhood Today.* https://www.scholastic.com/teachers/articles/teaching-content/infants-toddlers-activities-exploring-great-outdoors

Gartrell, D., & Sonsteng, K. (2008). Guidance matters: Promote physical activity—It's proactive guidance. *Young Children, 63*(2). https://drjuliejg.files.wordpress.com/2015/02/14-mar-08-yc-gm-phys-activity5.pdf

Honig, A. S. (n.d.). Infants & toddlers: Activities that support outdoor explorations. *Early Childhood Today.* https://www.scholastic.com/teachers/articles/teaching-content/infants-toddlers-activities-support-outdoor-explorations-0

Honig, A. S. (n.d.). Infants and toddlers: Let's go outside! *Early Childhood Today.* https://www.scholastic.com/teachers/articles/teaching-content/infants-toddlers-lets-go-outside

Honig, A. S. (n.d.). Outdoor summer activities for young children. *Early Childhood Today.* https://www.scholastic.com/teachers/articles/teaching-content/outdoor-summer-activities-young-children

Rivkin, M. S. (2001). Problem solving through outdoor play. *Early Childhood Today, 15*(7), 36–43.

Books

Bilton, H. (2010). *Outdoor learning in the early years: Management and innovation* (3rd ed.). Routledge.

Honig, A. S. (2015). *Experiencing nature with young children: Awakening delight, curiosity, and a sense of stewardship.* National Association for the Education of Young Children.

Nelson, E. M. (2012). *Cultivating outdoor classrooms: Designing and implementing child-centered learning environments.* Redleaf Press.

Rivkin, M. S., & Schein, D. (2014). *The great outdoors: Advocating for natural spaces for young children.* National Association for the Education of Young Children.

Sanders, S. (2002). *Active for life: Developmentally appropriate movement programs for young children.* Human Kinetics.

White, J. (2019). *Playing and learning outdoors: The practical guide and sourcebook for excellence in outdoor provision and practice with young children* (3rd ed.). Routledge.

Activities and Ideas to Try

B-Inspired Mama. (n.d.). Outdoor play ideas for kids. *Pinterest.* https://www.pinterest.com/binspiredmama/outdoor-play-ideas-for-kids

Bright Horizons. (n.d.). *17 Fun, low-cost outdoor activities for kids.* https://www.brighthorizons.com/family-resources/fun-outdoor-activities-families

Efe, B. (2015, April 18). 25 Ideas to make outdoor play fun. *Kids Activities Blog.* https://kidsactivitiesblog.com/65939/25-ideas-make-outdoor-play-fun

Cooper, S. (2018, July 3). 44 Preschool outdoor learning ideas. *Teaching 2 and 3 Year Olds.* https://teaching2and3yearolds.com/44-preschool-outdoor-learning-ideas

Gayle's Preschool Rainbow. (n.d.). *Outdoor play.* http://www.preschoolrainbow.org/preschool-outdoor.htm

Learning 4 Kids. (n.d.). *Active play.* https://www.learning4kids.net/category/active-play

McLennan, D. P. (2017). Math learning—and a touch of science—in the outdoor world. *Teaching Young Children, 10*(4). https://www.naeyc.org/resources/pubs/tyc/apr2017/math-learning-outdoors

No Time for Flash Cards. (2012, March 7). *50 Simple outdoor activities for kids.* https://www .notimeforflashcards.com/2012/03/50-simple-outdoor-activities-for-kids.html

Virtual Lab School. (n.d.). *Infants & toddlers learning environments—The outdoor environment: Designing for engagement.* https://www.virtuallabschool.org/infants-toddlers/learning-environments /lesson-3?module=4151

Virtual Lab School. (n.d.). *Preschool learning environments—The outdoor environment: Designing for learning.* https://www.virtuallabschool.org/preschool/learning-environments/lesson-3?module=3601

Virtual Lab School. (n.d.). *Preschool physical development—Supporting physical development: Outdoor environments and experiences.* https://www.virtuallabschool.org/preschool/physical-development /lesson-4?module=7541

Virtual Lab School. (n.d.). *School-age learning environments—The outdoor environment: Designing for learning.* https://www.virtuallabschool.org/school-age/learning-environments/lesson-3

Videos

McDaniel, L. (2014, August 17). *Video model of outside play* [Video]. YouTube. https://www.youtube.com /watch?v=PbcVe7fDu94

STARNET: Early Childhood. (2016, May 9). *Engaging young children in the outdoor environment* [Video]. YouTube. https://www.youtube.com/watch?v=FrEfhE5VuSQ

Arrival & Departure

Articles and Readings

Tours, S. B., & Dennis, L. R. (2015). Easing first day jitters: Strategies for successful home-to-school transitions. *Young Children, 70*(4): 84–89. https://www.naeyc.org/resources/pubs/yc/sep2015 /easing-first-day-jitters

Activities and Ideas to Try

Autism Classroom Resources. (n.d.). Creating learning opportunities during arrival and departure. https:// autismclassroomresources.com/5-incidental-teaching-opportunities-during-arrival-departure

Head Start Early Learning and Knowledge Center. (n.d.). *Supporting transitions: Resources for building collaboration.* https://eclkc.ohs.acf.hhs.gov/transitions/article/supporting-transitions-resources -building-collaboration

National Association for the Education of Young Children. (n.d.). *Routines and transitions.* https://www.naeyc.org/resources/topics/routines-and-transitions

Not Just Cute with Amanda Morgan. (2009, August 24). *Terrific transitions at preschool arrival and departure.* https://notjustcute.com/2009/08/24/terrific-transitions-at-preschool-arrival-and-departure

Preschool Plan-It. (n.d.). *5 Transition activities + tips for your preschool classroom.* https://www .preschool-plan-it.com/transition-activities.html

Videos

McDaniel, Lindy. *Goodbye ritual for a pre-K classroom* [Video]. YouTube:

- Option #1 (2014, September 1): https://www.youtube.com/watch?v=_8aZRPgK3yg

- Option #2 (2014, September 13): https://www.youtube.com/watch?v=jPAnZwEvJuk

- Option #3 (n.d.): https://www.youtube.com/watch?v=KaCsaYUA5PI

- Option #4 (n.d.): https://www.youtube.com/watch?v=f3m0h-Kgajw

McDaniel, Lindy. (n.d.). *Our ECSE classroom's schedule: Part one—Arrival & daily jobs* [Video]. YouTube. https://www.youtube.com/watch?v=uwFA7llHqXk

Seeing is Believing. (2012, February 9). *Arrival routines in action* [Video]. YouTube. https://www.youtube .com/watch?v=UlQQRVso4d8

Art

Articles and Readings

Bernstein, P. (2013). Why art and creativity are important. *Parents*. https://www.parents.com/toddlers-preschoolers/development/intellectual/why-art-and-creativity-are-important

Bongiorno, L. (2014). How process-focused art experiences support preschoolers. *Teaching Young Children, 7*(3). https://www.naeyc.org/resources/pubs/tyc/feb2014/process-art-experiences

PBS Kids for Parents. (n.d.). *Create Art!* https://www.pbs.org/parents/art

Books

Editors of Teaching Young Children. (2015). *Expressing creativity in preschool*. National Association for the Education of Young Children.

Koralek, D. (2005). *Spotlight on young children and the creative arts*. National Association for the Education of Young Children.

Activities and Ideas to Try

The Artful Parent. (n.d.). *500+ Kids arts and crafts activities*. https://artfulparent.com/kids-arts-crafts-activities-500-fun-artful-things-kids

Early Learning Ideas. (n.d.). *Art and crafts*. https://earlylearningideas.com/category/art-crafts

Education.com. (n.d.). *Preschool arts & crafts activities*. https://www.education.com/activity/preschool/arts-and-crafts

Gryphon House. (n.d.). *Free art activities for all ages*. https://www.gryphonhouse.com/activities/category/post-art

Hands On As We Grow. (n.d.). *What toddler crafts and art projects can we do? 30 Ideas*. https://handsonaswegrow.com/30-creative-toddler-craft-art-projects

JumpStart. (n.d.). *Art activities*. https://www.jumpstart.com/parents/activities/art-activities

Learning 4 Kids. (n.d.). *Craft*. https://www.learning4kids.net/category/craft

PBS Kids for Parents. (n.d.). *Arts*. https://www.pbs.org/parents/learn-grow/all-ages/arts

Play to Learn Preschool. (n.d.). *Art projects*. https://playtolearnpreschool.us/art

Preschool Learning Online. (n.d.). *PreK art activities, easy kids crafts & painting ideas*. https://www.preschoollearningonline.com/preschool-art.html

Teaching 2 and 3 Year Olds. (n.d.). *Archives: Art*. https://teaching2and3yearolds.com/category/art

Van't Hul, J. (2015, November 6). 7 Simple art activities for toddlers. *The Artful Parent*. https://artfulparent.com/7-simple-art-activities-for-toddlers

Videos

5-Minutes Crafts PLAY. (2018, February 10). *17 Educational crafts for preschoolers* [Video]. YouTube. https://www.youtube.com/watch?v=6CwFlhHZ97A

5-Minutes Crafts PLAY. (2018, October 5). *17 Fun educational crafts for toddlers* [Video]. YouTube. https://www.youtube.com/watch?v=FwdzRYbBh00

5-Minutes Crafts PLAY. (2019, June 17). *16 Creative drawing hacks for kids* [Video]. YouTube. https://www.youtube.com/watch?v=xSsdnC896pU

Clubbhouse Kids. (2017, May 14). *Ideas for art in the infant/toddler classroom* [Video]. YouTube. https://www.youtube.com/watch?v=X9F63Q6wcaQ

Preschool Learning Online. (n.d.). *Preschool kids art ideas: Pre K art activities* [Video]. YouTube. https://www.youtube.com/watch?v=9Y4HIiWMnGs

Bath Time

Activities and Ideas to Try

Alyssa. (n.d.). 18 Bath activities for kids. *Realistic Mama.* https://www.therealisticmama.com/bath-activities-for-kids

Braley, P. (2014, May 2). 10 Fun bath time activities for kids. *The Inspired Treehouse.* https://theinspiredtreehouse.com/?s=10+fun+bath

Block Play

Articles and Readings

Anderson, C. (2010). Blocks: A versatile learning tool for yesterday, today, and tomorrow. *Young Children, 65*(2).

Block building and make-believe for every child. (2010). *Teaching Young Children, 3*(3).

Blocks: Great learning tools from infancy through the primary grades. (2015). *Young Children, 70*(1). https://www.naeyc.org/resources/pubs/yc/mar2015

Kuder, B. N., & Hojnoski, R. L. (2016). Under construction: Strategic changes in the block area to promote engagement and learning. *Young Exceptional Children, 21*(2), 76–91. https://doi.org/10.1177/1096250616649224

Wise Lindeman, K., & McKendry Anderson, E. (2016). Does your block center promote 21st century skills? A checklist for teachers. *Teaching Young Children, 9*(3). https://www.naeyc.org/resources/pubs/tyc/feb2016/does-your-block-center-promote-21st-century

Books

Chalufour, I., & Worth, K. (2004). *Building structures with young children.* Redleaf Press.

Activities and Ideas to Try

Fun Learning for Kids. (n.d.). *7 Toddler learning activities with Mega Bloks.* https://funlearningforkids.com/7-toddler-learning-activities-with-mega-bloks

Hands On As We Grow. (n.d.). 47 Super fun block activities for preschoolers. *Pinterest.* https://www.pinterest.com/pin/283586107761540617

Hands On As We Grow. (n.d.). *Blocks of fun! 47 Block activities for preschoolers.* https://handsonaswegrow.com/lots-of-blocks-activities

Levin, V. (n.d.). Blocks center set up in preschool. *Pre-K Pages.* https://www.pre-kpages.com/blocks_center

Stephens, K. (2007). Block play activities for home, child care, or school. *Parenting Exchange.* https://www.easternflorida.edu/community-resources/child-development-centers/parent-resource-library/documents/block-play-activities.pdf

Teaching 2 and 3 Year Olds. (n.d.). *Archives: Blocks.* https://teaching2and3yearolds.com/category/blocks

Circle Time

Activities and Ideas to Try

Barton, E. E., Reichow, B., Wolery, M., & Chen, C.-I. (2011). We can all participate! Adapting circle time for children with autism. *Young Exceptional Children, 14*(2): 2–21. https://doi.org/10.1177/1096250610393681

Cooper, S. (2013, September 1). Circle time activities. *Teaching 2 and 3 Year Olds.* https://teaching2and3yearolds.com/circle-time-activities

FlannelBoardFun. (n.d.). Circle time activities. *Pinterest.* https://www.pinterest.com/FlannelBoardFun/circle-time-activities

Gayle's Preschool Rainbow. Preschool large group and circle activities. http://www.preschoolrainbow.org/activities-large.htm

Laura. (2011, February 15). Making circle time successful. *Teach Me to Talk!* https://teachmetotalk .com/2011/02/15/making-circle-time-successful

Levin, V. (n.d.). Circle time tips for preschool and pre-K teachers. *Pre-K Pages.* https://www.pre-kpages .com/circle_time

Luckenbill, J. (2011). Circle time puppets: Teaching social skills. *Teaching Young Children, 4*(4). https:// www.yumpu.com/en/document/read/4736782/circle-time-puppets-teaching-social-skills

Play to Learn Preschool. (n.d.). Circle time. https://playtolearnpreschool.us/category/circle-time

Teaching 2 and 3 Year Olds. (n.d.). *Archives: Circle time.* https://teaching2and3yearolds.com/category /circle-time

Videos

McDaniel, L. (n.d.). *Another way to set up large group in pre-K classrooms* [Video]. YouTube. https://www .youtube.com/watch?v=5rKsLZge8GI

McDaniel, L. (n.d.). *How to have successful large group sessions* [Video]. YouTube. https://www.youtube .com/watch?v=5svHUqvsCgI

Preschool Learning Online. (n.d.). *Preschool circle time songs, how to start circle time with a song, ideas, activities pre K* [Video]. YouTube. https://www.youtube.com/watch?v=6iWwLTS8IDI

Diapering, Toileting, & Handwashing

Articles and Readings

Suppo, J. L., & Mayton, M. R. (2012). A portable potty plan for children with autism. *Young Exceptional Children, 15*(4). https://doi.org/10.1177/1096250612451758

Books

Brucks, B. (2016). *Potty training in 3 days: The step-by-step plan for a clean break from dirty diapers.* Althea Publishers.

Capucilli, A. S. (2000). *The potty book for boys.* Barron's Educational Series.

Capucilli, A. S. (2000). *The potty book for girls.* Barron's Educational Series.

Patricelli, L. (2010). *Potty.* Candlewick Press.

Activities and Ideas to Try

Beck, C. (2016). Tips for how to teach kids potty training. *The OT Toolbox.* https://www.theottoolbox.com /tips-for-how-to-teach-kids-potty

Child Care Aware of North Dakota. (n.d.). *Diapering time activities.* https://www.ndchildcare.org/file _download/d84e8254-f9f7-41fe-b035-a30e8920d894

Child Care Aware of North Dakota. (n.d.). *Toilet (potty) training checklist.* https://ndchildcareorg .presencehost.net/file_download/a6ac918e-4075-4137-9dc1-6eac9df0493c

Parents. (n.d.). *Diapering.* https://www.parents.com/baby/diapers

Poole, C. (n.d.). Infants and toddlers/communication with families: How to create diapering and toileting routines. *Scholastic.* https://www.scholastic.com/teachers/articles/teaching-content/infants -toddlerscommunication-families-how-create-diapering-and-toileting-routines

Virtual Lab School. (n.d.). Staying healthy: Diapering and toileting. https://www.virtuallabschool.org /fcc/healthy-environments/lesson-3

Videos

Child Care Aware ND. (2017, December 18). Diapering [Video]. YouTube. https://www.youtube.com /playlist?list=PLsqrHdiqnOiuRgDvTLnxYRkyR9hUuvQOq

PBS Learning Media. (n.d.). *Hand washing* [Video]. https://www.pbslearningmedia.org/resource /eb12ac7a-a6fe-4758-80e2-7b12f588beba/hand-washing/#.WTtvq2grLIU

PBS Learning Media. (n.d.). *Prince Wednesday goes potty: Daniel Tiger's neighborhood* [Video]. https://www.pbslearningmedia.org/resource/36e64535-03e7-48cf-9d85-a7b890cb9938/prince -wednesday-goes-potty-daniel-tigers-neighborhood/#.WTtyk2jyvIU

PBS Learning Media. (n.d.). *When you have to go potty, stop and go right away! Daniel Tiger's neighborhood* [Video]. https://www.pbslearningmedia.org/resource/b6e14698-8253-44b6-acde-9c39b5d8280d /when-you-have-to-go-potty-stop-and-go-right-away-daniel-tigers-neighborhood/#.WTtyMmjyvIU

Virtual Lab School. (n.d.). *Stay healthy: Diapering and toileting* (infants and toddlers):

- *Helping children after accidents* [Video] (https://stream.virtuallabschool.org/healthy/3915/3915 -480.mp4)

- *Diapering correctly with sensitive interactions* [Video] (https://stream.virtuallabschool.org/healthy /5349/5349-480.mp4)

- *Changing diapers supports development* [Video] (https://stream.virtuallabschool.org/healthy/3743 /3743-480.mp4)

Virtual Lab School. (n.d.). *Stay healthy: Diapering and toileting* (preschool):

- *Restroom hygiene* [Video] (https://stream.virtuallabschool.org/healthy/3860/3860-480.mp4)

- *Helping children after accidents* [Video] (https://stream.virtuallabschool.org/healthy/3866/3866 -480.mp4)

Dramatic Play

Articles and Readings

Barton, E. E., & Pavilanis, R. (2012). Teaching pretend play to young children with autism. *Young Exceptional Children, 15*(1). https://doi.org/10.1177/1096250611424106?journalCode=yeca

Bright Horizons Education Team. *The importance of pretend play in child development.* https://www .brighthorizons.com/family-resources/importance-of-pretend-play-in-child-development

Early Learning Ideas. (n.d.). This is what you need to know about dramatic play. https://earlylearnin gideas.com/dramatic-play

McEntire, N. (2009). Pretend play in the early childhood classroom. *Childhood Education, 85*(3).

Books

Editors of Teaching Young Children. (2015). *Expressing creativity in preschool.* National Association for the Education of Young Children.

Koralek, D. (2005). *Spotlight on young children and the creative arts.* National Association for the Education of Young Children.

Activities and Ideas to Try

Dramatic play—Every day. (2005). *Texas Child Care.* https://www.childcarequarterly.com/winter05 _story2a.html

Illinois Early Learning Project. (n.d.). *Drama and young children.* https://illinoisearlylearning.org /tipsheets/drama

Learning 4 Kids. (n.d.). *Pretend.* https://www.learning4kids.net/category/pretend

Levin, V. (n.d.). Dramatic play. *Pre-K Pages.* https://www.pre-kpages.com/category/dramatic-play

PennState Extension. (n.d.). Dramatic play: Let's think beyond the housekeeping corner! https:// extension.psu.edu/programs/betterkidcare/knowledge-areas/environment-curriculum/activities /all-activities/dramatic-play-beyond-housekeeping-corner

Play to Learn Preschool. (n.d.). *Dramatic play.* https://playtolearnpreschool.us/dramatic-play

Preschool Learning Online. (n.d.). *Dramatic play preschool ideas & activities for children in preschool.* https://www.preschoollearningonline.com/dramatic-play.html

Teaching 2 and 3 Year Olds. (n.d.). *Archives: Dramatic play.* https://teaching2and3yearolds.com/category /dramatic-play

Videos

McDaniel, L. (n.d.). *Pretend play center in an early childhood classroom* [Video]. YouTube. https://www .youtube.com/watch?v=oh2agWaSSkU

Dressing

Activities and Ideas to Try

Beck, C. (2016, June 24). Functional skills for kids. *The OT Toolbox*. https://www.theottoolbox.com/functional-skills-for-kids

Brill, A. (2012, June 13). Giant list of self-care skills for babies, toddlers, and preschoolers. *Positive Parenting Connection*. https://www.positiveparentingconnection.net/giant-list-of-self-care-skills-for-babiestoddlers-and-preschoolers

Family Connect for Parents of Children with Visual Impairments. (n.d.). Teaching bathing and dressing skills for dual diagnosis children. https://familyconnect.org/multiple-disabilities/independent-living-skills/bathing-and-dressing/135

Videos

The Kids' Picture Show. (2013, April 22). *Getting dressed: How to put on a T-shirt* [Video]. YouTube. https://www.youtube.com/watch?v=WWNlgvtYcEs

The Kids' Picture Show. (2013, July 4). *Getting dressed: How to put on pants* [Video]. YouTube. https://www.youtube.com/watch?v=oMae4XZnxTw

Field Trips

Articles and Readings

National Association for the Education of Young Children. (2013). Get to know the NEW children's librarian. *Teaching Young Children, 7*(2), 28.

National Association for the Education of Young Children. (2016). Family field trips: Museums. *Teaching Young Children, 9*(4). https://www.naeyc.org/resources/pubs/tyc/apr2016/backpack/family-field-trips-museums

Resources for incorporating books throughout the curriculum. (2007). *Young Children, 62*(3).

Books

Abbot, E. A. (2020). *Family field trip: Explore art, food, music, and nature with kids*. Chronicle Books.

Brown, M. (2003). *D.W.'s library card*. Scholastic.

Buhr, E. (2018). *Little walks, big adventures: 50+ ideas for exploring with toddlers*. Gryphon House.

Cousins, L. (2013). *Maisy goes to the museum*. Candlewick.

Feldman, T. (2018). *Let's go to our zoo (Smithsonian Kids)*. Cottage Door Press.

Hill, E. (1996). *Spot goes to the park*. Puffin.

Jalongo, M. R. (2004). *Young children and picture books* (2nd ed.). National Association for the Education of Young Children.

McAnulty, S. (2018). *Max explains everything: Grocery store expert*. G.P. Putnam Sons.

Parish, H. (2013). *Amelia Bedelia's first field trip*. Greenwillow Books.

Parish, H., & Swear, L. (2005). *Amelia Bedelia, Bookworm*. Greenwillow Books.

Activities and Ideas to Try

Colorín Colorado. *Your library*. https://www.colorincolorado.org/your-library

Crouch, M. (2016, January 5). 4 Field trips that are perfect for preschoolers. *Parents*. https://www.parents.com/toddlers-preschoolers/activities/4-field-trips-that-are-perfect-for-preschoolers

Illinois Early Learning Project. (n.d.). *Outdoor field trips with preschoolers: Preparing with the children*. https://illinoisearlylearning.org/tipsheets/field-preparing

ilovelibraries. *For parents*. http://www.ilovelibraries.org/parents

Kiehl, K. L. (2016). Inspired by museums—Both outside and inside the classroom. *Teaching Young Children, 9*(4). https://www.naeyc.org/resources/pubs/tyc/apr2016/inspired-museums-outside-and-inside-classroom

Levin, V. (n.d.). Field trip ideas for preschool and kindergarten. *Pre-K Pages.* https://www.pre-kpages.com/field-trips

Levin, V. (n.d.). Preschool classroom library center. *Pre-K Pages.* https://www.pre-kpages.com/classlibrary

Not Just Cute with Amanda Morgan. (2010, August 16). Why don't you teach reading? A look at emergent literacy (series). https://notjustcute.com/2010/08/16/why-dont-you-teach-reading-a-look-at-emergent-literacy

SAG-AFTRA Foundation. (n.d.). *Storyline online.* https://www.storylineonline.net/library

Simply Daycare. (n.d.). *Field trip ideas.* https://www.simplydaycare.com/field-trip-ideas.html

U.S. Department of Education. *Helping your child use the library.* https://www2.ed.gov/pubs/parents/Library/Interested.html

Videos

Home Grown Books. (n.d.). *Resources* [series of videos for emergent readers]. https://homegrownbooksnyc.com/videos

South Florida PBS. (n.d.). Take a field trip [YouTube series]. https://www.youtube.com/c/WPBT2/search?query=kidvision

ZERO TO THREE. (2016, February 2). *Babies, toddlers, and early reading* [Video]. YouTube. https://www.zerotothree.org/resources/20-babies-toddlers-and-early-reading

Math

Articles and Readings

Burton, M. (2010). Five strategies for creating meaningful mathematics experiences in the primary years. *Young Children, 65*(6). https://www.researchgate.net/publication/285756551_Five_strategies_for_creating_meaningful_mathematics_experiences_in_the_primary_years

Geist, K., & Geist, E. (2008). Do re mi, 1-2-3 that's how easy math can be: Using music to support emergent mathematics. *Young Children, 63*(2). https://www.researchgate.net/publication/290004564_Do_re_mi_1-2-3_that%27s_how_easy_math_can_be_Using_music_to_support_emergent_mathematics

Moomaw, S., & Davis, J. A. (2010). STEM comes to preschool. *Young Children, 65*(5). https://www.researchgate.net/publication/292035679_STEM_comes_to_preschool

National Association for the Education of Young Children & National Council of Teachers of Mathematics. (2010). *Early childhood mathematics: Promoting good beginnings* [Position statement]. https://www.naeyc.org/sites/default/files/globally-shared/downloads/PDFs/resources/position-statements/psmath.pdf

National Association for the Education of Young Children. (2017). *Teaching Young Children, 11*(1). [October/November 2017 issue focused on math.]

Notari-Syverson, A., & Sadler, F. H. (2008). Math is for everyone: Strategies for supporting early mathematical competencies in young children. *Young Exceptional Children, 11*(3). https://www.researchgate.net/publication/240731670_Math_Is_for_Everyone_Strategies_for_Supporting_Early_Mathematical_Competencies_in_Young_Children

Pecaski McLennan, D. (2014). Making math meaningful for young children. *Teaching Young Children, 8*(1). https://www.naeyc.org/resources/pubs/tyc/oct2014/making-math-meaningful

Rosen, D., & Hoffman, J. (2009). Integrating concrete and virtual manipulatives in early childhood mathematics. *Young Children, 64*(3). https://www.researchgate.net/publication/287695795_Integrating_concrete_and_virtual_manipulatives_in_early_childhood_mathematics

Books

Copley, J. V. (2003). *Showcasing mathematics for the young child: Activities for three-, four-, and five-year-olds.* National Association for the Education of Young Children.

Copley, J. V. (2010). *The young child and mathematics.* National Association for the Education of Young Children.

Counsell, S., Escalada, L., Geiken, R., Sander, M., Uhlenberg, J., Meeteren, B. V., Yoshizawa, S., & Zan, B. (2016). *STEM learning with young children: Inquiry teaching with ramps and pathways.* National Association for the Education of Young Children.

Early Math Collaborative. (2013). *Big ideas of early mathematics: What teachers of young children need to know.* Pearson.

Editors of Teaching Young Children. (2015). *Exploring math and science in preschool.* National Association for the Education of Young Children.

Heroman, C. (2017). *Making and tinkering with STEM: Solving design challenges with young children.* National Association for the Education of Young Children.

Kotsopoulos, D., & Lee, J. (2014). *Let's talk about math: The LittleCounters approach to building early math skills.* Brookes Publishing Co.

Krogh, S., & Slentz, K. (2001). *The early childhood curriculum: Inquiry learning through integration.* Erlbaum.

Moomaw, S. (2011). *Teaching mathematics in early childhood.* Brookes Publishing Co.

Shillady, A. (2016). *Spotlight on young children: Exploring math.* National Association for the Education of Young Children.

Activities and Ideas to Try

Arkansas Child Development and Early Learning Standards. (2018). Mathematical thinking. In *Strategies and activities: Infant toddler.* https://ecep.uark.edu/_resources/pdf_other/06_division_materials/strategies_activities_infant_toddler2018.pdf

Cooper, S. (2020, March 6). The ultimate collection of preschool math activities. *Teaching 2 and 3 Year Olds.* https://teaching2and3yearolds.com/the-ultimate-collection-preschool-math-activities

Education.com. (n.d.). *Preschool math activities.* https://www.education.com/activity/preschool/math

Education.com. (n.d.). *Preschool math games.* https://www.education.com/games/preschool/math

Hanke, H. (n.d.). Fun activities to promote math skills. *BabyCenter.* https://www.babycenter.com/0_fun-activities-to-promote-math-skills_64460.bc

Institute of Education Sciences. (2014). *Educator's practice guide: Teaching math to young children.* What Works Clearinghouse. https://ies.ed.gov/ncee/wwc/Docs/PracticeGuide/early_math_pg_111313.pdf

JumpStart. (n.d.). *Math activities for kids.* https://www.jumpstart.com/parents/activities/math-activities

Learning 4 Kids. (n.d.). *Play categories: Numbers.* https://www.learning4kids.net/category/numbers

Levin, V. (n.d.). Math activities. *Pre-K Pages.* https://www.pre-kpages.com/math

National Association for the Education of Young Children. (n.d.). *Math talk with infants and toddlers.* https://www.naeyc.org/our-work/families/math-talk-infants-and-toddlers

PBS Kids. (n.d.). *Math games.* https://pbskids.org/games/math

PBS Kids for Parents. (n.d.). *Math.* https://www.pbs.org/parents/learn-grow/all-ages/math

Play to Learn Preschool. (n.d.). *Learning center: Math.* https://playtolearnpreschool.us/category/math

Teaching-Tiny-Tots.com. (n.d.). *Toddler math.* http://www.teaching-tiny-tots.com/toddler-math.html

Thayer, A. (n.d.). 15 Hands-on math activities for preschoolers. *Teaching Mama.* https://teachingmama.org/15-hands-on-math-activities-preschoolers

ZERO TO THREE. (n.d.). *Help your child develop early math skills.* https://www.zerotothree.org/resources/299-help-your-child-develop-early-math-skills

Videos

McDaniel, L. (n.d.). *Building a math center in an early childhood special needs classroom* [Video]. YouTube. https://www.youtube.com/watch?v=2i7XO0YJC3Y

PBS Learning Media. (n.d.). *Math resources* [Video series]. https://www.pbslearningmedia.org/math

ZERO TO THREE. (n.d.). Let's talk about math: Early math video series. https://www.zerotothree.org/resources/series/let-s-talk-about-math-early-math-video-series

Meals & Snacks

Articles and Readings

Bruns, D., & Thompson, S. D. (2011). Time to eat: Improving mealtimes of children with autism. *Young Exceptional Children, 14*(4). https://www.researchgate.net/publication/256447157_Time_to_Eat _Improving_Mealtimes_of_Young_Children_With_Autism

Bruns, D., & Thompson, S. D. (2014). Turning mealtimes into learning opportunities: Integrating feeding goals into IEPs. *Teaching Exceptional Children, 46*(6), 179–186. https://doi.org/10.1177/0040059914534619

Family Connect for Parents of Children with Visual Impairments. (n.d.). Supporting the development of eating skills for children with multiple disabilities. https://familyconnect.org/multiple-disabilities /independent-living-skills/eating-skills

Make mealtimes learning times. (2014). *Teaching Young Children, 7*(5). https://www.naeyc.org/resources /pubs/tyc/jun2014/backpack/make-mealtimes-learning-times

Thompson, S. D., Bruns, D., & Rains, K. W. (2010). Picky eating habits or sensory processing issues? Exploring feeding difficulties in infants and toddlers. *Young Exceptional Children, 13*(2). https://www .researchgate.net/publication/249836360_Picky_Eating_Habits_or_Sensory_Processing_Issues _Exploring_Feeding_Difficulties_in_Infants_and_Toddlers

Books

Bruns, D. A., & Thompson, S. D. (2012). *Feeding challenges in young children.* Brookes Publishing Co.

DK Publishing. (2012). *Baby touch and feel: Mealtime.* DK Children.

Fernando, N., & Potock, M. (2015). *Raising a healthy, happy eater: A parent's handbook: A stage-by-stage guide to setting your child on the path to adventurous eating.* The Experiment, LLC.

Satter, E. (1987). *How to get your kid to eat: But not too much.* Bull Publishing.

Verdick, E., & Heinlen, M. (2011). *Mealtime.* Toddler tools. Free Spirit Publishing.

Activities and Ideas to Try

New York State Department of Health. (2012). *Chatting with children at mealtimes: Creating a climate for communication.* https://www.health.ny.gov/prevention/nutrition/resources/chattingmeal.htm

Parents. (n.d.). *Eating and nutrition.* https://www.parents.com/kids/nutrition

Parents. (n.d.). *Feeding.* https://www.parents.com/baby/feeding

Play to Learn Preschool. (n.d.). *Preschool snack time.* https://playtolearnpreschool.us/preschool-snack -time-2

Virtual Lab School. (n.d.). *Infants & toddlers: Healthy environments | Staying healthy: Nutrition, feeding, and physical activity.* https://www.virtuallabschool.org/infants-toddlers/healthy/lesson-5?module=3446

Virtual Lab School. (n.d.). *Preschool: Healthy environments | Staying healthy: Nutrition and physical activity.* https://www.virtuallabschool.org/preschool/healthy/lesson-5?module=3076

ZERO TO THREE. (2010, February 20). *Creating routines for love and learning.* https://www.zerotothree .org/resources/223-creating-routines-for-love-and-learning

Videos

McDaniel, L. (n.d.). *Preparing for snack time in a pre-K classroom* [Video]. YouTube. https://www.youtube .com/watch?v=ebfVan-Byzc

PBS Learning Media. (n.d.). *Katerina finally tries a new food: Daniel Tiger's neighborhood* [Video]. https:// www.pbslearningmedia.org/resource/4f0c441c-2af8-437d-a102-b9b2c356fcce/katerina-finally -tries-a-new-food/#.WTtzlmgrLIU

PBS Learning Media. (n.d.). *Trying tomatoes: Daniel Tiger's neighborhood* [Video]. https://www.pbslearn ingmedia.org/resource/30c0868b-10fb-4f10-bfd5-31052d594d07/trying-tomatoes/#.WTtzV2grLIU

PBS Learning Media. (n.d.). *Trying veggie spaghetti: Daniel Tiger's neighborhood* [Video]. https://www .pbslearningmedia.org/resource/e3096f63-3d1f-4e16-bb0f-a46ca56e0ee3/trying-veggie -spaghetti/#.WTtwNmjyvIU

WUCF TV. (2018, June 14). *WUCF's Snack Hacks* [Video series]. https://www.wucf.org/learn/pbs-kids /snack-hacks

Music & Movement

Articles and Readings

Cooper, J. (2016). Integrating music, drama, and dance helps children explore and learn. *Teaching Young Children, 9*(4). https://www.naeyc.org/resources/pubs/tyc/apr2016/integrating-music-drama-and-dance-helps-children

National Association for the Education of Young Children. (2010). *Young Children, 65*(2). [March 2010 issue focused on music and other creative arts.]

Orlowski, M. A., & Hart, A. (2010). Go! Including movement during routines and transitions. *Young Children, 65*(5). https://www.researchgate.net/publication/294701367_Go_Movement_during_routines_and_transitions

PBS Kids for Parents. (n.d.). *Make and Play Music!* https://www.pbs.org/parents/music

Books

Editors of Teaching Young Children. (2015). *Expressing creativity in preschool.* National Association for the Education of Young Children.

Kotowicz, A. (2019). *Winter song: A day in the life of a kid.* ArtsKindred.

Koralek, D. (2005). *Spotlight on young children and the creative arts.* National Association for the Education of Young Children.

Activities and Ideas to Try

Arkansas Child Development and Early Learning Standards. (2018). Creativity and aesthetics. In *Strategies and activities: Infant toddler.* https://ecep.uark.edu/_resources/pdf_other/06_division_materials/strategies_activities_infant_toddler2018.pdf

Gryphon House. (2015, October 13). *Music and movement activities for infants, toddlers & preschoolers.* https://www.gryphonhouse.com/activities/music-and-movement-activities-for-infants-toddlers-preschoolers

Honig, A. S. (n.d.). Infants and toddlers/Activities: Musical activities *Scholastic.* https://www.scholastic.com/teachers/articles/teaching-content/infants-toddlersactivities-musical-activities

Illinois Early Learning Project. (n.d.). *Sing, play, and hear: Music's in the air.* https://illinoisearlylearning.org/tipsheets/sing

Kids Environment Kids Health, National Institute of Environmental Health Sciences. (n.d.). *Songs.* https://kids.niehs.nih.gov/games/songs/index.htm

Lerner, C., & Parlakian, R. (2016, August 11). Beyond Twinkle, Twinkle: Using music with infants and toddlers. *ZERO TO THREE.* https://www.zerotothree.org/resources/1514-beyond-twinkle-twinkle-using-music-with-infants-and-toddlers

Levin, V. (n.d.). Music in the classroom. *Pre-K Pages.* https://www.pre-kpages.com/music-in-the-classroom

Preschool Learning Online. *Learning songs for preschoolers.* https://www.preschoollearningonline.com/preschool-songs.html

Teaching 2 and 3 Year Olds. (n.d.). *Music and movement.* https://teaching2and3yearolds.com/category/music-and-movement

Nap & Sleep

Articles and Readings

Mendola, W. (2017). Nap time is for letting go. *Teaching Young Children, 10*(2). https://www.naeyc.org/resources/pubs/tyc/dec2016/nap-time-letting-go?utm_content=buffer8f76e&utm_medium=social&utm_source=facebook.com&utm_campaign=buffer

Pacheco, D. (2020, September 20). Children and sleep. *Sleep Foundation.* https://www.sleepfoundation.org/articles/children-and-sleep

Books

Verdick, E., & Heinlen, M. (2012). *Bedtime*. Toddler tools. Free Spirit Publishing.

Verdick, E., & Heinlen, M. (2011). *Naptime*. Toddler tools. Free Spirit Publishing.

Activities and Ideas to Try

Baby Sleep Site. (n.d.). *Baby and toddler sleep resources for childcare providers*. https://www.babysleepsite.com/childcare-resources

Ben-Joseph, E. P. (n.d.). All about sleep. *KidsHealth*. https://kidshealth.org/en/parents/sleep.html

Cleveland Clinic. (n.d.). *Sleep in toddlers and preschoolers*. https://my.clevelandclinic.org/health/articles/14302-sleep-in-toddlers–preschoolers

Harvey, H. (n.d.). Encouraging healthy sleep habits. *National Association for the Education of Young Children*. https://www.naeyc.org/our-work/families/encouraging-healthy-sleep-habits

Head Start Early Childhood Learning and Knowledge Center. (n.d.). *News you can use: The culture of sleep and child care*. https://eclkc.ohs.acf.hhs.gov/school-readiness/article/news-you-can-use-culture-sleep-child-care

Levin, V. (n.d.). Nap time tips for preschool teachers. *Pre-K Pages*. https://www.pre-kpages.com/nap-time-routine

Norman, R. (n.d.). *How to get your littles to sleep in and take longer naps*. https://amotherfarfromhome.com/help-babies-toddlers-sleep-later

Pantley, E. (n.d.). Eight sleep tips for toddlers & preschoolers. *Child Development Institute*. https://childdevelopmentinfo.com/ages-stages/toddler-preschooler-development-parenting/sleep-tips-toddlers-preschoolers/#gs.xhuf6w

Parents. (n.d.). *Napping*. https://www.parents.com/kids/sleep/naps

Parents. (n.d.). *Sleep*. https://www.parents.com/kids/sleep

Rachel. (2014, May 2). 16 Nap time play ideas. *Kids Activities Blog*. https://kidsactivitiesblog.com/52377/16-nap-time-play-ideas

Videos

PBS Learning Media. (n.d.). *The bedtime song: Daniel Tiger's neighborhood* [Video]. https://www.pbslearningmedia.org/resource/e4057574-ad19-48f3-811f-52d04f7afffc/the-bedtime-song/#.WTtxyWjyvIU

PBS Learning Media. (n.d.). *Finn's bedtime: Daniel Tiger's neighborhood* [Video]. https://www.pbslearningmedia.org/resource/44594303-a357-4b85-9f2b-700b4c45a0ff/finns-bedtime/#.WTtxhGgrLIU

PBS Learning Media. (n.d.). *Storytime: Daniel Tiger's neighborhood* [Video]. https://www.pbslearningmedia.org/resource/2ea5c444-11a9-4a84-b3ab-38c6a1b268c0/storytime/#.WTtxfWgrLIU

Science (Growing and Ready levels only)

Articles and Readings

Head Start Early Childhood Learning and Knowledge Center. (n.d.). *News you can use: Early science learning for infants and toddlers*. https://eclkc.ohs.acf.hhs.gov/school-readiness/article/news-you-can-use-early-science-learning-infants-toddlers

Moomaw, S., & Davis, J. A. (2010). STEM Comes to Preschool. *Young Children, 65*(5). https://www.researchgate.net/publication/292035679_STEM_comes_to_preschool

National Association for the Education of Young Children. (2009). *Young Children, 64*(6). [November 2009 issue focused on science.] https://www.naeyc.org/resources/topics/science

National Institute of Environmental Health Sciences. (n.d.). *Science—How it works*. https://kids.niehs.nih.gov/topics/how-science-works/index.htm

Patrick, H., Mantzicopoulos, P. Y., & Samarapungavan, A. (2009). Reading, writing, and conducting inquiry about science in kindergarten. *Young Children, 64*(6). https://www.researchgate.net/publication/257981023_Reading_writing_and_conducting_inquiry_about_science_in_kindergarten

Books

Ashbrook, P. (2003). *Science is simple: Over 250 activities for preschoolers.* Gryphon House.

Counsell, S., Escalada, L., Geiken, R., Sander, M., Uhlenberg, J., Meeteren, B. V., Yoshizawa, S., & Zan, B. (2016). *STEM learning with young children: Inquiry teaching with ramps and pathways.* National Association for the Education of Young Children.

Dziengel, A. (2018). *STEAM play & learn: 20 Fun step-by-step preschool projects about science, technology, engineering, arts, and math!* Walter Foster Jr.

Editors of Teaching Young Children. (2015). *Exploring math and science in preschool.* The preschool teacher's library of playful practice set. National Association for the Education of Young Children.

Gelman, R., Brenneman, K., MacDonald, G., & Roman, M. (2009). *Preschool pathways to science.* Brookes Publishing Co.

Heroman, C. (2017). *Making and tinkering with STEM: Solving design challenges with young children.* National Association for the Education of Young Children.

Shillady, A. (2013). *Spotlight on young children: Exploring science.* National Association for the Education of Young Children.

Activities and Ideas to Try

Arkansas Child Development and Early Learning Standards. (2018). Science and technology. In *Strategies and activities: Infant toddler.* https://ecep.uark.edu/_resources/pdf_other/06_division_materials/strategies_activities_infant_toddler2018.pdf

Education.com. (n.d.). *Preschool science activities and experiments.* https://www.education.com/activity/preschool/science

Education.com. (n.d.). *Preschool science lesson plans.* https://www.education.com/lesson-plans/preschool/science

Fun Learning for Kids. (n.d.). *30 Science activities for preschoolers that are totally awesome.* https://funlearningforkids.com/science-activities-preschoolers

Hands On As We Grow. (n.d.). *Science activities for kids.* https://handsonaswegrow.com/kids-activities/learning-activities/science

Holly. (2020, September 27). 15 Fun science activities for kids. *Kids Activities Blog.* https://kidsactivitiesblog.com/50127/fun-science-activities

JumpStart. (n.d.). *Online science resources.* https://www.jumpstart.com/parents/resources/science-resources

Learning 4 Kids. (n.d.). *Science.* https://www.learning4kids.net/category/science

Levin, V. (n.d.). Science center. *Pre-K Pages.* https://www.pre-kpages.com/tag/science-center

National Association for the Education of Young Children. (2016, June 14). Supporting the scientific thinking and inquiry of toddlers and preschoolers through play. *Smithsonian National Air and Space Museum.* https://scienceinprek.si.edu/resource/document/naeyc-supporting-scientific-thinking-and-inquiry-toddlers-and-preschoolers-through

Play to Learn Preschool. (n.d.). *Learning center: Science.* https://playtolearnpreschool.us/category/science

Play to Learn Preschool. (n.d.). Science experiments—Preschool. *Pinterest.* https://www.pinterest.com/PlayToLearnPS/science-experiments-preschool

Preschool Learning Online. *Science activities for preschoolers.* https://www.preschoollearningonline.com/science-activities-for-preschoolers.html

Teaching 2 and 3 Year Olds. (n.d.). *Toddler science.* https://teaching2and3yearolds.com/category/science/toddler-science

Videos

PBS Learning Media. (n.d.). *Science* [Video series]. https://www.pbslearningmedia.org/science

ZERO TO THREE. (n.d.). *Everyday fun with science: Let's talk about STEM Video* [Video]. https://www.zerotothree.org/resources/1573-everyday-fun-with-science-let-s-talk-about-stem-video

Sensory

Articles and Readings

Howe, M. B., Brittain, L. A., & McCathren, R. B. (2004). Meeting the sensory needs of young children in classrooms. *Young Exceptional Children, 8*(1). https://www.researchgate.net/publication/234559569 _Meeting_the_Sensory_Needs_of_Young_Children_in_Classrooms

Lynch, S. A., & Simpson, C. G. (2004). Sensory processing: Meeting individual needs using the seven senses. *Young Exceptional Children, 7*(4). https://www.researchgate.net/publication/249836322 _Sensory_Processing_Meeting_Individual_Needs_Using_the_Seven_Senses

Not Just Cute with Amanda Morgan. (2009, February 11). *How to find sensory materials on the cheap.* https://notjustcute.com/2009/02/11/how-to-find-sensory-materials-on-the-cheap

Thompson, S. D., & Rain, K. W. (2008). Learning about sensory integration dysfunction: Strategies to meet young children's sensory needs at home. *Young Exceptional Children, 12*(2). https://www.researchgate .net/publication/249836110_Learning_About_Sensory_Integration_Dysfunction_Strategies_to _Meet_Young_Children%27s_Sensory_Needs_at_Home

Thompson, S. D., & Raisor, J. M. (2013). Meeting the sensory needs of young children. *Young Children, 68*(2). https://www.researchgate.net/publication/289814027_Meeting_the_sensory_needs_of_young _children

Activities and Ideas to Try

Cherry, M. (n.d.). *40 Plus awesome sensory play activities for babies and toddlers.* https://mericherry .com/2015/02/03/sensory-play-babies-toddlers

Growing a Jeweled Rose. (n.d.). *Sensory play activities for babies.* https://www.growingajeweledrose .com/2013/04/sensory-activities-potato-flakes.html

Hands On As We Grow. (n.d.). *25 Sensory activities for kids.* https://handsonaswegrow.com/sensory -activities-for-kids

Learning 4 Kids. (n.d.). *List of sensory play activities.* https://www.learning4kids.net/play-categories /list-of-sensory-play-ideas

Levin, V. (n.d.). Sensory bins. *Pre-K Pages.* https://www.pre-kpages.com/category/sensory-bins

Play to Learn Preschool. (n.d.). *Non-food sensory bin ideas for preschoolers.* https://playtolearnpreschool .us/category/sensory

Teaching 2 and 3 Year Olds. (n.d.). *Sensory bins.* https://teaching2and3yearolds.com/category/sensory -bins

Technology (Growing and Ready levels only)

Articles and Readings

Judge, S. (2001). Integrating computer technology within early childhood classrooms. *Young Exceptional Children, 5*(1). https://www.researchgate.net/publication/234642140_Integrating_Computer _Technology_Within_Early_Childhood_Classrooms

Moomaw, S., & Davis, J. A. (2010). STEM comes to preschool. *Young Children, 65*(5). https://www .researchgate.net/publication/292035679_STEM_comes_to_preschool

National Association for the Education of Young Children and Fred Rogers Center for Early Learning and Children's Media at Saint Vincent College. (2012). *Joint position statement: Technology and interactive media as tools in early childhood programs serving children from birth through age 8.* https://www.naeyc .org/sites/default/files/globally-shared/downloads/PDFs/resources/topics/PS_technology_WEB.pdf

Pecaski McLennan, D. (2017). Creating coding stories and games. *Teaching Young Children, 10*(3). https://www.naeyc.org/resources/pubs/tyc/feb2017/creating-coding-stories-and-games

Books

Counsell, S., Escalada, L., Geiken, R., Sander, M., Uhlenberg, J., Meeteren, B. V., Yoshizawa, S., & Zan, B. (2015). *STEM learning with young children: Inquiry teaching with ramps and pathways.* National Association for the Education of Young Children.

Donohue, C. (2014). *Technology and digital media in the early years: Tools for teaching and learning.* Routledge.

Donohue, C. (2016). *Family engagement in the digital age: Early childhood educators as media mentors.* National Association for the Education of Young Children.

Heroman, C. (2017). *Making and tinkering with STEM: Solving design challenges with young children.* National Association for the Education of Young Children.

Parette, H. P., & Blum, C. (2013). *Instructional technology in early childhood.* Brookes Publishing Co.

Sadao, K. C., & Robinson, N. B. (2010). *Assistive technology for young children: Creating inclusive learning environments.* Brookes Publishing Co.

Shillady, A., & Muccio, L. S. (2012). *Spotlight on young children and technology.* National Association for the Education of Young Children.

Stone-MacDonald, A., Wendell, K. B., Douglass, A., & Love, M. L. (2015). *Engaging young engineers: Teaching problem-solving skills through STEM.* Brookes Publishing Co.

Activities and Ideas to Try

ABCmouse.com. (n.d.). *Full online curriculum for children ages 2–8.* https://www.abcmouse.com/abt/homepage?8a08850bc2=T410032292.1595259042.8049

Arkansas Child Development and Early Learning Standards. (2018). Science and technology. In *Strategies and activities: Infant toddler.* https://ecep.uark.edu/_resources/pdf_other/06_division_materials/strategies_activities_infant_toddler2018.pdf

Colorín Colorado. (n.d.). *For families: Technology at home.* https://www.colorincolorado.org/technology-home

Early Childhood Teacher. (n.d.). *ECE technology: 10 Trending tools for teachers.* https://www.earlychildhoodteacher.org/blog/ece-technology-10-trending-tools-for-teachers

National Association for the Education of Young Children. (n.d.). *Technology and young children: Online resources and position statement.* https://www.naeyc.org/resources/topics/technology-and-media/resources

Videos

Colorado Department of Education. (n.d.). Results matter video library: iPads in early childhood [Video series]. https://www.cde.state.co.us/resultsmatter/RMVideoSeries_iPadsInEarlyChildhood

Writing

Articles and Readings

Baghban, M. (2007). Scribbles, labels, and stories: The role of drawing in the development of writing. *Young Children, 62*(1). https://www.researchgate.net/publication/234723247_Scribbles_Labels_and_Stories_The_Role_of_Drawing_in_the_Development_of_Writing

Early Childhood Teacher. (n.d.). *How to teach children to be successful writers.* https://www.earlychildhoodteacher.org/blog/how-to-teach-children-to-be-successful-writers

Love, A., Burns, M. S., & Buell, M. J. (2007). Writing: Empowering literacy. *Young Children, 62*(1). https://www.researchgate.net/publication/234757182_Writing_Empowering_Literacy

Not Just Cute with Amanda Morgan. (2010, August 27). *The write way to read.* https://notjustcute.com/2010/08/27/the-write-way-to-read

Books

Neuman, S. B., Copple, C., & Bredekamp, S. (2000). *Learning to read and write: Developmentally appropriate practices for young children.* National Association for the Education of Young Children.

Schickedanz, J. A., & Casbergue, R. (2009). *Writing in preschool: Learning to orchestrate meaning and marks.* National Association for the Education of Young Children.

Schickedanz, J. A., & Collins, M. F. (2012). *So much more than ABCs: The early phases of reading and writing.* National Association for the Education of Young Children.

Activities and Ideas to Try

Cincinnati Children's Blog. (2013, April 13). *5 Pre-writing activities for your 3-year-old.* https://blog.cincinnatichildrens.org/learning-and-growing/pre-writing-activities

Education.com. *Preschool writing.* https://www.education.com/resources/preschool/writing

Hanke, H. (2019, January 26). Fun activities to promote writing skills. *BabyCenter.* https://www.babycenter.com/0_fun-activities-to-promote-writing-skills_64524.bc

Levin, V. (n.d.). Writing center for preschool and pre-K. *Pre-K Pages.* https://www.pre-kpages.com/writing_center

National Writing Project. (n.d.). *Resources.* https://archive.nwp.org/cs/public/print/doc/resources.csp

Reading Rockets. (n.d.). *Writing.* https://www.readingrockets.org/teaching/reading-basics/writing

Thayer, A. (n.d.). 10 Pre-writing activities for preschoolers. *Teaching Mama.* https://teachingmama.org/prewriting-activities-for-preschoolers

The OT Toolbox. (n.d.). *Handwriting.* https://www.theottoolbox.com/handwriting

U.S. Department of Education. (n.d.). 25 Activities for reading and writing fun. *Reading Rockets.* https://www.readingrockets.org/article/25-activities-reading-and-writing-fun

AEPS®-3 Skills Matrix

APPENDIX B: AEPS-3 SKILLS MATRIX

Fine Motor

AEPS-3 Test Item

A. Reach, Grasp, and Release

AEPS-3 Test Item	Active & Outdoor Play	Arrival & Departure	Art	Bath Time	Block Play	Circle Time	Diapering, Toileting, & Handwashing	Dramatic Play	Dressing	Field Trips	Math	Meals & Snacks	Music & Movement	Nap & Sleep	Science	Sensory	Technology	Writing
1. Makes directed batting or swiping movements with each hand	B	B	B	B	B		B		B	B			B	B				
1.1 Brings hands together near midline	B	B	B		B	B	B	B	B	B		B	B					
1.2 Makes directed movements with arms	B		B	B	B	B	B		B	B			B	B		B		
FS 1.2a Child makes nondirected movements with arms.	B																	
2. Grasps pea-size object	B					B	B	B	B	B	B	B						
FS 2a Child grasps pea-size object with either hand, using tip of index finger and thumb with hand and/or arm resting on surface for support. Thumb is to side of index finger (inferior pincer grasp).																		
2.1 Grasps hand-size object	B	B	B	B	B	B	B	B	B	B	B	B	B			B		B
FS 2.1a Child grasps hand-size object with either hand, holding object at base of index finger and thumb.																		
2.2 Grasps small cylindrical object								B		B	B	B	B			B		B
2.3 Grasps pea-size object using fingers in raking or scratching movement								B			B	B				B		
2.4 Grasps hand-size object using whole hand			B		B			B		B	B	B	B			B		
FS 2.4a Child grasps hand-size object with either hand, holding object on side of hand near little finger and against palm. Thumb is not holding object (ulnar palmar grasp).																		
FS 2.4b Child briefly holds object placed in either hand.																		
3. Stacks objects	B	B			B	B	B	B	B	B	B	B	B					
FS 3a Child places small object on top of another small object with or without releasing it.																		
3.1 Releases object into targeted space	B	B	B	B	B	B		B		B	B		B			B		
FS 3.1a Child uses either hand to release handheld object onto or into large target while resting hand.																		

APPENDIX B: AEPS-3 SKILLS MATRIX

Fine Motor (continued)

AEPS-3 Test Item	AEPS-3 Curriculum Routine/Activity																	
	Active & Outdoor Play	Arrival & Departure	Art	Bath Time	Block Play	Circle Time	Diapering, Toileting, & Handwashing	Dramatic Play	Dressing	Field Trips	Math	Meals & Snacks	Music & Movement	Nap & Sleep	Science	Sensory	Technology	Writing
3.2 Releases object into nondefined space																		
FS 3.2a Child releases handheld object with either hand by pushing or pulling object against surface.	B	B	B	B	B			B	B	B			B			B		
B. Functional Skill Use																		
1. Activates object with finger																		
FS 1a Child touches or attempts to manipulate button, key, or switch to activate mechanical toy.	B	B					B	B	B	B	B	B	B	B		B		
FS 1b Child touches switch or other part of mechanical toy that produces movement or sound (e.g., child touches tail of toy animal that wags when wound up).	G	G					G	G		G	G	G	G		G	G	G	
1.1 Uses finger to point or touch																		
FS 1.1a Child isolates own index finger by pointing or touching (not necessarily with intent).	B	B	B		B	B		B	B	B	B	B	B	B		B		B
FS 1.1b Child uses thumb or fingers to poke.																		
1.2 Uses hand to activate object	B	B			B			B		B	B		B	B		B		
1.3 Uses fingers to explore object	B	B	B		B			B	B	B	B	B	B		G	G		
2. Rotates wrist to manipulate object	G	G	G	G	G	G	G	G	G	G	G	G	G	G	G	G		
2.1 Turns object using either hand	B	B	B	B	B	B	B	B	B	B	B	B	B			B		
FS 2.1a Child turns hand and arm from palm-down position to face midline while holding object (e.g., child holds block in each hand with hands palm-down and turns them toward each other).																		
FS 2.1b Child turns wrist and arm over when not holding an object (clasps fingers together and turns wrists and hand; turns one arm and hand while examining fingers).																		
3. Manipulates object with two hands, each performing different action RS 1	G	G	G		G	G	G	G	G	G	G	G	G	G	G	G		G
3.1 Assembles toy					G						G				G			
FS 3.1a Child takes apart toy or object that has pieces.																		

APPENDIX B: AEPS-3 SKILLS MATRIX

Fine Motor *(continued)*

AEPS-3 Curriculum Routine/Activity

AEPS-3 Test Item	Active & Outdoor Play	Arrival & Departure	Art	Bath Time	Block Play	Circle Time	Diapering, Toileting, & Handwashing	Dramatic Play	Dressing	Field Trips	Math	Meals & Snacks	Music & Movement	Nap & Sleep	Science	Sensory	Technology	Writing
3.2 Aligns objects	G			G	G					G	G	G		G	G			
3.3 Fits variety of shapes into corresponding spaces																		
FS 3.3a Child places round object into corresponding space (e.g., child puts plug in drain, cup in holder, toy people in vehicles).					G						G				G			
FS 3.3b Child puts object into defined space so that object fits partially in intended space.																		
FS 3.3c Child removes variety of shapes from corresponding spaces (e.g., child removes pieces from puzzle or form board, takes plug out of tub).																		
FS 3.3d Child takes object out of defined space (e.g., child removes block from dump truck, cars from toy garage, cup and toothbrush from holder).																		
3.4 Holds object with one hand and manipulates object or produces action with other hand	B	B	B	B	B			B	B	B	B	B	B			B		
FS 3.4a Child manipulates or produces action with object while adult steadies object.	B	B	B															
3.5 Transfers object from hand to hand	B	B	B	B	B		B	B	B	B	B		B	B		B		B
C. Mechanics of Writing																		
1. Holds writing tool using three-finger grasp to write or draw RS 2	R	R	R	R		R		R		R	R				R		R	R
FS 1a Child uses three-finger grasp to hold writing tool.																		
1.1 Writes or draws using mixed strokes			G	G				G			G				G		G	G
FS 1.1a Child draws simple shapes (e.g., circle, X).																		
1.2 Writes or draws using curved lines			G	G				G			G				G		G	G
FS 1.2a Child makes circular or curved shape with writing tool.																		
1.3 Writes or draws using straight lines			G	G				G			G				G		G	G
FS 1.3a Child makes horizontal stroke with crayon, marker, or pencil.																		
FS 1.3b Child makes vertical stroke with crayon, marker, or pencil.																		
1.4 Scribbles		G	G	G				G			G				G		G	G
FS 1.4a Child makes mark on paper.																		

Assessment, Evaluation, and Programming System for Infants and Children, Third Edition (AEPS®-3), by Bricker, Dionne, Grisham, Johnson, Macy, Slentz, & Waddell. © 2022 Brookes Publishing Co. All rights reserved.

APPENDIX B: AEPS-3 SKILLS MATRIX

Fine Motor (*continued*)

AEPS-3 Test Item	Active & Outdoor Play	Arrival & Departure	Art	Bath Time	Block Play	Circle Time	Diapering, Toileting, & Handwashing	Dramatic Play	Dressing	Field Trips	Math	Meals & Snacks	Music & Movement	Nap & Sleep	Science	Sensory	Technology	Writing
D. Use of Electronic Devices																		
1. Uses finger to interact with electronic device						G					G						G	G
1.1 Uses finger to interact with simple electronic game											G						G	
1.2 Uses finger to interact with touch screen																		
FS 1.2a Child uses hand or part of hand to interact with touch screen.		B																

APPENDIX B: AEPS-3 SKILLS MATRIX

Gross Motor

AEPS-3 Test Item

AEPS-3 Curriculum Routine/Activity

AEPS-3 Test Item	Active & Outdoor Play	Arrival & Departure	Art	Bath Time	Block Play	Circle Time	Diapering, Toileting, & Handwashing	Dramatic Play	Dressing	Field Trips	Math	Meals & Snacks	Music & Movement	Nap & Sleep	Science	Sensory	Technology	Writing
A. Body Control and Weight Transfer																		
1. Turns head, moves arms, and kicks legs independently of each other	B	B			B		B		B	B			B			B		
1.1 Kicks legs	B			B	B		B		B	B			B					
FS 1.1a Child kicks both legs together.																		
1.2 Waves arms	B	B		B	B				B	B			B			B		
1.3 Turns head side to side	B			B	B				B	B			B	B		B		
2. Puts weight on one hand or arm while reaching with opposite hand	B	B			B					B		B				B		
2.1 Remains propped on extended arms with head lifted	B				B					B		B				B		
FS 2.1a Child assumes swimming posture with weight primarily on abdomen with arms and legs stretched out above weight-bearing surface.																		
2.2 Remains propped on nonextended forearms with head lifted	B								B	B		B				B		
FS 2.2a Child lifts head and shoulders off surface when lying on stomach.																		
FS 2.2b Child uses arms to propel body backward when lying on stomach.																		
FS 2.2c Child lifts head off surface when lying on stomach.																		
3. Rolls from back to stomach		B			B				B	B				B				
3.1 Rolls from stomach to back					B					B				B				
3.2 Rolls from back or stomach to side		B			B				B	B				B				
FS 3.2a Child rolls from side to back.																		
FS 3.2b When lying on stomach or back, child positions self on verge of rolling in direction of one extended arm with face turned toward extended arm.																		

APPENDIX B: AEPS-3 SKILLS MATRIX

Gross Motor (*continued*)

AEPS-3 Curriculum Routine/Activity

AEPS-3 Test Item	Active & Outdoor Play	Arrival & Departure	Art	Bath Time	Block Play	Circle Time	Diapering, Toileting, & Handwashing	Dramatic Play	Dressing	Field Trips	Math	Meals & Snacks	Music & Movement	Nap & Sleep	Science	Sensory	Technology	Writing
4. Assumes balanced sitting position	B	B		B	B	B		B	B	B		B	B			B		B
FS 4a When standing, child lowers body, bends knees, and shifts weight backward to sitting position.																		
FS 4b When on hands and knees, child rotates body while extending and pushing with arms and shifts weight to sitting position.																		
FS 4c When on hands and knees, child shifts weight to lean back and sit on legs, then extends legs out in front to sit on buttocks.																		
FS 4d When in side-lying position, child moves to sitting position by bending at waist while extending and pushing with arms, bearing weight on hips to raise body off ground.																		
FS 4e When sitting, child leans to left and right, then regains balanced, upright sitting position.																		
4.1 Assumes hands-and-knees position from sitting	B	B		B	B	B				B			B			B		
4.2 Regains balanced, upright sitting position after reaching across body	B	B		B	B	B				B		B	B			B		
4.3 Regains balanced, upright sitting position after leaning left, right, and forward	B	B		B	B	B				B		B	B			B		
FS 4.3a When sitting, child leans forward, then regains balanced, upright sitting position.																		
4.4 Sits balanced without support	B	B	B	B	B	B		B	B	B		B	B			B		B
4.5 Sits balanced using hands for support	B	B	B	B	B	B		B	B	B			B					
4.6 Holds head in midline when sitting supported	B	B	B	B	B			B	B	B		B	B			B		B
FS 4.6a When sitting in supported position, child lifts head momentarily.																		
FS 4.6b When sitting in supported position, child holds upper back straight.																		
5. Gets out of chair	B	B	B					B	B	B	B	B	B					B
5.1 Sits down in chair	B	B	B					B	B	B	B	B						B
5.2 Maintains sitting position in chair	B	B	B					B	B	B	B	B						B

Assessment, Evaluation, and Programming System for Infants and Children, Third Edition (AEPS®-3), by Bricker, Dionne, Grisham, Johnson, Macy, Slentz, & Waddell. © 2022 Brookes Publishing Co. All rights reserved.

APPENDIX B: AEPS-3 SKILLS MATRIX

Gross Motor (*continued*)

AEPS-3 Test Item

B. Movement and Coordination

AEPS-3 Test Item	Active & Outdoor Play	Arrival & Departure	Art	Bath Time	Block Play	Circle Time	Diapering, Toileting, & Handwashing	Dramatic Play	Dressing	Field Trips	Math	Meals & Snacks	Music & Movement	Nap & Sleep	Science	Sensory	Technology	Writing
1. Creeps forward using alternating arm and leg movements	B																	
FS 1a Child reaches with one arm while maintaining weight on other hand and both knees.		B	B		B					B		B						
FS 1b Child moves under obstacles.																		
1.1 Rocks while in creeping position	B	B			B					B								
1.2 Assumes creeping position	B	B			B					B								
1.3 Crawls forward on stomach	B	B			B					B		B				B		
1.4 Pivots on stomach	B	B			B					B						B		
2. Stoops and regains balanced standing position	B	B	B		B	B		B	B	B			B			B		
FS 2a Child regains standing position after squatting or stooping by using support (e.g., furniture, wall, person).												B						
2.1 Rises from sitting to standing position	B	B	B		B	B		B	B	B		B	B			B		
FS 2.1a Child leans forward from sitting position, bears weight on hands, and shifts weight from buttocks to knees.																		
2.2 Stands unsupported	B	B	B		B			B	B	B	B		B			B		
FS 2.2a Child stands bearing own full weight with one-hand support.																		
FS 2.2b Child stands bearing own full weight with two-hand support.																		
2.3 Pulls to standing position	B	B			B			B	B	B		B		B		B		
FS 2.3a Child uses support to pull up one foot from kneeling position by shifting weight to one foot and one knee.																		
2.4 Pulls to kneeling position					B			B					B	B		B		

Assessment, Evaluation, and Programming System for Infants and Children, Third Edition (AEPS®-3), by Bricker, Dionne, Grisham, Johnson, Macy, Slentz, & Waddell. © 2022 Brookes Publishing Co. All rights reserved.

APPENDIX B: AEPS-3 SKILLS MATRIX

Gross Motor (continued)

AEPS-3 Curriculum Routine/Activity

AEPS-3 Test Item	Active & Outdoor Play	Arrival & Departure	Art	Bath Time	Block Play	Circle Time	Diapering, Toileting, & Handwashing	Dramatic Play	Dressing	Field Trips	Math	Meals & Snacks	Music & Movement	Nap & Sleep	Science	Sensory	Technology	Writing
3. Walks avoiding people, furniture, or objects	G	G	G		G	G	G	G	G	G		G	G	G	G			G
FS 3.1a Child walks unsupported for short distance and changes direction without falling.	B	B	B		B	B	B	B	B	B		B	B	B				B
FS 3.1b Child walks unsupported for short distance without falling.	G	G	G		G	G	G	B	B			G	G	G	G		G	G
3.2 Walks with one-hand support	B	B	B		B	B	B	B	B	B		B	B	B				B
3.3 Walks with two-hand support	B	B	B		B	B	B	B	B	B		B	B	B				B
3.4 Cruises	B	B	B		B					B		B						
FS 3.4a Child rises from sitting to standing position with support.																		
4. Alternates feet going up and down stairs	G	G								G	G				G	G		G
FS 4a Child walks up and down stairs without support. Child does not alternate feet.																		
4.1 Walks up and down stairs using support	G	G								G	G				G	G		G
FS 4.1a Child walks up stairs holding rail or wall with one hand.																		
FS 4.1b Child walks up stairs using two-hand support.																		
4.2 Moves up and down stairs	G	G					G			G	G				G	G		G
FS 4.2a Child moves up stairs.																		
FS 4.2b Child climbs onto adult-size furniture (e.g., chair, couch, bed) or low play structure.	G						G											
4.3 Gets up and down from low structure	G	G	G		G	G	G			G			G		G	G		G
FS 4.3a Child moves over obstacles.																		
FS 4.3b Child climbs onto low, stable structure (e.g., low step, raised platform).																		
FS 4.3c Child climbs down from adult-size furniture (e.g., chair, couch, bed) or low play structure.																		
5. Runs while avoiding people, furniture, or other objects	G	G								G					G			
FS 5a Child turns corner while running.																		
FS 5b Child stops and starts again while running.																		

APPENDIX B: AEPS-3 SKILLS MATRIX

Gross Motor (continued)

AEPS-3 Curriculum Routine/Activity

AEPS-3 Test Item	Active & Outdoor Play	Arrival & Departure	Art	Bath Time	Block Play	Circle Time	Diapering, Toileting, & Handwashing	Dramatic Play	Dressing	Field Trips	Math	Meals & Snacks	Music & Movement	Nap & Sleep	Science	Sensory	Technology	Writing
5.1 Runs	G	G								G					G		G	
5.2 Walks fast	G	G		G			G			G					G		G	
6. Jumps forward RS 3	G			G						G			G		G		G	
FS 6a Child jumps forward, landing with one foot at a time.																		
6.1 Jumps up and down in place	G									G	G		G		G		G	
FS 6.1a Child bends at knees, rises up on feet or toes, and jumps up with one foot leading.																		
FS 6.1b Child bends at knees and rises up on toes while feet remain on ground (i.e., child "jumps up" without feet leaving ground).																		
6.2 Jumps down from low structure	G									G					G			
FS 6.2a Child step-jumps or hops (leads with one foot) from low, stable structure to supporting surface.																		
6.3 Jumps down with support	B									B								
7. Skips RS 4	R	R								R			R		R	R	R	
7.1 Gallops	R	R								R	R		R		R	R	R	
7.2 Hops forward on one foot	R	R		R						R	R		R		R	R	R	R
FS 7.2a Child balances on one foot.																		
C. Active Play																		
1. Swings bat, club, or stick to strike stationary object	R									R					R	R		
1.1 Bounces ball with one hand	R									R	R				R	R		
1.2 Bounces ball with two hands	G									G	G				G	G		
1.3 Catches ball	G									G	G				G	G		
FS 1.3a When large object is tossed to child, child stretches out two arms in front.																		

(page 9 of 42)

APPENDIX B: AEPS-3 SKILLS MATRIX

Gross Motor (continued)

AEPS-3 Test Item — AEPS-3 Curriculum Routine/Activity

AEPS-3 Test Item	Active & Outdoor Play	Arrival & Departure	Art	Bath Time	Block Play	Circle Time	Diapering, Toileting, & Handwashing	Dramatic Play	Dressing	Field Trips	Math	Meals & Snacks	Music & Movement	Nap & Sleep	Science	Sensory	Technology	Writing
1.4 Kicks ball	G														G	G		
FS 1.4a When object is in front of child's feet, child walks into object and moves object forward (e.g., child walks into large foam block to move it forward).																		
FS 1.4b Child kicks ball or similar object while holding onto support (e.g., adult's leg, wall, railing).																		
1.5 Throws ball overhand at target with one hand	G									G	G				G	G		
1.6 Throws or rolls ball at target with two hands	B				B					B	B				B	B		
FS 1.6a Child throws object forward with one or two hands, not necessarily at target.	G				G					G	G				G	G		
FS 1.6b Child flings object with one hand.																		
FS 1.6c Child rolls ball, not necessarily at target.																		
FS 1.6d Child moves ball forward (e.g., bats at it).																		
2. Uses hands to hang on play equipment with bars `RS 5`	R									R					R			
2.1 Moves swing back and forth	R									R	R							
2.2 Climbs play equipment	G									G					G			
FS 2.2a Child climbs play equipment without alternating arms and legs in coordinated fashion.																		
FS 2.2b Child moves up incline.																		
2.3 Goes down small slide	G									G	G				G			
FS 2.3a Child moves down incline.																		
3. Rides and steers bicycle	R									R					R			
3.1 Pedals and steers bicycle with training wheels	G									G					G			
3.2 Pedals and steers tricycle	G									G					G			
FS 3.2a While sitting on tricycle with feet on pedals, child pedals tricycle forward and backward.																		

APPENDIX B: AEPS-3 SKILLS MATRIX

Gross Motor (*continued*)

AEPS-3 Test Item	Active & Outdoor Play	Arrival & Departure	Art	Bath Time	Block Play	Circle Time	Diapering, Toileting, & Handwashing	Dramatic Play	Dressing	Field Trips	Math	Meals & Snacks	Music & Movement	Nap & Sleep	Science	Sensory	Technology	Writing
3.3 Pushes riding toy with feet while steering	B							B		B								
FS 3.3a While sitting on riding toy with feet on surface, child pushes forward with feet.	G							G		G								
FS 3.3b While sitting on riding toy with feet on surface, child pushes backward with feet.																		
3.4 Sits on riding toy or in wagon while in motion	B	B						B		B								

AEPS-3 Curriculum Routine/Activity

Assessment, Evaluation, and Programming System for Infants and Children, Third Edition (AEPS®-3), by Bricker, Dionne, Grisham, Johnson, Macy, Slentz, & Waddell. © 2022 Brookes Publishing Co. All rights reserved.

APPENDIX B: AEPS-3 SKILLS MATRIX

Adaptive

AEPS-3 Test Item	AEPS-3 Curriculum Routine/Activity																	
	Active & Outdoor Play	Arrival & Departure	Art	Bath Time	Block Play	Circle Time	Diapering, Toileting, & Handwashing	Dramatic Play	Dressing	Field Trips	Math	Meals & Snacks	Music & Movement	Nap & Sleep	Science	Sensory	Technology	Writing
A. Eating and Drinking																		
1. Uses lips to take semisolid foods off eating utensil										B		B						
1.1 Swallows semisolid foods										B		B						
1.2 Swallows liquids										B		B		B				
2. Eats foods from variety of food groups with variety of textures										G		G			G	G		
2.1 Eats hard and chewy foods										G		G			G	G		
2.2 Eats crisp foods										B		B			B	B		
2.3 Eats soft and dissolvable foods										B		B				B		
3. Eats with eating utensils										G		G			G	G		
3.1 Brings food to mouth with eating utensil										R		R			R	R		
FS 3.1a Child eats by spearing food with utensil (e.g., fork, chopsticks).																		
FS 3.1b Child eats by scooping food with utensil (e.g., spoon, naan, fork, tortilla).																		
3.2 Eats with fingers										B		B				B		
3.3 Accepts food presented on eating utensils										B		B						
4. Drinks from open-mouth container										G		G			G	G		
4.1 Drinks from cup with spouted lid	B									B		B		B				
4.2 Drinks from container held by adult	B									B		B		B		B		
FS 4.2a Child drinks from cup using some lip closure on rim of container.																		

Assessment, Evaluation, and Programming System for Infants and Children, Third Edition (AEPS®-3), by Bricker, Dionne, Grisham, Johnson, Macy, Slentz, & Waddell. © 2022 Brookes Publishing Co. All rights reserved.

APPENDIX B: AEPS-3 SKILLS MATRIX

Adaptive (continued)

AEPS-3 Test Item	Active & Outdoor Play	Arrival & Departure	Art	Bath Time	Block Play	Circle Time	Diapering, Toileting, & Handwashing	Dramatic Play	Dressing	Field Trips	Math	Meals & Snacks	Music & Movement	Nap & Sleep	Science	Sensory	Technology	Writing
5. Uses culturally appropriate social dining skills (RS 6)								R		R		R				G		
5.1 Puts appropriate amount of food in mouth, chews, and swallows before taking another bite										G		G				R		
5.2 Takes in appropriate amount of liquid and returns cup to surface										R		R				G		
6. Prepares food for eating										G		G				G		
6.1 Pours liquid into variety of containers				G						R		R			G	G		
6.2 Serves food with utensil										G		G			G	G		
B. Personal Care Routines																		
1. Carries out all toileting functions	G						R			R								
1.1 Indicates need to use toilet	G	G		G			G			G				G				
1.2 Has bowel and bladder control	G	G		G			G			G				G				
FS 1.2a Child sits on toilet or potty chair regularly and accomplishes bowel and bladder functions some of the time.																		
FS 1.2b Child sits on toilet or potty chair regularly without accomplishing bowel or bladder function.																		
1.3 Indicates awareness of soiled and wet pants or diapers	G	G					G			G				G				
2. Bathes and dries self				R						R						R		
FS 2a Child cooperates with bathing.																		
2.1 Washes and dries face			G	G														
2.2 Washes and dries hands			G				G					G		G	G	G		G

APPENDIX B: AEPS-3 SKILLS MATRIX

Adaptive (continued)

AEPS-3 Curriculum Routine/Activity

AEPS-3 Test Item	Active & Outdoor Play	Arrival & Departure	Art	Bath Time	Block Play	Circle Time	Diapering, Toileting, & Handwashing	Dramatic Play	Dressing	Field Trips	Math	Meals & Snacks	Music & Movement	Nap & Sleep	Science	Sensory	Technology	Writing
3. Completes all steps for personal hygiene, including brushing teeth, combing hair, and wiping nose				R					R	R		R		R		R		
FS 3a Child completes all steps for brushing teeth.																		
FS 3b Child completes all steps for brushing or combing hair.																		
FS 3c Child completes all steps for using tissue to clean nose.																		
3.1 Completes some steps to brush teeth, comb hair, and wipe nose				G								G		G		G		
FS 3.1a Child completes some steps for using tissue to clean nose.																		
FS 3.1a.1 Child wipes nose.																		
FS 3.1a.2 Child blows nose when adult wipes it.																		
FS 3.1a.3 Child tolerates adult wiping nose.																		
FS 3.1b Child completes some steps for brushing teeth.																		
FS 3.1b.1 Child moves toothbrush around in mouth with bristles briefly contacting teeth.																		
FS 3.1b.2 Child puts toothbrush in mouth and chews on bristles.																		
FS 3.1b.3 Child tolerates adult lightly brushing teeth and gums.																		
FS 3.1b.4 Child tolerates rubber tip of toothbrush or adult's finger covered with cloth moving over gums and teeth.																		
FS 3.1b.5 Child opens mouth on request.																		
FS 3.1c Child completes some steps for brushing or combing hair.																		
FS 3.1c.1 Child cooperates when adult brushes or combs hair.																		
C. Dressing and Undressing																		
1. Undresses self by removing all clothing		R		R				R	R					R		R		
1.1 Unfastens clothing				R			R	R	R							R		R
1.2 Takes off pullover clothing over head																		
FS 1.2a Child removes pullover clothing part way.		G	G	G				G	G			G		G		G		G
FS 1.2b Child indicates desire to remove pullover clothing.		R	R	R				R	R			R		R		R		R

Assessment, Evaluation, and Programming System for Infants and Children, Third Edition (AEPS®-3), by Bricker, Dionne, Grisham, Johnson, Macy, Slentz, & Waddell. © 2022 Brookes Publishing Co. All rights reserved.

APPENDIX B: AEPS-3 SKILLS MATRIX

Adaptive (continued)

AEPS-3 Test Item	Active & Outdoor Play	Arrival & Departure	Art	Bath Time	Block Play	Circle Time	Diapering, Toileting, & Handwashing	Dramatic Play	Dressing	Field Trips	Math	Meals & Snacks	Music & Movement	Nap & Sleep	Science	Sensory	Technology	Writing
1.3 Takes off front-opening coat, jacket, or shirt		G	G	G				G	G						G	G		G
FS 1.3a Child removes coat, jacket, or shirt part way.																		
FS 1.3b Child indicates desire to remove coat, jacket, or shirt.																		
1.4 Takes off pants				G			G	G	G					G		G		
FS 1.4a Child removes pants part way.																		
FS 1.4b Child indicates desire to remove pants.																		
1.5 Takes off shoes	B							B	B					B				
FS 1.5a Child removes shoes part way.																		
FS 1.5b Child indicates desire to remove shoes.																		
1.6 Takes off socks	B							B	B	B				B				
FS 1.6a Child removes socks part way.																		
FS 1.6b Child indicates desire to remove socks.																		
1.7 Takes off hat	B							B	B	B								
FS 1.7a Child removes hat part way.																		
FS 1.7b Child indicates desire to remove hat.																		
2. Selects appropriate clothing and dresses self	R	R	R	R				R	R					R		R		R
2.1 Fastens clothing	R	R	R	R					R									
FS 2.1a Child assists in fastening clothing.																		
2.2 Puts on front-opening clothing		G	G					G	G							G		G
FS 2.2a Child assists in putting on front-opening clothing.																		
2.3 Puts on pullover clothing		G	G	G			G	G	G					G		G		G
FS 2.3a Child assists in putting on pullover clothing.																		
2.4 Puts on pull-up clothing		G	G	G			G	G	G					G		G		
FS 2.4a Child assists in putting on pull-up clothing.																		

Adaptive (continued)

AEPS-3 Test Item	Active & Outdoor Play	Arrival & Departure	Art	Bath Time	Block Play	Circle Time	Diapering, Toileting, & Handwashing	Dramatic Play	Dressing	Field Trips	Math	Meals & Snacks	Music & Movement	Nap & Sleep	Science	Sensory	Technology	Writing
2.5 Puts on socks	G	G		G				G	G					G		G		
FS 2.5a Child tries to put on socks.																		
2.6 Puts on shoes		G						G	G						G	G		
FS 2.6a Child tries to put on shoes.																		
D. Personal Safety																		
1. Takes independent action to alleviate distress, discomfort, and pain	G	G			G	G	G	G	G	G	G	G	G			G		
1.1 Communicates internal distress, discomfort, or pain to adult	G	G		G	G	G	G	G	G	G	G	G	G			G		
2. Complies with common home and community safety rules	R	R	R	R	R		R	R		R	R	R	R	R	R	R	R	R
2.1 Complies with graphic or written warning signs and symbols	R	R	R	R	R					R	R			R	R	R	R	R
3. Takes independent action when faced with dangerous conditions or substances	R	R					R			R		R		R	R	R		
3.1 Responds appropriately to warnings of dangerous conditions or substances	G	G			R		G			G		G			G	G		
4. Recognizes and reports information regarding safety RS 7													R		R			
4.1 States or produces personal information to promote/maintain personal safety	R	R			R		R	R		R					R	R		R
4.2 Reports inappropriate events, actions, or language by others	R	R	R	R	R	R	R	R		R		R	R		R	R	R	R

Assessment, Evaluation, and Programming System for Infants and Children, Third Edition (AEPS®-3), by Bricker, Dionne, Grisham, Johnson, Macy, Slentz, & Waddell. © 2022 Brookes Publishing Co. All rights reserved.

APPENDIX B: AEPS-3 SKILLS MATRIX

Social-Emotional

A. Interactions with Adults

AEPS-3 Test Item	Active & Outdoor Play	Arrival & Departure	Art	Bath Time	Block Play	Circle Time	Diapering, Toileting, & Handwashing	Dramatic Play	Dressing	Field Trips	Math	Meals & Snacks	Music & Movement	Nap & Sleep	Science	Sensory	Technology	Writing
1. Initiates positive social behavior toward familiar adult	B	B	B	B	B	B	B			B		B	B	B				
1.1 Responds appropriately to familiar adult's affective tone	B	B	B	B	B	B	B			B		B	B	B				
1.2 Responds to familiar adult's positive social behavior	B	B	B	B	B	B	B			B		B	B					
FS 1.2a Child responds to familiar adult's social behavior by maintaining or continuing interaction (e.g., child knocks down block tower that adult built and waits for or helps adult to rebuild tower).																		
FS 1.2b Child shows interest in communication from familiar adult (e.g., child stops crying when adult talks soothingly, increases motor action when adult speaks playfully, looks at adult who is talking, watches adult as adult sings).																		
2. Maintains social interaction with familiar adult	B	B	B		B		B		B	B	B	B	B					
FS 2a Child responds to communication from familiar adult and maintains interaction (e.g., adult asks child to tell about pictures in book, and child makes vocalizations about pictures; then adult supplies words for pictures, and child vocalizes again or points to picture).																		
2.1 Initiates simple social interaction with familiar adult	B	B	B	B	B	B	B		B	B	B	B	B	B				
FS 2.1a Child assumes active role in drawing attention of or getting close to familiar adult to continue social game (e.g., child crawls after father, tugs at grandma's clothes, or climbs into mother's lap).																		
2.2 Repeats part of interactive game or action in order to continue game or action	B		B	B	B	B		B	B	B	B	B	B					
2.3 Responds to familiar game or action	B		B	B	B	B		B	B	B	B							
FS 2.3a Child interacts with familiar adult in vocally similar manner by matching patterns of vocal exchanges (e.g., child gurgles when adult gurgles, child stops vocalizing when adult stops vocalizing, child varies length of vocalizations as function of length of adult's verbalizations, child changes rhythm of vocalizations when adult sings to child).																		

Assessment, Evaluation, and Programming System for Infants and Children, Third Edition (AEPS®-3), by Bricker, Dionne, Grisham, Johnson, Macy, Slentz, & Waddell. © 2022 Brookes Publishing Co. All rights reserved.

APPENDIX B: AEPS-3 SKILLS MATRIX

Social-Emotional (*continued*)

AEPS-3 Test Item	Active & Outdoor Play	Arrival & Departure	Art	Bath Time	Block Play	Circle Time	Diapering, Toileting, & Handwashing	Dramatic Play	Dressing	Field Trips	Math	Meals & Snacks	Music & Movement	Nap & Sleep	Science	Sensory	Technology	Writing
3. Participates in familiar social routines with caregivers				G								G	G	G			G	
3.1 Initiates next step of familiar social routine		G	G	G		G	G		G			G	G	G	G			G
3.2 Follows familiar social routines with familiar adults		G	G	G	G	G	G	G	G	G		G	G	G	G			G
FS 3.2a Child responds to established social routines.																		
B. Social-Emotional Expression and Regulation																		
1. Responds appropriately to others' emotions	G	G		G	G	G	G	G		G		G						G
FS 1a Child responds appropriately to familiar adult's affect.																		
FS 1b Child displays affection toward familiar adult.																		
FS 1c Child returns affection modeled by adult.																		
FS 1d Child smiles in response to familiar adult.																		
FS 1e Child reacts differently to familiar and unfamiliar adults.																		
FS 1f Child stops crying in response to familiar adult (e.g., approach, vocalization, smile, appearance).																		
1.1 Identifies/labels emotions in others	G	G		G	G	G	G	G		G			G			G	G	G
1.2 Identifies/labels own emotions	G	G		G	G	G	G	G		G			G			G	G	G
2. Uses appropriate strategies to manage emotional states	G	G		G			G	G		G		G	G	G	G	G		
FS 2a Child shows awareness of external physical needs such as being cold, hot, dirty, wet, or hurt. Child demonstrates discomfort by frowning or whining while wearing dirty or wet clothes.																		
FS 2b Child uses pacifier, own thumb, or adult's finger for nonnutritive sucking.																		
FS 2c Child can be soothed by familiar adult caregiver.																		
2.1 Responds appropriately to soothing by peer	G	G			G	G		G		G			G		G	G		G

APPENDIX B: AEPS-3 SKILLS MATRIX

Social-Emotional (*continued*)

AEPS-3 Test Item	Active & Outdoor Play	Arrival & Departure	Art	Bath Time	Block Play	Circle Time	Diapering, Toileting, & Handwashing	Dramatic Play	Dressing	Field Trips	Math	Meals & Snacks	Music & Movement	Nap & Sleep	Science	Sensory	Technology	Writing
2.2 Seeks comfort, closeness, or physical contact from familiar adult	B	B				B	B		B	B		B	B	B		B		
FS 2.2a Child responds in attempt to prolong positive interaction (e.g., when mother looks away from child, child touches mother's face to get her to look back again).																		
FS 2.2b Child uses familiar adults for comfort, closeness, or physical contact.																		
FS 2.2c Child differentiates between familiar and unfamiliar adults for comfort, closeness, or physical contact.																		
2.3 Responds appropriately to soothing by adult	B	B			B	B	B		B	B		B	B	B		B		
FS 2.3a Child shows interest in familiar adult's social behavior (e.g., child looks at adult when adult plays Peekaboo or smiles when adult peeks around corner).																		
3. Makes positive statements about self or accomplishments	G	G	G	G	G	G	G	G	G	G	G	G	G	G	G	G	G	G
3.1 Explains or shows others how to do tasks mastered	R	R	R	R	R	R	R	R	R	R	R	R	G	R	R	R	R	R
3.2 Shares accomplishment with familiar caregiver	G	G	G	G	G	G	G	G	G	G	G	G	G	G	G	G	G	G
C. Interactions with Peers																		
1. Maintains interaction with peer	G	G	G		G	G	G	G		G	G	G	G	G	G	G	G	G
1.1 Initiates social behavior toward peer	G	G	G		G		G	G		G	G	G	G	G	G	G	G	G
1.2 Responds appropriately to peer social behavior	G	G	G			G	G	G		G	G	G	G	G	G	G	G	G
FS 1.2a Child shows interest in peer's social behavior (e.g., child looks at toy offered by peer, child waves arms and smiles while watching peer on swing).																		

APPENDIX B: AEPS-3 SKILLS MATRIX

Social-Emotional (*continued*)

AEPS-3 Test Item / AEPS-3 Curriculum Routine/Activity

AEPS-3 Test Item	Active & Outdoor Play	Arrival & Departure	Art	Bath Time	Block Play	Circle Time	Diapering, Toileting, & Handwashing	Dramatic Play	Dressing	Field Trips	Math	Meals & Snacks	Music & Movement	Nap & Sleep	Science	Sensory	Technology	Writing
1.3 Plays near one or two peers	B	B			B			B		B	B		B			B		B
FS 1.3a Child plays near one or two peers in presence of familiar adult (e.g., child plays with Legos in proximity of teacher reading a story to a peer).																		
FS 1.3b Child observes peers or siblings (e.g., child watches older sibling playing with friend).																		
FS 1.3c Child entertains self by playing appropriately with toys.																		
2. Plans and acts out recognizable event, theme, or storyline in imaginary play	R																	
FS 2a Child uses action associated with common object, but object is absent; focus of child's play is on action rather than imaginary object (e.g., child kicks imaginary ball, eats imaginary cookie, throws imaginary ball).				R	R			R	R									
2.1 Enacts roles or identities in imaginary play	R			R				R	R									
FS 2.1a Child enacts typical action of familiar character or animal by using real object associated with character or animal (e.g., child sits in baby brother's chair and pretends to cry, child takes mother's keys and pretends to go bye-bye).																		
FS 2.1b Child enacts imaginary events related to daily routine activities (e.g., child pretends to sleep on bed, drink from empty cup).																		
2.2 Uses imaginary props in play	R				R			R		R								
FS 2.2a Child uses imaginary objects in play.																		
3. Maintains cooperative activity [RS 8]	R		R	R	R			R		R	R						R	
3.1 Initiates cooperative activity	G		G		G			G	G	G							G	
3.2 Joins others in cooperative activity	G		G		G			G	G	G	G				G		G	
3.3 Shares or exchanges objects			G		G			G	G	G			G					G
4. Maintains engagement in games with rules	R							R		R	R	R	R				R	
4.1 Knows and follows game rules	R							R		R	R	R	R				R	
4.2 Participates in game	R			R				R		R	R	R	R				R	

Assessment, Evaluation, and Programming System for Infants and Children, Third Edition (AEPS®3), by Bricker, Dionne, Grisham, Johnson, Macy, Slentz, & Waddell. © 2022 Brookes Publishing Co. All rights reserved.

APPENDIX B: AEPS-3 SKILLS MATRIX

Social-Emotional (continued)

AEPS-3 Test Item

D. Independent and Group Participation

AEPS-3 Test Item	Active & Outdoor Play	Arrival & Departure	Art	Bath Time	Block Play	Circle Time	Diapering, Toileting, & Handwashing	Dramatic Play	Dressing	Field Trips	Math	Meals & Snacks	Music & Movement	Nap & Sleep	Science	Sensory	Technology	Writing
1. Interacts appropriately with others during small-group activities *(RS 9)*	G	G	G		G	G		G		G	G	G	G		G	G		G
1.1 Interacts appropriately with materials during small-group activities		G	G	G	G	G		G		G	G	G	G		G	G	G	G
1.2 Responds appropriately to directions during small-group activities	G	G	G	G	G	G		G		G	G	G	G		G	G	G	G
1.3 Remains with group during small-group activities	G		G	G		G				G	G	G	G		G	G	G	G
2. Interacts appropriately with others during large-group activities *(RS 10)*	G				G	G				G	G	G	G		G	G	G	G
2.1 Interacts appropriately with materials during large-group activities						G				G	G	G	G	G	G	G	G	G
2.2 Responds appropriately to directions during large-group activities	G					G				G	G	G	G		G	G	G	G
2.3 Remains with group during large-group activities	G			G	G	G				G	G	G	G		G	G		G
3. Initiates and completes independent activities *(RS 11)*	G	G	G		G	G	G	G	G	G	G	G	G	G			G	B
3.1 Responds to request to finish activity			B		B		G	B	G	B	B			G			G	G
3.2 Responds to request to begin activity	G	G	G	G	G		G	G	G	G	G	G		G			G	G
3.3 Entertains self by playing with toys	B	B	B	B	B			B		B	B			B				B
4. Resolves conflicts using negotiation *(RS 12)*	G	G	G		G	G	G	G		G	G	G	G	G	G		G	G
4.1 Uses strategies to resolve conflicts	G	B						B					B				G	G
4.2 Claims and defends possessions	B	G	G		B			G		B	B	B	B		G			B

APPENDIX B: AEPS-3 SKILLS MATRIX

Social-Emotional (continued)

AEPS-3 Test Item

AEPS-3 Curriculum Routine/Activity

E. Meeting Social Expectations

AEPS-3 Test Item		Active & Outdoor Play	Arrival & Departure	Art	Bath Time	Block Play	Circle Time	Diapering, Toileting, & Handwashing	Dramatic Play	Dressing	Field Trips	Math	Meals & Snacks	Music & Movement	Nap & Sleep	Science	Sensory	Technology	Writing
1. Meets observable physical needs in socially appropriate ways	RS 13	R	R														G		
1.1 Meets internal physical needs of hunger and thirst		G			R	R	R	R	G	R	R	R	R	R	R	R	R		
2. Meets accepted social norms in community settings		R	R			G	R	R	R	R	G	R	G	R	R	R	R		
2.1 Meets behavioral expectations in familiar environments		G	G	G	G	R	G	G	G		R	G	R	R	G	R	G	G	R
2.2 Adjusts behavior based on feedback from others or environment		G	G	G	G	G	G	G	G		G	G	G	G	G		G	G	R
FS 2.2a Child understands how own behavior affects others.																			
3. Follows context-specific rules	RS 14	R	R		R	R	R	G	R		R	G	R	R	R	R	R		R
3.1 Seeks adult permission when appropriate		G	G	G				G		G	G			G				G	
3.2 Follows established social rules in familiar environments		G	G	G			G	G	R	G	G	G	G	G	G		G		G
4. Relates identifying information about self	RS 15	R	R		R		R		R		R		R		R	R		R	R
4.1 States birthday					R				R				R		R	R	R		R
4.2 States age							G		G									G	
4.3 Provides given name or nickname of self and others			G	G			G		G									G	

(page 22 of 42)

APPENDIX B: AEPS-3 SKILLS MATRIX

Social-Communication

AEPS-3 Test Item — A. Early Social Communication

AEPS-3 Test Item	Active & Outdoor Play	Arrival & Departure	Art	Bath Time	Block Play	Circle Time	Diapering, Toileting, & Handwashing	Dramatic Play	Dressing	Field Trips	Math	Meals & Snacks	Music & Movement	Nap & Sleep	Science	Sensory	Technology	Writing
1. Turns and looks toward person speaking																		
FS 1a Child turns and looks toward noise-producing object.	B	B	B	B	B	B	B	B	B	B		B	B			B		
1.1 Quiets to familiar voice		B	B	B	B	B	B		B	B		B	B	B				
2. Produces speech sounds		B	B	B	B	B	B	B	B	B		B	B			B		B
2.1 Coos and gurgles		B	B	B	B	B	B		B	B		B	B			B		
3. Engages in vocal exchanges FS 3a Child uses behaviors similar to communication skills (e.g., while awake in crib, child uses vocalizations, gestures, and expressions similar to those used to communicate).	B	B	B	B	B	B	B	B	B	B		B	B			B		
3.1 Vocalizes to another person expressing positive affective state	B	B	B	B	B	B	B	B	B	B		B	B			B		
3.2 Vocalizes to another person expressing negative affective state	B	B	B	B	B	B	B	B	B	B		B	B			B		
4. Uses intentional gestures, vocalizations, and objects to communicate	B	B	B	B	B	B	B	B	B	B	B	B	B			B		
FS 4a Child demonstrates greeting function of communication by gesturing or vocalizing (e.g., when sibling enters room, child vocalizes or uses waving gesture; adult enters room and child vocalizes or uses "up" reaching gesture).											B							
FS 4b Child demonstrates confirmation function of communication by gesturing or vocalizing (e.g., when adult says "There's the ball," child points to ball).																		
FS 4c Child demonstrates comment/reply function of communication by gesturing or vocalizing (e.g., when adult asks "What happened?" child points to spilled milk).																		
FS 4d Child demonstrates information function of communication by gesturing or vocalizing (e.g., when adult asks "Where's your teddy?" child points to teddy bear).																		
FS 4e Child demonstrates attention function of communication by gesturing or vocalizing (e.g., child points to sibling jumping in swimming pool; adult says "There's Billy").																		
FS 4f Child demonstrates question function of communication by gesturing or vocalizing (e.g., child points to new stuffed animal; adult says "What's that?").																		
FS 4g Child demonstrates comment/describe function of communication by gesturing or vocalizing (e.g., child points to truck; adult says "That's a truck").																		

Assessment, Evaluation, and Programming System for Infants and Children, Third Edition (AEPS®-3), by Bricker, Dionne, Grisham, Johnson, Macy, Slentz, & Waddell. © 2022 Brookes Publishing Co. All rights reserved.

APPENDIX B: AEPS-3 SKILLS MATRIX

Social-Communication (continued)

Legend: B = B marker; G = G marker (as shown in the original AEPS-3 Curriculum Routine/Activity grid).

AEPS-3 Test Item	Active & Outdoor Play	Arrival & Departure	Art	Bath Time	Block Play	Circle Time	Diapering, Toileting, & Handwashing	Dramatic Play	Dressing	Field Trips	Math	Meals & Snacks	Music & Movement	Nap & Sleep	Science	Sensory	Technology	Writing
4.1 Makes requests of others		B	B	B	B	B		B	B	B	B	B	B	B				
4.2 Makes choices to express preferences		B	B	B	B	B		B	B	B	B	B	B	B		B		B
4.3 Expresses desire to continue activity	B	B	B	B	B	B		B		B		B	B			B		
FS 4.3a Child reproduces action (e.g., waves arms, vocalizes, smiles) after an adult is attentive to child's initial behavior.																		
FS 4.3b Child indicates desire for adult to continue game or action by touching part of adult's body used to produce game or action (e.g., child touches adult's hand or eyes to indicate desire to continue playing Peekaboo).																		
FS 4.3c Child indicates desire to continue familiar game or action (e.g., child waves arms, bounces, vocalizes, laughs, smiles, kicks legs).																		
4.4 Expresses negation or protests	B	B	B	B	B	B	B	B	B	B		B	B	B		B		
FS 4.4a Child demonstrates protest function of communication by gesturing or vocalizing displeasure (e.g., adult puts child in crib, child cries).																		
FS 4.4b Child demonstrates rejection function of communication by gesturing or vocalizing refusal (e.g., when adult puts bottle to child's mouth, child closes mouth and turns away; when adult offers child toy, child pushes toy away; when adult gives child cracker, child turns head away).																		

B. Communicative Understanding

AEPS-3 Test Item	Active & Outdoor Play	Arrival & Departure	Art	Bath Time	Block Play	Circle Time	Diapering, Toileting, & Handwashing	Dramatic Play	Dressing	Field Trips	Math	Meals & Snacks	Music & Movement	Nap & Sleep	Science	Sensory	Technology	Writing
1. Follows gaze to establish joint attention	B	B	B	B	B	B	B	B	B	B	B	B	B					B
1.1 Follows pointing gestures with eyes	B	B	B	B	B	B	B	B	B	B	B	B	B					B
1.2 Looks toward object	G	G	G	G	B	G	G	G	G	G	G	G	G					B
2. Locates common objects, people, or events	B	B	B	B	B	G	G	G	G	B	G	G	G		G	G	G	G
FS 2a Child locates common objects, people, or events in familiar pictures.															G	G	G	G
FS 2b Child locates common objects, people, events, or actions with contextual cues.																G		
2.1 Recognizes own and familiar names	B	B	B	B	B	B		B	B	B	B	B	B					
2.2 Responds to single-word directive	B	B	B	B	B	B	B	B	B	B	B	B	B					

APPENDIX B: AEPS-3 SKILLS MATRIX

Social-Communication (continued)

AEPS-3 Test Item	Active & Outdoor Play	Arrival & Departure	Art	Bath Time	Block Play	Circle Time	Diapering, Toileting, & Handwashing	Dramatic Play	Dressing	Field Trips	Math	Meals & Snacks	Music & Movement	Nap & Sleep	Science	Sensory	Technology	Writing
3. Follows multistep directions without contextual cues	G	G	G	G	G	G	G	G	G	G	G	G	G	G	G	G	G	G
3.1 Follows multistep directions with contextual cues	G	G	G	G	G	G	G	G	G	G	G	G	G	G	G	G	G	G
3.2 Follows one-step direction without contextual cues	G	G	G	G	G	G	G	G	G	G	G	G	G	G	G	G	G	G
3.3 Follows one-step direction with contextual cues	G	G	G	G	G	G	G	G	G	G	G	G	G	G	G	G	G	G
FS 3.3a Child participates in verbal and gestural social routines (e.g., child responds to requests to "Come here" or "Sit down").																		
4. Responds to comprehension questions related to *why, how,* and *when*	R	R		R	R	R	R	R	R	R	R	R	R	R	R	R	R	R
4.1 Answers *who, what,* and *where* questions	G	G		G	G	G	G	G	G	G	G	G		G	G	G	G	G
FS 4.1a Child responds with vocalization or gesture to simple questions.																		
C. Communicative Expression																		
1. Produces multiple-word sentences to communicate	G	G	G	G	G	G	G	G	G	G	G	G	G	G	G	G		G
1.1 Uses two-word utterances	G	G	G	G	G	G	G	G	G	G	G	G	G	G	G	G	G	G
1.2 Uses 50 single words, signs, or symbols	G	B	G	G	B	G	G	G	G	B	G	G	B	G	G	G	G	G
1.3 Uses consistent approximations for words or signs	B	B	B	B	B	B	B	B	B	B	B	B	B	B	B	B		B
1.4 Uses consistent consonant-vowel combinations	B	B	B	B	B	B	B	B	B	B	B	B	B	B		B	B	B
2. Uses plural pronouns to indicate subjects, objects, and possession in multiple-word sentences	G	G	G	G	G	G	G	G	G	G	G	G	G	G	G	G	G	G
2.1 Uses irregular plural nouns in multiple-word sentences✲	R	R	R	G	R	R	R	R	R	R	R	R	R	R	R	R	R	R
2.2 Uses regular plural nouns✲	G	G	G	G	G	G	G	G	G	G	G	G	G	G	G	G	G	G

✲ This item is modified in Spanish. See Volume 2, *AEPS-3 Assessment,* Chapter 3, for details.

APPENDIX B: AEPS-3 SKILLS MATRIX

Social-Communication *(continued)*

AEPS-3 Test Item	Active & Outdoor Play	Arrival & Departure	Art	Bath Time	Block Play	Circle Time	Diapering, Toileting, & Handwashing	Dramatic Play	Dressing	Field Trips	Math	Meals & Snacks	Music & Movement	Nap & Sleep	Science	Sensory	Technology	Writing
3. Uses helping verbs*	G	G	G	G	G	G	G	G	G	G				G	G		G	
3.1 Uses irregular past tense of common verbs*	R	R		R	R	R	R	R	R	R	R	R	R	R	R	R	R	R
3.2 Uses regular past tense of common verbs	G	G		G	G	G	G	G	G	G	G	G	G	G	G		G	G
3.3 Uses *to be* verbs*	G	G	G	G	G	G	G	G	G	G	G	G		G	G	R	G	G
4. Asks questions using inverted auxiliary*	G	G	G	G	G	G	G	G	G	G	G	G	R	G	G		G	G
4.1 Asks *wh-* questions	G	G	G	G	G	G	G	G	G	G	G	G		G	G		G	G
D. Social Use of Language																		
1. Uses language to initiate and sustain social interaction (RS 16)	G	G	G	G	G	G	G	G	G	G	G	G		G	G	G	G	G
1.1 Follows social conventions of language	G	G	G	G	G		G	G	G	G	G	G	R	G	G	G	G	G
2. Provides and seeks information while conversing using words, phrases, or sentences (RS 17)	G	G	G	G	G	G	G	G	G	G	G	G	G		G	G	G	G
2.1 Asks questions to obtain information	G	G	G	G	G	G	G	G	G	G					G	G		G
2.2 Describes objects, people, and events as part of social exchange	G	G	G	G	G	G	G	G	G	G	G	G		G	G	G	G	G
3. Uses conversational rules when communicating with others (RS 18)	R	R	R	R	R	R	R	R	R	R	R	R	R	R	G	R	G	R
3.1 Uses socially appropriate physical orientation	R	R	R			R	R	R	R	R	R	R	R					
3.2 Varies voice to impart meaning and recognize social or environmental conditions	R	R	R	R	R	R	G	R	R	R		R	R	R	R	R	R	R

Assessment, Evaluation, and Programming System for Infants and Children, Third Edition (AEPS®-3), by Bricker, Dionne, Grisham, Johnson, Macy, Slentz, & Waddell. © 2022 Brookes Publishing Co. All rights reserved.

* This item is modified in Spanish. See Volume 2, AEPS-3 Assessment, Chapter 3, for details.

APPENDIX B: AEPS-3 SKILLS MATRIX

Social-Communication *(continued)*

AEPS-3 Test Item	AEPS-3 Curriculum Routine/Activity																					
	Active & Outdoor Play	Arrival & Departure	Art	Bath Time	Block Play	Circle Time	Diapering, Toileting, & Handwashing	Dramatic Play	Dressing	Field Trips	Math	Meals & Snacks	Music & Movement	Nap & Sleep	Science	Sensory	Technology	Writing
3.3 Responds to topic initiations from others	G R		G R		G R	G R		G R	G R	G R	G R	G R						
3.4 Alternates between speaker and listener roles during conversations with others	G	G		G	G	G	G	G	G	G	G	G		G	G	G		G
3.5 Responds to contingent questions from others	G	G	G	G	G	G	G	G	G	G	G	G		G	G	G		G

(page 27 of 42)

APPENDIX B: AEPS-3 SKILLS MATRIX

Cognitive

AEPS-3 Test Item

A. Sensory Exploration

AEPS-3 Test Item	Active & Outdoor Play	Arrival & Departure	Art	Bath Time	Block Play	Circle Time	Diapering, Toileting, & Handwashing	Dramatic Play	Dressing	Field Trips	Math	Meals & Snacks	Music & Movement	Nap & Sleep	Science	Sensory	Technology	Writing
1. Orients to events or stimulation																		
FS 1a Child displays reflexive responses to tactile events, such as rooting response and grasp.	B	B	B	B	B	B	B	B	B	B	B	B	B			B		
FS 1b Child visually follows object moving in a circular direction.																		
FS 1c Child visually follows object moving in a vertical direction.																		
FS 1d Child visually follows object moving in a horizontal direction.																		
1.1 Reacts to events or stimulation																		
FS 1.1a Child displays reflexive pupillary and blinking responses when facing bright lights.	B	B	B	B	B	B	B	B	B	B	B	B	B			B		
2. Combines simple actions to examine people, animals, and objects	B	B	B	B	B	B		B		B	B	B	B			B		
2.1 Uses sensory means to explore people, animals, and objects	B	B	B	B	B	B	B	B		B	B	B	B			B		
FS 2.1a Child explores and plays with parts of own body (e.g., child sucks fingers or watches hands and feet).																		
FS 2.1b Child explores or plays with objects that satisfy physical needs (e.g., mother's breast, nipple on bottle, pacifier, blanket, clothing).																		

B. Imitation and Memory

AEPS-3 Test Item	Active & Outdoor Play	Arrival & Departure	Art	Bath Time	Block Play	Circle Time	Diapering, Toileting, & Handwashing	Dramatic Play	Dressing	Field Trips	Math	Meals & Snacks	Music & Movement	Nap & Sleep	Science	Sensory	Technology	Writing
1. Imitates novel coordinated motor actions	G	G	G	G	G	G	G	G	G	G	G	G	G		G	G	G	G
1.1 Imitates novel simple motor action not already in repertoire	B	B	B	B	B	B	B	B	B	B	B	B	B			G	G	B
1.2 Imitates familiar simple motor action	B	B	B	B	B	B	B	B	B	B	B	B	B					B
FS 1.2a Child reproduces motor action similar to, but different from, adult's modeling (e.g., adult opens and closes fingers, child waves own hand).																		
FS 1.2b Child initiates action, adult imitates child's action, and child repeats action by imitating adult (e.g., child sticks out tongue, adult imitates, child repeats action within turn-taking interaction).																		

Assessment, Evaluation, and Programming System for Infants and Children, Third Edition (AEPS®-3), by Bricker, Dionne, Grisham, Johnson, Macy, Slentz, & Waddell. © 2022 Brookes Publishing Co. All rights reserved.

APPENDIX B: AEPS-3 SKILLS MATRIX

Cognitive (continued)

AEPS-3 Test Item	Active & Outdoor Play	Arrival & Departure	Art	Bath Time	Block Play	Circle Time	Diapering, Toileting, & Handwashing	Dramatic Play	Dressing	Field Trips	Math	Meals & Snacks	Music & Movement	Nap & Sleep	Science	Sensory	Technology	Writing
2. Imitates novel words	G	G	G	G	G	G	G	G	G	G	G	G	G	G	G	G	G	G
FS 2a Child says a sound or word, adult responds with novel word that is modification of child-initiated sound or word, child imitates novel word (e.g., child says "Baba," adult responds "Bobbie," child imitates "Bobbie").																		
FS 2b Child says simple, familiar consonant-vowel word, adult imitates word, child repeats word by imitating adult (e.g., child says "Go," adult says "Go," child imitates "Go").																		
2.1 Imitates novel vocalizations	B	B		B	B	B	B	B	B	B	B	B	B					
2.2 Imitates familiar vocalizations	B	B		B	B	B	B	B	B	B	B	B	B					
3. Relates past events	R	R	R	R	R	R	R	R	R	R		R	R	R	R	R		R
3.1 Relates recent events without contextual cues	G	G	G	G	G	G	G	G	G	G		G	G	G	G	G		G
3.2 Relates recent events with contextual cues	R	R	R	G	G	R	R	G	R	R			R	R	G	R		R
3.3 Relates events immediately after they occur		G	G	G	G	G	G	G	G	G			G	G	G	G		G
C. Conceptual Knowledge																		
1. Maintains search for object not in its usual location	R			R	R		R	R	R			R			R	R	R	R
FS 1a Child asks adult for object when object is not found in its usual location.																		
FS 1b Child maintains search for object in its usual location (e.g., child searches second time in toy box for favorite toy).																		
FS 1c Child looks for object in its usual location.																		
FS 1d Child looks for object in proximity of its usual location (e.g., child goes into kitchen and requests cracker, child looks for ball in corner where toys are kept).																		

Assessment, Evaluation, and Programming System for Infants and Children, Third Edition (AEPS®-3), by Bricker, Dionne, Grisham, Johnson, Macy, Slentz, & Waddell. © 2022 Brookes Publishing Co. All rights reserved.

APPENDIX B: AEPS-3 SKILLS MATRIX

Cognitive (continued)

AEPS-3 Test Item	Writing	Technology	Sensory	Science	Nap & Sleep	Music & Movement	Meals & Snacks	Math	Field Trips	Dressing	Dramatic Play	Diapering, Toileting, & Handwashing	Circle Time	Block Play	Bath Time	Art	Arrival & Departure	Active & Outdoor Play
1.1 Locates object in second of two hiding places		G	G	G							G			G				G
FS 1.1a After child sees object hidden first in one place, then another, child searches for object in first hiding place, then in next hiding place.																		
FS 1.1b After child sees object hidden first in one place, then another, child searches for object in first hiding place.																		
FS 1.1c Child searches for object by continuing to follow object's path after it disappears (e.g., child looks for toy train at end of tunnel through which train has disappeared).																		
FS 1.1d Child looks for hidden object where object was last seen before it disappeared (e.g., adult takes doll from child's lap and covers it with blanket, child searches for doll in lap or in adult's hand).																		
1.2 Locates hidden object							B			B	B			B	B		B	B
2. Recognizes symbols				G					G		G			G	G			G
FS 2a Child labels familiar people, actions, objects, and events in pictures.																		
FS 2b Child indicates recognition of familiar people, actions, objects, and events by pointing to, touching, or picking up picture.																		
2.1 Uses object to represent another object		G		G		G			G	G	G	G	G	G			G	G
FS 2.1a Child uses representational actions with objects (e.g., child pretends to peel and eat plastic banana).																		
FS 2.1b Child uses picture or toy to represent real object (e.g., child makes barking noise while holding picture of dog).																		
FS 2.1c Child uses functionally similar object as substitute for another object to perform game or action (e.g., child feeds doll with bottle, then takes cup and gives doll drink).																		
FS 2.1d Child uses functionally appropriate actions with objects (e.g., child pretends to talk on toy phone).																		
FS 2.1e Child differentiates actions on objects according to response of object (e.g., bangs together hard objects; rolls, rattles, or shakes round objects; chews on soft objects).																		
FS 2.1f Child uses simple motor actions on different objects.																		
FS 2.1g Child produces simple, undifferentiated action on all objects (e.g., drops or bangs objects).																		

(page 30 of 42)

APPENDIX B: AEPS-3 SKILLS MATRIX

Cognitive *(continued)*

AEPS-3 Curriculum Routine/Activity

AEPS-3 Test Item	Active & Outdoor Play	Arrival & Departure	Art	Bath Time	Block Play	Circle Time	Diapering, Toileting, & Handwashing	Dramatic Play	Dressing	Field Trips	Math	Meals & Snacks	Music & Movement	Nap & Sleep	Science	Sensory	Technology	Writing
3. Classifies using multiple attributes																		
3.1 Classifies according to function	G				R	R			R	R	G	R			R		R	
FS 3.1a Child groups two functionally related objects (e.g., diaper and pin, doll and blanket).	R		R	G	G	G		G	G	G	G	G			G	R	G	R
FS 3.1b Child functionally relates one object to succession of similar objects from another class (e.g., child gives each of three dolls drink, in turn, from toy cup).				R				R	R			R			R	R	R	R
3.2 Classifies according to physical attribute	G			G	G	G		G	G	G	G	G			G		G	
FS 3.2a Child groups together two or more similar objects (e.g., child chooses toy airplanes, child chooses two spoons from drawer).																		
3.3 Discriminates between objects or people using common attributes	G			G	G	G		G		G	G	G	G		G	G	G	
FS 3.3a Child recognizes familiar object, person, or event by responding in same way to similar object, person, or event over time (e.g., child looks into all mirrors and smiles, child poses in front of camera).				G	G	G		G		G	G	G			G	G	G	
4. Uses early conceptual comparisons	G	G	G	G	G	G	G	G	G	G	G	G	G	G	G	G	G	G
4.1 Identifies common concepts	R	R	R	R	R	R	R	R		R	R			R	R	R	R	R
FS 4.1a Child demonstrates understanding of at least six pairs of early opposite concepts by sorting, labeling, or selecting objects with appropriate quality from at least six pairs (e.g., hot/cold, top/bottom, in/out, wet/dry, full/empty, up/down, stop/go, fast/slow, clean/dirty).	G	G	G	G	G	G		G	G	G	G	G	G	G	G	G		G
4.2 Identifies concrete concepts	G	G	G	G	G	G		G	G	G	G	G	G	G	G	G		G

APPENDIX B: AEPS-3 SKILLS MATRIX

Cognitive (continued)

AEPS-3 Test Item

AEPS-3 Curriculum Routine/Activity

AEPS-3 Test Item	Active & Outdoor Play	Arrival & Departure	Art	Bath Time	Block Play	Circle Time	Diapering, Toileting, & Handwashing	Dramatic Play	Dressing	Field Trips	Math	Meals & Snacks	Music & Movement	Nap & Sleep	Science	Sensory	Technology	Writing
D. Reasoning																		
1. Uses object to obtain another object	B				B			B	B			B						B
1.1 Uses part of object or support to obtain another object	G			G	G			G	G			G			G			G
FS 1.1a Child uses object to act upon another object (e.g., child hits drum with stick or draws line with stick in wet sand).																		
FS 1.1b Child acts on part of object or support to produce visible or auditory effect (e.g., child pulls placemat and dish rattles, child pulls string and toy moves).																		
FS 1.1c Child moves own body parts to produce effect on object (e.g., child kicks crib mobile).																		
1.2 Retains one object when second object is obtained	B	B	B	B	B			B								B		
FS 1.2a Child retains object with one hand while acting on second object (e.g., child holds block while banging another block with other hand).																		
FS 1.2b Child retains one object while looking at second object.																		
2. Coordinates actions with objects to achieve new outcomes	B	B	B	B	B			B	B	B		B				B		
2.1 Tries different simple actions to achieve goal	B	B	B	B	B			B	B	B		B						
2.2 Uses simple actions on objects	B	B	B	B	B			B	B	B		B				B		

APPENDIX B: AEPS-3 SKILLS MATRIX

Cognitive (continued)

AEPS-3 Test Item

AEPS-3 Test Item	Active & Outdoor Play	Arrival & Departure	Art	Bath Time	Block Play	Circle Time	Diapering, Toileting, & Handwashing	Dramatic Play	Dressing	Field Trips	Math	Meals & Snacks	Music & Movement	Nap & Sleep	Science	Sensory	Technology	Writing
3. Solves problems using multiple strategies [RS 19]	R		R	R	R	R		R			R	R	R		R	R		R
3.1 Evaluates common solutions to solve problems or reach goals					G	G	G	G	G		G	G	G		G			
FS 3.1a Child solves common problems (e.g., child pulls stool to cabinet to reach items on higher shelf).																		
FS 3.1b Child suggests acceptable solutions to problems (e.g., when adult says she is cold, child offers, "We could turn up the heat").																		
FS 3.1c Child uses adult to assist with solving common problem (e.g., child hands container to adult to help open it).																		
FS 3.1d Child uses more than one strategy in attempt to solve common problem (e.g., child tugs on mother's pants to get attention, mother doesn't respond, child cries).																		
FS 3.1e Child repeats same strategy to attempt to solve common problem (e.g., child tugs on mother's pants to get attention, mother doesn't respond, child tugs again).																		
4. Draws plausible conclusions about events beyond personal experience [RS 20]	R				R	R		R								R		R
4.1 Draws conclusions about causes of events based on personal experience						G	G	G		G					G			
E. Scientific Discovery																		
1. Expands simple observations and explorations into further inquiry [RS 21]		G		G	G	G		G		G					G	G		
1.1 Uses simple tools to gather information	G																	
1.2 Uses senses to explore	B	B	B	B	B	B	B	B	B	B	B	B	B		B	B		B

(page 33 of 42)

Assessment, Evaluation, and Programming System for Infants and Children, Third Edition (AEPS®-3), by Bricker, Dionne, Grisham, Johnson, Macy, Slentz, & Waddell. © 2022 Brookes Publishing Co. All rights reserved.

APPENDIX B: AEPS-3 SKILLS MATRIX

Cognitive *(continued)*

AEPS-3 Test Item

AEPS-3 Test Item	Active & Outdoor Play	Arrival & Departure	Art	Bath Time	Block Play	Circle Time	Diapering, Toileting, & Handwashing	Dramatic Play	Dressing	Field Trips	Math	Meals & Snacks	Music & Movement	Nap & Sleep	Science	Sensory	Technology	Writing
2. Anticipates outcome of investigation (RS 22)	G									G					G			
2.1 Generates specific questions for investigation		G								G					G			
2.2 Demonstrates knowledge about natural happenings				G		G				G		G			G			
2.3 Makes observations	B	B	B		B	B		B		B	B	B	B			B		B
3. Investigates to test hypotheses (RS 23)															G			
3.1 Draws on prior knowledge to guide investigations					G					G					G			
3.2 Manipulates materials to cause change (RS 24)	G		G		G					G	G		G		G	G		G
4. Transfers knowledge	R	R	R	R	R	R		R		R	R		R		R	R	R	G
4.1 Communicates results of investigations		R	R		R	R				R	R				R	R		
4.2 Demonstrates knowledge of properties of change resulting from investigations		R	R		R					R					R			R
4.3 Shows awareness that manipulation of materials or processes prompted change in those materials or processes		R	R		R					R					R			R

AEPS-3 Curriculum Routine/Activity

Assessment, Evaluation, and Programming System for Infants and Children, Third Edition (AEPS®-3), by Bricker, Dionne, Grisham, Johnson, Macy, Slentz, & Waddell. © 2022 Brookes Publishing Co. All rights reserved.

APPENDIX B: AEPS-3 SKILLS MATRIX

Literacy

AEPS-3 Test Item

A. Awareness of Print Concepts

AEPS-3 Curriculum Routine/Activity

AEPS-3 Test Item	Active & Outdoor Play	Arrival & Departure	Art	Bath Time	Block Play	Circle Time	Diapering, Toileting, & Handwashing	Dramatic Play	Dressing	Field Trips	Math	Meals & Snacks	Music & Movement	Nap & Sleep	Science	Sensory	Technology	Writing
1. Participates in shared group reading																		
1.1 Participates in shared one-on-one reading						G				G					G	G	G	
FS 1.1a Child demonstrates functional use of reading materials while looking at picture books.				B		B		B		B				B		B		B
FS 1.1b Child orally fills in or completes familiar text while looking at picture books.																		B
FS 1.1c Child indicates awareness that familiar text is left out or skipped over while looking at picture books.																		
FS 1.1d Child points to objects and answers questions while looking at picture books.																		
FS 1.1e Child responds to request to sit and read book with adult.																		
2. Demonstrates understanding that text is read in one direction and from top to bottom of page				G	G	G		G		G	G			G	G	G	G	
2.1 Turns pages of book from beginning toward end				G		G		G		G	G			G	G		G	
FS 2.1a Child attempts to turn pages.																		
2.2 Holds book or other printed material with pictures correctly oriented				G	G	G	G	G		G	G			G	G	G	G	
FS 2.2a Child holds books or other printed materials with or without pictures using both hands. Book does not need to be correctly oriented.																		
3. Recognizes print words for common or familiar people, objects, or pictures		R	R	R	R	R	R	R		R	R	R		R	R	R	R	R
3.1 Recognizes own first name in print		G	G			G	G	G		G	G	G			G		G	G
3.2 Recognizes common signs and logos	G	G	G	G	G	G	G	G		G	G	G		G	G	G	G	G

B. Phonological Awareness

AEPS-3 Test Item	Active & Outdoor Play	Arrival & Departure	Art	Bath Time	Block Play	Circle Time	Diapering, Toileting, & Handwashing	Dramatic Play	Dressing	Field Trips	Math	Meals & Snacks	Music & Movement	Nap & Sleep	Science	Sensory	Technology	Writing
1. Produces rhyming words given oral prompt ▶ RS 25						R												
FS 1a Child produces some rhyming words in familiar rhymes.													R					

APPENDIX B: AEPS-3 SKILLS MATRIX

Literacy *(continued)*

AEPS-3 Curriculum Routine/Activity

AEPS-3 Test Item	Writing	Technology	Sensory	Science	Nap & Sleep	Music & Movement	Meals & Snacks	Math	Field Trips	Dressing	Dramatic Play	Diapering, Toileting, & Handwashing	Circle Time	Block Play	Bath Time	Art	Arrival & Departure	Active & Outdoor Play
1.1 Identifies rhyming words						R							R					
FS 1.1a Child repeats simple nursery rhymes.																		
FS 1.1b Child says nursery rhymes along with familiar adult.																		
1.2 Participates in repetitive verbal play						G	G	G	G	G	G	G	G	G	G		G	G
FS 1.2a Child indicates interest in hearing or repeating nursery rhymes.																		
2. Segments compound words into component words *RS 26*		R			R	R							R					
2.1 Blends two simple words into compound words						R							R					
2.2 Claps for words in sentences						R							R					
3. Segments syllables of two- and three-syllable words *RS 27*		R			R	R												
3.1 Blends syllables into two- and three-syllable words						R							R					
3.2 Claps for each syllable in two- and three-syllable words						R							R					
4. Segments CVC words into individual sounds *RS 28*		R			R	R							R					
4.1 Blends separate CVC sounds into simple words		R			R	R												
4.2 Identifies middle sounds in CVC words		R			R	R												
4.3 Identifies last sounds in CVC words					R	R							R					
4.4 Identifies beginning sounds in CVC words		R			R	R							R					
4.5 Produces words that begin with specified sound						R							R					

Assessment, Evaluation, and Programming System for Infants and Children, Third Edition (AEPS®-3), by Bricker, Dionne, Grisham, Johnson, Macy, Slentz, & Waddell. © 2022 Brookes Publishing Co. All rights reserved.

APPENDIX B: AEPS-3 SKILLS MATRIX

Literacy (continued)

AEPS-3 Curriculum Routine/Activity

AEPS-3 Test Item	Active & Outdoor Play	Arrival & Departure	Art	Bath Time	Block Play	Circle Time	Diapering, Toileting, & Handwashing	Dramatic Play	Dressing	Field Trips	Math	Meals & Snacks	Music & Movement	Nap & Sleep	Science	Sensory	Technology	Writing
C. Alphabet Knowledge																		
1. Names all uppercase and lowercase letters of alphabet [RS 29]	R	R		R	R	R	R	R	R	R		R	R				R	R
1.1 Matches frequently occurring lowercase letters with uppercase counterparts		R		R	R		R	R	R			R	R				R	R
1.2 Names 12 frequently occurring letters	R	R		R	R	R	R	R	R	R		R		R			R	R
1.3 Recognizes five frequently occurring letters not in first name			R			R		R	R	R								R
1.4 Names letters in own first name	R	R	R	R	R	R		R	R	R		R			R		R	R
1.5 Recognizes three letters in own first name	R	R	R	R	R			R	R	R		R					R	
2. Reads simple CVC and sight word text [RS 30]	R	R		R						R	R	R		R			R	
2.1 Sounds out CVC words	R	R		R						R	R		R				R	
2.2 Reads frequently occurring sight words	R	R								R	R	R	R	R	R		R	
FS 2.2a Child recognizes own name in print.																		
2.3 Produces correct sounds for 20 letters of alphabet		R		R	R									R			R	
2.4 Produces correct sounds for six letters of alphabet		R		R	R							R	R	R	R		R	
D. Vocabulary and Story Comprehension																		
1. Demonstrates understanding that pictures represent text				G		G		G		G				G	G		G	G
1.1 Labels familiar people, actions, objects, and events in picture books				G		G				G				G	G	G	G	
1.2 Locates familiar objects, people, events, and actions in picture books				G		G				G				G	G		G	
FS 1.2a Child locates common actions and events in familiar books or pictures.																		
FS 1.2b Child locates common objects and people in familiar books or pictures.																		
1.3 Matches pictures to actual objects, people, or actions			G			G					G					G		G

Assessment, Evaluation, and Programming System for Infants and Children, Third Edition (AEPS®-3), by Bricker, Dionne, Grisham, Johnson, Macy, Slentz, & Waddell. © 2022 Brookes Publishing Co. All rights reserved.

APPENDIX B: AEPS-3 SKILLS MATRIX

Literacy (continued)

AEPS-3 Test Item	Active & Outdoor Play	Arrival & Departure	Art	Bath Time	Block Play	Circle Time	Diapering, Toileting, & Handwashing	Dramatic Play	Dressing	Field Trips	Math	Meals & Snacks	Music & Movement	Nap & Sleep	Science	Sensory	Technology	Writing
2. Retells simple story [RS31]			G	G		G				G				G	G		G	
2.1 Makes predictions about what will happen next in story						G				G				G	G		G	
2.2 Answers and asks questions related to story — FS 2.2a Child makes comments related to story while looking at book (e.g., child points to lion in book and says "I went to the zoo").						G				G				G	G		G	
2.3 Tells story associated with series of pictures			G			G								G	G		G	
3. Demonstrates understanding of abstract story vocabulary [RS32]			G			G		G										
3.1 Demonstrates understanding of key vocabulary in picture books			R			R		R		G					G		G	
3.2 Demonstrates understanding of title, author, and illustrator						G				R				R	R		R	
3.3 Demonstrates understanding of vocabulary associated with early literacy concepts						R				G				G	G		G	
E. Writing																		
1. "Reads" back own dictation to label or caption picture [RS33]			R	R				R		G					R		R	R
1.1 Dictates description of drawing			G	G						R					G		G	G
1.2 Verbally labels representational drawings			G	R						G					R		R	R

Assessment, Evaluation, and Programming System for Infants and Children, Third Edition (AEPS®-3), by Bricker, Dionne, Grisham, Johnson, Macy, Slentz, & Waddell. © 2022 Brookes Publishing Co. All rights reserved.

APPENDIX B: AEPS-3 SKILLS MATRIX

Literacy *(continued)*

AEPS-3 Curriculum Routine/Activity

AEPS-3 Test Item	Active & Outdoor Play	Arrival & Departure	Art	Bath Time	Block Play	Circle Time	Diapering, Toileting, & Handwashing	Dramatic Play	Dressing	Field Trips	Math	Meals & Snacks	Music & Movement	Nap & Sleep	Science	Sensory	Technology	Writing
1.3 Verbally labels nonrepresentational drawings			G	G						G					G			G
		R	R	R				R		R					R		R	R
2. Writes and draws for a variety of purposes [RS 34]	G		G	G				G		R					R		R	G
2.1 Makes representational drawings	G		G	G				G							G		G	G
3. Writes words using conventional spelling	R		R	R				R		R	R				R		R	R
3.1 Writes using developmental spelling	R		R	R				R		R	R				R		R	R
3.2 Prints first name	R	R	R	R				R		R					R		R	R
FS 3.2a Child prints three letters.																		
3.3 Copies entire first name		R	R	R				R							R		R	R
FS 3.3a Child copies three letters.																		
FS 3.3b Child copies complex shapes.																		
FS 3.3c Child copies simple shapes.																		
3.4 Writes using "scribble writing"	R	R	R	R				R							R		R	R

Assessment, Evaluation, and Programming System for Infants and Children, Third Edition (AEPS®-3), by Bricker, Dionne, Grisham, Johnson, Macy, Slentz, & Waddell. © 2022 Brookes Publishing Co. All rights reserved.

APPENDIX B: AEPS-3 SKILLS MATRIX

Math

AEPS-3 Test Item — AEPS-3 Curriculum Routine/Activity

AEPS-3 Test Item	Active & Outdoor Play	Arrival & Departure	Art	Bath Time	Block Play	Circle Time	Diapering, Toileting, & Handwashing	Dramatic Play	Dressing	Field Trips	Math	Meals & Snacks	Music & Movement	Nap & Sleep	Science	Sensory	Technology	Writing
A. Counting																		
1. Counts out 3 items	G	G	G	G	G	G		G	G	G	G	G		G	G	G	G	G
1.1 Counts 3 items to determine "How many?"	G	G	G	G	G	G		G	G	G	G	G		G	G	G	G	G
FS 1.1a Child demonstrates one-to-one correspondence by assigning one of two objects to another person and keeping other object (e.g., child gives one of two daisies to father, keeps other daisy).																		
FS 1.1b Child demonstrates concept of one (e.g., when told child can have one cookie, child takes only one).																		
1.2 Recites numbers 1–3	B	B	B	B	B	B	B	B	B	B	B	B	B	B	B	B	B	B
2. Counts out 10 items	R	R	R	R	R	R		R	R	R	R	R		R	R	R	R	R
2.1 Counts 10 items to determine "How many?"	R		R			R	R	R	G	R	R	R		R	R	R	R	
2.2 Recites numbers 1–10	R	R	R	R	R	G	G	G		R	R	R	R	R	R	R		R
3. Counts out 20 items	R	R	R	R	R	R	R	R	R	R	R	R		R	R	R		R
3.1 Counts 20 items to determine "How many?"	R	R	R	R	R	R		R		R	R	R		R	R	R	R	R
3.2 Recites numbers 1–20	R	R		R	R	R	R			R	R	R	R	R	R	R	R	R
4. Skip counts by tens to 100	R	R	R	R	R	R	R	R	R	R	R	R		R	R	R		
4.1 Recites numbers 31–100	R	R					R		R	R	R			R	R	R	R	R
4.2 Recites numbers 1–30	R	R	R	R		R	R		R	R	R	R	R	R	R	R	R	R
B. Quantitative Relations																		
1. Compares items in sets to 5 by counting		G		G	G			G		G	G	G		G	G	G	G	
1.1 Compares items in sets to 5 by matching		G		G	G			G		G	G			G	G	G	G	

APPENDIX B: AEPS-3 SKILLS MATRIX

Math (continued)

AEPS-3 Test Item

AEPS-3 Test Item	Active & Outdoor Play	Arrival & Departure	Art	Bath Time	Block Play	Circle Time	Diapering, Toileting, & Handwashing	Dramatic Play	Dressing	Field Trips	Math	Meals & Snacks	Music & Movement	Nap & Sleep	Science	Sensory	Technology	Writing
1.2 Creates equivalent sets of 5 items	R	G	G		G	G		G	G	G	G	G			G	G	G	
1.3 Uses quantity comparison words — FS 1.3a Child demonstrates understanding of quantity words (e.g., child points to person at table who has more).	R		G		G	G		G	G	G	G	G			G	G		G
2. Compares items in sets of 6 to 10 by counting	R	R	R	R	R	R		R			R				R	R	R	
2.1 Compares items in sets of 6 to 10 by matching	R	R	R	R	R			R			R				R	R	R	
2.2 Creates equivalent sets of 10 items	R		R		R	R		R			R				R	R	R	
3. Compares items in sets of 11 to 20 by counting RS 35	R	R	R	R	R	R		R			R				R	R		
3.1 Compares items in sets of 11 to 20 by matching	R		R		R			R			R				R	R		
3.2 Compares items in sets of 11 to 20 by visual examination	R		R		R	R		R			R				R	R		

C. Reading and Writing Numbers

AEPS-3 Test Item	Active & Outdoor Play	Arrival & Departure	Art	Bath Time	Block Play	Circle Time	Diapering, Toileting, & Handwashing	Dramatic Play	Dressing	Field Trips	Math	Meals & Snacks	Music & Movement	Nap & Sleep	Science	Sensory	Technology	Writing
1. Reads and writes numerals for quantities to 5 RS 36	R	R	R	R	R	R		R		R	R	R		R	R	R	R	R
1.1 Demonstrates understanding of mathematical meaning of written numerals *1–5*	R	R	R	R	R	R		R		R	R	R		R	R	R	R	R
1.2 Labels numerals *1–5*	R	R	R	R	R	R		R		R	R	R		R	R	R	R	R
2. Reads and writes numerals for quantities 6–10 RS 37	R	R	R	R	R	R		R		R	R	R		R	R	R	R	R
2.1 Demonstrates understanding of mathematical meaning of written numerals *6–10*	R	R	R	R	R	R		R		R	R	R		R	R	R	R	R
2.2 Labels numerals 6–10	R	R	R	R	R	R		R		R	R	R		R	R	R	R	R
3. Reads and writes numerals for quantities 11–20 RS 38	R	R	R	R	R	R		R		R	R	R		R	R	R	R	R
3.1 Demonstrates understanding of mathematical meaning of written numerals *11–20*	R		R		R	R		R		R	R	R		R	R	R		R
3.2 Labels numerals 11–20	R	R	R	R	R	R		R		R	R	R		R	R	R	R	R

Assessment, Evaluation, and Programming System for Infants and Children, Third Edition (AEPS®-3), by Bricker, Dionne, Grisham, Johnson, Macy, Slentz, & Waddell. © 2022 Brookes Publishing Co. All rights reserved.

APPENDIX B: AEPS-3 SKILLS MATRIX

Math (*continued*)

AEPS-3 Test Item

D. Addition and Subtraction

AEPS-3 Test Item	Active & Outdoor Play	Arrival & Departure	Art	Bath Time	Block Play	Circle Time	Diapering, Toileting, & Handwashing	Dramatic Play	Dressing	Field Trips	Math	Meals & Snacks	Music & Movement	Nap & Sleep	Science	Sensory	Technology	Writing
1. Reads and writes symbols for addition (+) and equals (=) [RS 39]				R							R				R		R	R
1.1 Solves picture or object addition problems using shortcut sum strategy			R	R							R				R		R	R
1.2 Counts forward to 10	R		R	R	R	R	R	R	R	R	R			R	R	R	R	R
1.3 Solves picture or object problems using count all strategy			R	R	R	R	R				R				R		R	R
1.4 Says number after 1–10	R		R	R	R	R	R			R	R		R	R	R	R	R	R
1.5 Demonstrates understanding of concept of addition			R	R	R	R					R	R		R	R	R	R	R
2. Reads and writes symbols for subtraction (−) and equals (=) [RS 40]								R			R				R		R	R
2.1 Solves picture or object subtraction problems with set of 10 or less			R				R			R	R	R		R	R	R	R	R
2.2 Says number before 2–10	R		R	R	R	R					R	R	R	R	R	R	R	R
2.3 Demonstrates understanding of concept of subtraction			R	R				R			R			R	R	R	R	R

Assessment, Evaluation, and Programming System for Infants and Children, Third Edition (AEPS®-3), by Bricker, Dionne, Grisham, Johnson, Macy, Slentz, & Waddell. © 2022 Brookes Publishing Co. All rights reserved.

(page 42 of 42)

Index

Page numbers followed by *f* and *t* indicate figures and tables, respectively.